REA

"If I had to describe Sharon Salzberg's work in only two words, they might be 'only connect.' If there was only one word, that would be even easier: 'love.' In *Real Love*, one of the world's leading authorities on love tells us how to find it, how to nurture it, how to honor it, and most of all how to rethink it. Salzberg shows us how to experience love not as an emotion, not as the byproduct of a particular romantic or familial relationship, but as an ability that all of us can cultivate. This book has the power to set your heart at peace."
—Susan Cain, author of *Quiet*

"Sharon Salzberg is an amazing teacher, and her words and inspiration in *Real Love* illuminate the way to love wisely. A treasure for your heart." —Jack Kornfield, author of *A Path with Heart*

"This expert's guidebook cuts deftly through layers of modern confusion to the core of what it means to love and be loved. Salzberg has penned a treasure house of practical tools and rituals mined from her own tenure mending wounded hearts in the trenches of human relationships. This book offers up frank, practical stories and wisdom about love, communication, and relationships indispensable to all." —Amanda Palmer

"Written with compassion and keen insight. *Real Love* opens the heart, helping everyone understand love as revolutionary spiritual practice." —bell hooks

"In a most lively and inspiring way, Sharon Salzberg shows that unconditional love—for ourselves, for our dear ones, for all sentient beings—is naturally present within our hearts. Even when love from others and to others seems out of reach, what we really need to do is to let it come to the surface and express itself inexhaustibly. *Real Love* is a precious guide to experience the most supreme of all emotions." —Matthieu Ricard, author of *Altruism*

"In *Real Love*, Sharon Salzberg combines the brilliance of her understanding, the depth of her compassion, and the incisive friend-liness of her writing skills to create a book that illuminates the many subtleties and nuances of love. Real love is not an abstraction, and Sharon brings it to life in ways that can uplift us all." —Joseph Goldstein, author of *Mindfulness*

"Sharon Salzberg's *Real Love* is a genuine offering of love that im-mediately befriends the reader. It is a practical how-to guide for unearthing the love within oneself, no matter how buried. It's also a gentle but insistent invitation—both clear-eyed and kind—to find the real love in others and in our world, at a time when it is most urgently needed." —Sarah Jones, Tony and Obie Award–winning playwright and actress

"Sharon Salzberg is the superstar of lovingkindness meditation. No one has done more to spread this powerful method for kindling universal love in our hearts." —Daniel Goleman

"Sharon's teachings on awakening a loving heart have touched stu-dents and readers around the world. In addition to her wonderful wisdom, Sharon's very presence inspires: She is generous and kind, through and through." —Tara Brach, author of *Radical Acceptance*

REAL LOVE

REAL LOVE

THE

ART OF

MINDFUL

CONNECTION

✳

SHARON SALZBERG

FLATIRON
BOOKS
NEW YORK

www.flatironbooks.com

Grateful acknowledgment is made for permission to reproduce from the following:

Extract from "Our Weddings, Our Worth" by Frank Bruni, published in *The New York Times*, June 26, 2015. All rights reserved. Used by permission and protected by the Copyright Laws of the United States. The printing, copying, redistribution, or retransmission of this Content without express written permission is prohibited.

Extract from "Even as I Hold You" from *Good Night, Willie Lee, I'll See You in the Morning* by Alice Walker. Copyright © 1978 by Alice Walker. Used by permission of Doubleday, an imprint of the Knopf Doubleday Publishing Group, a division of Penguin Random House LLC. All rights reserved.

Extract from *Honeybee: Poems and Short Prose* by Naomi Shihab Nye. Text copyright © 2008 by Naomi Shihab Nye. Used by permission of HarperCollins Publishers.

Extract from "Rich People Just Care Less" by Daniel Goleman, published in *The New York Times*, October 5, 2013. All rights reserved. Used by permission and protected by the Copyright Laws of the United States. The printing, copying, redistribution, or retransmission of this Content without express written permission is prohibited.

The Library of Congress has cataloged the hardcover edition as follows:

Names: Salzberg, Sharon, [author].
Title: Real love : the art of mindful connection / Sharon Salzberg.
Description: First edition. | New York : Flatiron Books, 2017.
Identifiers: LCCN 2017289071 | ISBN 9781250076502 (hardcover) | ISBN 9781250076526 (ebook)
Subjects: LCSH: Love. | Mindfulness (Psychology) | Meditation. | Self-actualization (Psychology)
Classification: LCC BF575.L8 S325 2017 | DDC 152.4'1—dc23
LC record available at https://lccn.loc.gov/2017289071

ISBN 978-1-250-07651-9 (trade paperback)

Our books may be purchased in bulk for promotional, educational, or business use. Please contact your local bookseller or the Macmillan Corporate and Premium Sales Department at 1-800-221-7945, extension 5442, or by email at MacmillanSpecial Markets@macmillan.com.

First Flatiron Books Paperback Edition: May 2018

To my teacher, Nani Bala Barua (Dipa Ma),
who went through so much loss and
came to the power of boundless love.

CONTENTS

❋

Introduction: Looking for Love   1

SECTION 1

Introduction: Beyond the Cliché   9

1. The Stories We Tell Ourselves   25
2. The Stories Others Tell About Us   34
3. Welcoming Our Emotions   45
4. Meeting the Inner Critic   55
5. Letting Go of Perfection   65
6. Becoming Embodied   73
7. Moving Beyond Shame   78
8. Taking a Stand on Happiness   85
9. Following Your Ethical Compass   90

SECTION 2

Introduction: Love as a Verb   101
10. Barriers to Finding Real Love   111
11. Cultivate Curiosity and Awe   121

12. Authentic Communication   130

13. Playing Fair: A Win-Win Proposition   143

14. Navigate the Space Between   153

15. Letting Go   162

16. Healing, Not Victory   173

17. The Heart Is a Generous Muscle   182

18. Forgiveness and Reconciliation   192

SECTION 3

Introduction: The Wide Lens of Compassion   211

19. Priming the Pump   223

20. Challenging Our Assumptions   233

21. Love Everybody   247

22. Creating Community   256

23. From Anger to Love   266

24. Say Yes to Life   279

TAKEAWAYS FROM EACH SECTION   292

ACKNOWLEDGMENTS   295

NOTES   297

REAL LOVE

INTRODUCTION

✳

Looking for Love

Love takes off masks that we fear we cannot live
without and know we cannot live within.

—JAMES BALDWIN

SINCE WE WERE CHILDREN, we have been told a patchwork of stories about love. We expect love to give us exaltation, bliss, affection, fire, sweetness, tenderness, comfort, security, and so very much more—all at once.

Our minds are too often clouded by pop-culture images that equate love with sex and romance, delivered in thunderbolts and moonbeams. This idea of love makes us say things and do things we do not mean. It makes us cling frantically to relationships that are bound to change, challenge us, or slip away. Major bookstores often have a love section that's actually just a romantic relationship section—volumes on how to get a relationship, how to keep a relationship, and how to cure a relationship. As one publisher said to me, "The love market is saturated."

Perhaps we think we're getting the portion of love we deserve, which is not very much at all: "I'm just not lucky in love," or "I've been too damaged to love." We may feel so cynical (sometimes as a mask to hide heartbreak or loneliness) that we dismiss love as a sorry illusion. Some of us decide we are through with love because it takes much more from us than it ever gives back. At those wounded moments when we most need love, a hardened heart can seem like the best defense.

Many of us have been told that if we loved others enough and sacrificed, it wouldn't matter that we didn't love ourselves, and that we could keep that up forever. Or if we loved a friend or a child enough, that love itself could cure all ills, meaning no more painful setbacks or defeats. If there is such pain, it implies we were bad at love. Or maybe it was suggested to us that all we needed in this world was love and that we didn't have to fight what is wrong or call out what is cruel or unjust.

But apart from all these stories, as human beings we naturally live our lives wanting belonging, connection, a home in this world. We yearn for warmth, for possibility, for the more abundant life that love seems to promise. We sense there is a quality of real love that is possible beyond the narrow straits we have been told to navigate, a possibility that's not idealized or merely abstract. We have an intuition that we can connect so much more deeply to ourselves and to one another.

One of my own turning points came in 1985 when I did a meditation retreat in Burma. I was practicing intensive lovingkindness meditation, offering phrases of wishing well to myself and others all day long, like, "May I be happy; may you be happy." As I practiced, at one point it felt as though I came to a threshold. On one side was the conventional idea of who I had thought myself to be—that is, someone completely dependent on another person to feel any love in my life. It was as though I considered love to be like a package, in the hands of the all-powerful delivery person, and if that person changed their mind at my doorstep and walked away, I would be bereft—irredeemably incomplete, lacking the love I so longed for. On the other side of the threshold was the reflection of who I suspected I actually was—someone with an inner capacity for love, no matter who was present or what was happening, someone who could access love that another person might enhance or challenge, but there was no one who could either bestow that capacity on me or take it away. I stepped over.

I saw I couldn't flourish as a human being as long as I saw myself as the passive recipient of love. (There's an awful lot of waiting in that position, and then damage control when it doesn't work out, and also numbness.) But I could certainly flourish as love's embodiment.

This book is an exploration of real love—the innate capacity we each have to love—in everyday life. I see real love as the most fundamental of our innate capacities, never destroyed no matter what we might have gone through or might yet go through. It may be buried, obscured from view, hard to find, and hard to trust . . . but it is there. Faintly pulsing, like a heartbeat, beneath the words we use to greet one another, as we ponder how to critique others' work without hurting them, as we gather the courage to stand up for ourselves or realize we have to let go of a relationship—real love seeks to find authentic life, to uncurl and blossom.

I believe that there is only one kind of love—*real love*—trying to come alive in us despite our limiting assumptions, the distortions of our culture, and the habits of fear, self-condemnation, and isolation that we tend to acquire just by living a life. All of us have the capacity to experience real love. When we see love from this expanded perspective, we can find it in the smallest moments of connection: with a clerk in the grocery store, a child, a pet, a walk in the woods. We can find it within ourselves.

Real love comes with a powerful recognition that we are fully alive and whole, despite our wounds or our fears or our loneliness. It is a state where we allow ourselves to be seen clearly by ourselves and by others, and in turn, we offer clear seeing to the world around us. It is a love that heals.

The how of this book is based on a tool kit of mindfulness techniques and other practices cultivating lovingkindness and compassion that I have been teaching for over forty years. Mindfulness practice helps create space between our actual experiences and the reflexive stories we tend to tell about them (e.g., "This is all I deserve"). Lovingkindness practice helps us move out of the terrain of our default narratives if they tend to be based on fear or disconnection. We become authors of brand-new stories about love.

There are meditations, reflections, and interactive exercises designed to be suitable for anybody. They outline a path of exploration that is exciting, creative, and even playful. I draw from my own experience and from that of the many meditation students I have guided, several of whom have generously offered their stories here. The meditations in particular are meant to be done more than just once—over time, practicing them will create a steady foundation in mindfulness and lovingkindness in our lives.

Our exploration begins with that often-forgotten recipient who is missing real love: ourselves. We expand the exploration to include working with lovers, parents, spouses, children, best friends, and work friends, divorce, dying, forgiveness—the challenges and opportunities of daily life. And we move on to exploring the possibility of abiding in a sense of profound connection to all beings, even those around whom we draw strong boundaries or have tried in the past to block. We may not at all like them, but we can wish them to be free (and us to be free of their actions defining us). This vast sense of interconnection, within and without, leads us to love life itself.

I am writing this book for all who find that yearning within to be happier, who dare to imagine they might be capable of much, much more in the matter of love. And I am writing for those who at times suffer in feeling, as I once did, unloved and incapable of changing their fate. My hope is that through this book I can help you cultivate real love, that beautiful space of caring where you come into harmony with all of your life.

SECTION 1

INTRODUCTION

✳

Beyond the Cliché

Y OU ARE A PERSON WORTHY of love. You don't have to do anything to prove that. You don't have to climb Mt. Everest, write a catchy tune that goes viral on YouTube, or be the CEO of a tech start-up who cooks every meal from scratch using ingredients plucked from your organic garden. If you've never received an award and there are no plaques proclaiming your exceptional gifts hanging on your walls, you still deserve all the love in the world. You do not have to earn love. You simply have to exist. When we see ourselves and see life more clearly, we come to rely on that. We remember that we do deserve the blessing of love.

A lack of real love for ourselves is one of the most constricting, painful conditions we can know. It cuts us off from our deepest potential for connecting and caring; it is enslavement to powerful—but surmountable—conditioning.

And yet, no matter what bravery we show to the world, most of us have recurring doubts about our worth. We worry that we're not desirable enough, good enough, successful enough. We fear we're not enough, period. Intellectually, we may appreciate that loving ourselves would give us a firm foundation, one from which we could extend love out into the world. But for most of us this is a leap of logic, not a leap of the heart. We don't easily leap toward things we don't trust, and most of us don't trust that we are worth loving.

Nora expresses her confusion: "You always hear that you need to practice self-love in order to love others. But no one tells you *how* to love yourself. On the one hand, it feels like a cure-all: I need to love myself to find a lover. On the other hand, I think a lot of people seek out romance as a way of not loving themselves. In some sense, self-love is the most difficult. You're also the most convenient person to hate."

Michelle describes a wake-up call: "One day, when I was in my late twenties, a dear platonic friend said to me, 'Do you know how much I love you?' I instantly felt a wave of sadness. 'No,' I said, 'I don't know how much you love me.' 'I know,' he replied gently. At that moment, I became aware that I had never even thought of myself as being lovable. And I realized that it was not possible for me to receive love either."

Why is it so difficult for us to love ourselves? Why is it so much harder to offer ourselves the same sort of care and kindness that we readily dispense to our friends?

For one thing, the notion of loving oneself has gotten an undeservedly bad rap, which goes something like this: self-love is narcissistic, selfish, self-indulgent, the supreme delusion of a runaway ego looking out for "number one."

In fact, just the opposite is true. When the airplane cabin pressure is dropping, no one would call it selfish when a father secures his own oxygen mask before turning to help his child. More broadly, to love oneself genuinely is to come into harmony with life itself—including all others. Psychotherapist and meditator Linda Carroll explained the difference to me this way: "Loving yourself is holding yourself accountable to be the best you can be in your life. Narcissistic love has nothing to do with accountability." In other words, when we cultivate tenderness and compassion for the whole of our experiences—the difficult and hurtful parts, in addition to the triumphs—we naturally behave more kindly and responsibly toward others. Our hearts soften and we see that each of us is, in our own way, grappling with this human life that Zorba the Greek called "the full catastrophe"—replete with wonder and sorrow.

And so we begin with ourselves.

We are born ready to love and be loved. It is our birthright. Our ability to connect with others is innate, wired into our nervous systems, and we need connection as much as we need physical nourishment. But we're also born to learn, and from our earliest days, we begin to create our map of the world and our place in it. We form simple expectations: if I cry, someone will come—or not. Soon we start to weave fragments of our experiences into stories to explain what is happening to us and in the world around us. When we're very young, most of these expectations and stories are *implicit*, encoded in our bodies and nervous systems. But as we grow older, they become more *explicit*, and we may be able to recall where and when we first received a particular message about our worth and about our ability to love and be loved.

MESSAGES FROM OUR FAMILIES AND
LIFE HISTORY

EACH OF US has our own individual histories, families, and life events that broadcast messages like a twenty-four-hour cable news channel. Some of these messages penetrate our conscious minds, while the majority are received by our unconscious and may take years to retrieve and articulate. Elliott recalls that, as a small boy, whenever he expressed sadness or fear, his father tried to talk him out of his feelings. "You're not sad," his dad would say. Or "You don't look like a chicken, so why are you acting so scared?" Without being aware of it, Elliott internalized the message that it was unsafe to reveal his emotions. It wasn't until the near breakup of his marriage—averted by a combination of psychotherapy and meditation—that he finally felt free enough to express his true feelings.

For most of us, life experiences are a rich mix of positive and negative, but evolutionary biologists tell us we have a "negativity bias" that makes us especially alert to danger and threat, lest we get eaten by a tiger (or so our nervous systems tell us). In order to ensure our survival, our brains remember negative events more strongly than positive ones (all the better to recall where the tiger was hiding). So when we're feeling lost or discouraged, it can be very hard to conjure up memories and feelings of happiness and ease.

While this default response is essential to our survival when we're in real danger, it can also be the source of great suffering when we're not. With meditation, however, we can actually retrain our nervous systems away from this fight-or-flight response. We learn to identify our thoughts and feelings for what they are, without getting swept away by them.

MESSAGES FROM OUR CULTURE

FRIENDS RAISED WITH a notion of original sin often tell me that guilt has shadowed them from the time they were very young. Common thoughts include things like, *I was born bad; I was born broken; there is something fundamentally wrong with me.* Even if such concepts weren't part of our religious or family backgrounds, they persist in our culture and can result in a pervasive sense of defeat: nothing I am or do will ever be good enough.

For some, the sin is being born the "wrong" gender, ethnicity, race, or sexual orientation, all of which can lead to feelings of not belonging. These cultural messages not only impede our ability to love and care for ourselves but can inhibit our potential by causing us to lower our expectations and rein in our dreams. At the same time, the opportunities available to us may realistically be diminished because of society's projections onto us. We may even become the target of outright hatred and threats to our safety.

James Baldwin, the late, brilliant, gay African American author, described his process of coming to terms with such messages in his essay "They Can't Turn Back": "It took many years of vomiting up all the filth I'd been taught about myself, and half-believed, before I was able to walk on the earth as though I had a right to be here."

We may also be swamped by the pervasive messages of our materialistic culture, which stresses competition, status, and "success" over character and emotional intelligence. This makes it easy to fall into the lose-lose trap of comparing ourselves to others. But, as psychologist Sonja Lyubomirsky points out in her book *The How of Happiness*, "The more social comparisons you make, the more likely you are to encounter unfavorable comparisons, and the more sensitive you are to social comparisons, the more likely you are to suffer their negative consequences . . . No matter how successful, wealthy, or fortunate we become, there's always someone who can best us."

When we constantly hear that we should be smarter, better connected, more productive, wealthier—you name it—it takes real courage to claim the time and space to follow the currents of our talents, our aspirations, and our hearts, which may lead in a very different direction.

MESSAGES FROM THE MEDIA

HAVE YOU EVER wakened in the morning feeling contented and quiet, and then, within fifteen minutes of checking your phone, felt out of sorts and jealous? Longing for something more?

Many of us now spend as much time immersed in images on a screen as participating in the world outside our devices. Whether subtly or blatantly, ads tell us that our bodies need making over, our clothes just won't do, our living room is a mess, and we're not invited to the right parties—all as a way to sell us more and more. Along the way, what might be a source of pleasure becomes infused with anxiety.

Social activist Jerry Mander hypothesizes that media is deliberately designed to induce self-hatred, negative body image, and dejection, with advertising drummed up—and sold—to offer the cure.

Regardless of the source of these messages, we can become more aware of them. We can see which messages we've adopted as our own beliefs and learn instead to hold them more loosely; in time, we can even replace them with an inquiring mind, an open heart, an enhanced sense of vitality. We may not be able to make the messages disappear, but we can question them. The more we do so, the less intrusive and limiting they become. In turn, we become freer to connect more authentically with others, as well as to our own deepest yearnings.

START WHERE YOU ARE

I HAVE NEVER believed that you must completely love yourself first before you can love another. I know many people who are hard on themselves, yet love their friends and family deeply and are loved in return—though they might have difficulty in receiving that love. But it's hard to sustain love for others over the long haul until we have a sense of inner abundance and sufficiency.

When we experience inner impoverishment, love for another too easily becomes hunger: for reassurance, for acclaim, for affirmation of our worth. Feeling incomplete inside ourselves, we search for others to complete us. But the equation doesn't work that way: we can't gain from others what we're unable to give ourselves.

It's important to recognize that self-love is an unfolding process that gains strength over time, not a goal with a fixed end point. When we start to pay attention, we see that we're challenged daily to act lovingly on our own behalf. Simple gestures of respect—care of the body, rest for the mind, and beauty for the soul in the form of music and art or nature—are all ways of showing ourselves love. Really, all of our actions—from how we respond when we can't fit into our favorite pair of jeans to the choice of foods we eat—can signify self-love or self-sabotage. So can the way we react when a stranger cuts us off in line, a friend does something hurtful, or we get an unwelcome medical diagnosis.

As Maya Angelou said in her book *Letter to My Daughter*, "You may not control all the events that happen to you, but you can decide not to be reduced by them." I started meditation practice, as many do, with the need to turn around that tendency to feel reduced by life.

Still, it takes a special courage to challenge the rigid confines of our accustomed story. It's not that easy to radically alter our views about where happiness comes from, or what brings us joy. But it's eminently possible. We truly can reconfigure how we see ourselves and reclaim the love for ourselves that we're innately capable of. That's why I invite students to set out on this path in the spirit of adventure, instead of feeling that real love is a pass/fail exam that they're scared to take.

Although love is often depicted as starry-eyed and sweet, love for the self is made of tougher stuff. It's not a sappy form of denial. You might still feel rage, desire, and shame like everyone else in the world, but you can learn to hold these emotions in a context of caring.

Real love allows for failure and suffering. All of us have made mistakes, and some of those mistakes were consequential, but you can find a way to relate to them with kindness. No matter what troubles have befallen you or what difficulties you have caused yourself or others, with love for yourself you can change, grow, make amends, and learn. Real love is not about letting yourself off the hook. Real love does not encourage you to ignore your problems or deny your mistakes and imperfections. You see them clearly and still opt to love.

THE COMPASSION MUSCLE

WE BEGIN TO cultivate real love for ourselves when we treat ourselves with compassion. In a sense, self-compassion is like a muscle. The more we practice flexing it, especially when life doesn't go exactly according to plan (a frequent scenario for most of us), the stronger and more resilient our compassion muscle becomes.

Katherine says: "The hardest part of this practice for me has been listening to, feeling, and grieving the intense pain of my child-hood and teen years. Avoiding this pain gradually closed down my life and awareness, but my heart has begun to warm back to life. I'm able to be present in new ways for myself, my husband, my children, and my grandchildren."

When Katherine says her heart has warmed, it's not just a metaphor. As psychologist Kristin Neff (Self-Compassion.org) writes in one of her blog posts, "When we soothe our painful feelings with the healing balm of self-compassion, not only are we changing our mental and emotional experience, we're also changing our body chemistry." She reports on research that suggests while self-criticism triggers increases in blood pressure, adrenaline, and the hormone cortisol—all results of the fight-or-flight response—self-compassion triggers the release of oxytocin, the "bonding hormone," which increases feelings of trust, calm, safety, and generosity.

The starting place for this radical reimagining of love is mindfulness. By sitting quietly and focusing on the steady rhythm of the breath as you draw it in and release it, you create room to relate to yourself with compassion. The breath is the first tool for opening the space between the story you tell yourself about love and your capacity to tap into the deep well of love inside you and all around you.

Nina grew up with rigid parents who thought play was frivolous, so they kept her busy with assigned tasks. And though Nina loved to sing, her mom and dad shamed her because she had less-than-perfect pitch. When I first met Nina at a meditation class, she reported that her life was all demanding work, with no time for play, including singing, her passion. But over many months, she began to experiment with the very things that she'd once been told not to do. She recently wrote me: "I am here to stretch a toe into an area of fear . . . Singing has become a joy—I am learning to play."

Admonishment for play is a message that would cause anyone to approach any feelings of love with fists readied and a clenched heart. It creates fear. It blocks your voice, your life force, and prevents you from showing yourself to the world as you truly are—off-key notes and all.

LOVINGKINDNESS MEDITATION

FOR MANY OF us, real love for ourselves may be a possibility we pretty much gave up on long ago. So as we explore new ways of thinking, we need to be willing to investigate, experiment, take some risks with our attention, and stretch. We are going to try a new approach to this matter of love we may have been closed to, assuming we already know it inside and out.

The practice of lovingkindness is about cultivating love as a transformative strength, enabling us to feel love that is not attached to the illusion of people (including ourselves) being static, frozen, disconnected. As a result, lovingkindness challenges those states that tend to arise when we think of ourselves as isolated from everyone else—fear, a sense of deficiency, alienation, loneliness. This practice forcefully penetrates these states, and it begins, in fact, with befriending—rather than making an enemy out of—ourselves.

Unlike our pop-cultural ideas of love as mushy, related to wanting, owning, and possessing, lovingkindness is open, free, unconditional, and abundant. Lovingkindness is the practice of offering to oneself and others wishes to be happy, peaceful, healthy, strong.

We use the repetition of certain phrases to express these wishes and as the vehicle to change the way we pay attention to ourselves and others. There are three main arenas in which we experiment through lovingkindness meditation:

How do we pay attention? With the practice, we learn to be more fully present and whole in our attention, rather than fragmented or distracted.

What do we pay attention to? If we are fixated on our flaws and the faults of others, without falling into denial, we learn to admit the other side, the good within us, the capacity for change still alive in us even if unrealized or covered over.

Who do we pay attention to? We learn to include those we have tended to exclude, we learn to look at rather than right through those we have previously unconsciously decided do not matter, do not count. The spirit of these wishes is that they connect us all in our common urge toward happiness.

Cultivating lovingkindness for ourselves is the foundation of real love for our friends and family, for new people we encounter in our daily lives, for all beings and for life itself. The classical progression of lovingkindness meditation is that you start with offering loving-kindness to yourself and move on to others with whom you have varying degrees of difficulty. After ourselves, over time we will meditate on someone we admire and respect, then a friend, then a neutral person such as your dry cleaner or a shopkeeper, then a person who is somewhat challenging for you, and then all beings. In this section, we will focus on lovingkindness for ourselves and move on to complete the arc of the practice in the following two sections.

—Traditionally, the phrases used are ones like, "May I be safe," "Be happy," "Be healthy," "Live with ease."

—Some people prefer to say, "May I *feel* safe, *feel* happy . . ." The last phrase, "May I live with ease," means in the things of everyday life, like livelihood and relationships. "May it not be such a struggle."

—Feel free to experiment with these phrases, or replace them altogether with different phrases that might work better for you. Some common replacements are "May I be peaceful" or "May I be filled with lovingkindness" or "May I have ease of heart."

—The phrase needs to be general enough, open enough so that it can be the conduit for paying attention to yourself and others in a different way. The spirit is one of gift-giving, of offering. It's a sense of blessing—we're not goal-setting or parsing areas of self-improvement, like, "May I get better at public speaking." What would happen when we then focused on our neighbor or grandmother? Instead, we're practicing generosity of the spirit with each phrase.

The power of concentration we want to be developing is challenged by constantly needing to think of new phrases for each new recipient. While you shouldn't feel imprisoned by the phrases, it's good to mostly keep the same phrases toward the varied recipients if you can. The aspirations we repeat should be deep and somewhat enduring—rather than something fleeting like, "May I find a good parking space."

INTRODUCTION PRACTICES

Introducing lovingkindness

1. Begin by sitting comfortably. You can close your eyes or not, however you feel most at ease. You can set the time you plan to sit for, using an app or an alarm. If you are newer to meditation, five or ten minutes would be my suggestion. Choose the three or four phrases that express what you most deeply wish for yourself, and begin to repeat them silently.

2. Repeat the phrases, like, "May I be happy," with enough space and enough silence so that it is a rhythm that's pleasing to you. I have a friend who thought he'd get extra credit for saying more phrases—you don't need to be in a rush. Gather all of your attention around one phrase at a time.

3. You don't need to manufacture or fabricate a special feeling. The power of the practice comes from our full, wholehearted presence behind each phrase, from being willing to pay attention to ourselves and others in truthful, though perhaps unaccustomed ways. If you fear sen-

timentality or phoniness, this is an especially important reminder.

4. This is different from affirmations that tell us we are getting better and better, or insist that we're perfect just as we are. If it feels phony, or like you are begging or imploring ("May I please, please be happy already"), remind yourself that it is a practice of generosity—you are giving yourself a gift of loving attention.

5. You may decide it is helpful to coordinate these phrases with the breath, or simply have your mind rest in the phrases.

6. When you find your attention has wandered, see if you can let go of the distraction gently, and return to the repetition of the phrases. Don't worry if it happens a lot.

7. When you feel ready, you can open your eyes.

Receiving lovingkindness

An alternative practice to experiment with is imagining someone who represents the force of love for you. Perhaps they've helped you directly, or perhaps you've never met them but you've been inspired by them from afar. Maybe they exist now or they've existed historically or even mythically. It could be an adult, a child, or even a pet. See if you can bring them here, get a sense of their presence—you might visualize them or say their name to yourself.

Then experience yourself as the recipient of their energy, attention, care, or regard as you silently repeat whatever phrases are expressive of that which you would wish the most for yourself. But say them as though from them to you: "May you be safe," "Be happy," "Be healthy," "Live with ease of heart."

All kinds of different emotions may arise. You may feel gratitude and awe. You might feel shy or embarrassed. Whatever emotion arises, just let it pass through you. Your touchstone is those phrases: "May you be happy," "May you be peaceful," or whatever phrases you've chosen. Imagine your skin is porous and receiving this energy coming in. There's nothing special you need to do to deserve this kind of acknowledgment or care: it is coming simply because you exist.

You can end the session by allowing that quality of lovingkindness and care to flow right back out toward all beings everywhere. That which you received, you can now transform into giving. The quality of care and kindness that does exist in this world can become part of you and part of what you express in return.

And when you feel ready, you can open your eyes and relax.

Being love

When we opened the Insight Meditation Society in February 1976, we didn't have any programming scheduled for the first month. Those of us who were there decided to do a retreat ourselves. I decided to do intensive lovingkindness practice, which I had long wanted to do. Even though I didn't have a teacher to guide me, I relied on my knowledge of the structure of the practice (beginning with offering lovingkindness to yourself, etc.) and began.

I spent the whole first week offering lovingkindness to myself, and I just felt nothing. No bolts of lightning, no great breakthrough moment—it felt pretty dreary. Then something happened to a friend of ours in Boston, so several of us suddenly had to leave the retreat. I was upstairs in one of the bathrooms, getting ready to go, when I dropped a large jar of something on the tile floor, and the jar shattered. To my amazement, I noticed the first thought that came to me was *You are really a klutz, but I love you*. Look at that! I thought. You could have given me anything in the course of that week to persuade me something was happening, and I would have said no. Yet all along, something deep and profound was shifting.

That's how we know if the practice is working or not. Our

efforts likely won't show results in the formal period we dedicate to meditation each day; rather, they will show in our lives, which of course is where it counts. When we make a mistake, when we feel unseen, when we want to celebrate our ability to care. We will see the effects when we meet a stranger, when we face adversity. The results reveal themselves both as a result of our dedicated practice and because lovingkindness is an accessible tool no matter what situation we are in.

The difference between a life laced through with frustration and one sustained by happiness depends on whether it is motivated by self-hatred or by real love for oneself. There are several specific factors that either limit or increase our ability to come from a genuine place of real love for ourselves.

Kaia wrote her thoughts about this to me: "Through experiences of fear, rejection, and pain—the experiences that for most of us are part of a 'normal' childhood and adult life—I eventually shut myself off from that pure love, at least part of the time. I believe that for most of us, a great deal of the time, love feels painful, vulnerable, like a golden nugget we know is contained deep inside of us, but that we feel compelled to guard at all costs. And we're often doing this without even noticing it."

1

THE STORIES WE TELL
OURSELVES

✳

We tell ourselves stories in order to live.

—JOAN DIDION

O UR MINDS ARE WIRED TO create order, a cohesive narrative, and our stories are our anchors. They tell us who we are,
what matters most, what we're capable of, what our lives are all
about.

Something happens to us in childhood—say, a dog bites us—
and suddenly we have a story. We become terrified of all dogs, and
for years afterward, we break into a sweat whenever a dog comes
close. If we pay attention, one day we realize we've spun a story in

our minds about an entire species based on a single incident with a single animal—and that our story is not really true.

The tales we tell ourselves are the central themes in our psyches. If we're the child of an emotionally needy, alcoholic parent, we might conclude—unconsciously—that it's our job to take care of absolutely everyone, even to our own detriment. If as adults we're diagnosed with a serious illness, we may believe it's our fault and create a story around that: We didn't eat right. We stayed too long in a toxic relationship. Until we begin to question our basic assumptions about ourselves and view them as fluid, not fixed, it's easy to repeat established patterns and, out of habit, reenact old stories that limit our ability to live and love ourselves with an open heart.

Fortunately, as soon as we ask whether or not a story is true in the present moment, we empower ourselves to reframe it. We begin to notice that nearly all of our stories can be cast in various lights, depending on our point of view. Sometimes we may be the hero of our story; at other times, the victim.

I think of Jonah, who was the first in his family to attend college. Even the first step of applying was daunting, and once he was admitted, he had to find a way to finance his education himself. That meant juggling long shifts at work and a heavy course load at school. He struggled to keep up in his classes. Still, as he proudly tells his story, the obstacles he overcame were a key to his success. Jonah graduated and got a good job, where he met his partner. A decade after graduation, Jonah says, "Look at me now."

But Jonah might tell his story in a different way, with pain taking a more central role. There would be more memories of lonely nights, feelings of exclusion, worries about being an impostor. Jonah might describe how the world was stacked against him and linger over the people who had slighted him. It would still be a hero's story, but one marked by frustration and bitterness.

Many of the stories we tell ourselves about love are like the painful version of Jonah's story. We're more inclined to regard past losses with self-blame than with compassion. And when it comes to the present, we tend to speculate and fill in the blanks: A friend doesn't call at the appointed hour and we're convinced he's forgotten us, when in fact he had to take his sick child to the doctor. Our boss asks to speak to us and we're convinced we've done something wrong, when instead we're given a new project. Since we're not aware that we're spinning a story, these narratives can contribute to anxiety and depression, while constricting our hope for the future and eating away at our self-worth.

One of my students attributes his painful marriage and divorce, as well as other "failed" relationships, to his own feelings of unworthiness and self-blame. "I am so thin-skinned because I'm beating myself up 24-7," he says. "Had I been more compassionate with myself in my past relationships, perhaps I would've had better coping mechanisms." Through psychotherapy and meditation, this student has learned to question his negative storytelling and tune out the constant chatter of his inner critic.

Diane, whose partner had recently broken off their engagement, immediately blamed herself for being "unlovable," even though she, too, harbored serious doubts about the future of the relationship. But instead of pausing and investigating the source of her story of unlovability with mindfulness and self-compassion, Diane leaped to a negative conclusion carried over from childhood.

If we heard a friend say, "I'm not worth much. I'm not interesting, I've failed at so much, and that's why no one loves me," we would probably leap to her defense. "But I love you," we'd insist. "Your other friends love you, too. You're a good person." Yet so often we don't counter the negative statements that crowd our own minds every day.

Instead, we might ask ourselves: If I look at what's happening through the eyes of love, how would I tell this story?

TAPPING INTO BURIED NARRATIVES

OUR SENSES ARE often the gateway to our stories, triggering memories from long ago. We catch a whiff of fresh blueberry muffins, which reminds us of our childhood—the blueberries growing wild in our garden when the family had a beach house. And then we're gone: we smell the sea, taste the clams we ate sitting on high stools at the boardwalk, and are transported back to that horrible night when Dad got drunk. The sharp memory of that night might bring up the sad thought that Dad probably never really loved us, followed by a leap into the present: *Maybe I'm spoiled for love. Maybe I'll never be loved.*

This process is largely unconscious. The unconscious mind is a vast repository of experiences and associations that sorts things out much faster than the slow-moving conscious mind, which has to work hard to connect the dots. Moreover, the unconscious mind operates with some very powerful biases, and tends to underscore our pain.

In some cases, the limiting stories we have woven about ourselves don't even belong to us. Unconsciously, we may be reliving our mother's anxiety, our father's disappointments, or the unresolved traumas suffered by our grandparents. "Just as we inherit our eye color and blood type, we may also inherit the residue of traumatic events that have taken place in our family," explains therapist Mark Wolynn, author of *It Didn't Start with You*. Wolynn tells the story of a client who suddenly became paralyzed with the fear of being "suffocated" when she turned forty. It was only when she investigated her family history that she discovered that a grandmother whom she'd been told had "died young" of vague causes had actually been put to death in the gas chamber at Auschwitz when she was forty years old.

The idea that traumatic residues—or unresolved stories—can be inherited is groundbreaking. Research in the rapidly developing field of epigenetics—the biological science of alterations in gene expression—shows that traits can be transmitted from one generation to as many as three generations of descendants. For example, a landmark study in Sweden found that a grandparent's experience of either famine or plenty had implications for the life span of the next generation—and the one after that. Another study, this one conducted by Rachel Yehuda, a professor of psychiatry and neuroscience at Mount Sinai Hospital in New York, found that offspring of Holocaust survivors were three times more likely to respond to a traumatic event with post-traumatic stress disorder (PTSD) than children whose parents did not survive the Holocaust. What's more, Yehuda and her team found that the children of pregnant women who were near the World Trade Center when the buildings came down were also more prone to PTSD.

If you think you may be unconsciously living out someone else's story, Wolynn suggests asking yourself—or family members—some key questions. These include: Who died early? Who left? Who was abandoned or excluded from the family? Who died in childbirth? Who committed suicide? Who experienced a significant trauma?

Whether the stories we tell ourselves arise directly from our own life experiences or were unconsciously inherited from previous generations, identifying the source of our personal narratives helps us to release its negative aspects and reframe it in ways that promote wholeness.

REWRITING OUR STORY

AS WE CONSTRUCT our identities, we tend to reinforce certain interpretations of our experiences, such as, "No one was there for me, so I must be unlovable." These interpretations become ingrained in our minds and validated by the heated reactions of our bodies. And so they begin to define us. We forget that we're constantly changing and that we have the power to make and remake the story of who we are. But when we do remember, the results can be dramatic and turn our lives around.

For years, Stephanie struggled with insomnia. When she was in her early thirties, her doctor prescribed a blood-pressure-lowering medication for her persistent migraines. The trouble was, Stephanie already had low blood pressure, and the drug made it drop even further, making her so anxious that she felt as if she would die if she let herself fall asleep. Instead of identifying the real source of the problem, her physician prescribed sleeping pills. By the time Stephanie consulted another doctor (who discontinued the blood pressure medication immediately), she was hooked on sleeping pills—and remained addicted to them for the next twenty years.

"I hated myself for taking them and tried so many times to stop, but I just couldn't," she recalls. "I truly believed that there was something inherently wrong with me and that my body no longer had the capacity to sleep without chemicals. The nights I tried not to take the pills, I'd lie awake for hours, panicking, drenched in sweat, until I finally just gave up and reached for the drug."

But two years ago, when Stephanie started reading news stories about the dangers of sleeping pills, she became determined to stop taking them. She began meditating more regularly and tried every imaginable herbal remedy; still, she struggled and relapsed off and on for months. It wasn't until she identified—and questioned—the story she'd been telling herself about how she couldn't sleep unaided by drugs that she successfully weaned herself off them. "When I finally saw clearly that I'd been held captive by this story that was just a story and not the truth, it was as if a lightbulb went on. For the first time in twenty years, I was able to trust my ability to let go and fall asleep on my own," she says.

Ultimately, we're the only ones who can take a familiar story, one that is encoded in our bodies and minds, and turn it around.

Nancy Napier, a trauma therapist, talks about working with people who have been through what she calls "shock trauma," a huge life disruption—from dangerous situations, like a terrible car accident or plane crash, to more everyday events, like getting laid off or a break up in a relationship that are perceived as huge. The key piece, Napier tells me, is that people's ordinary lives have been destabilized, and their expectations feel like they have been ripped apart. One of the first things she often says to her clients who have experienced trauma is *You survived*. "You'd be amazed at how many people for whom that is a real surprise," she explains. "It's a news flash to the nervous system and psyche."

If I were choosing captions for snapshots of my early life, they would look like this: "Motherless child," "Abandoned," "My mentally ill father," "Raised by first-generation immigrants," "I don't know how to be like everyone else." Pain, upheaval, and fear brought me to seek a new story through meditation.

One of my meditation teachers was an extraordinary Indian woman named Dipa Ma. She became my role model of someone who endured crushing loss and came through it with enormous love. Her whole path of meditation was propelled by loss—first, the deaths of two of her children, then the sudden death of her beloved husband. She was so grief-stricken that she just gave up and went to bed, even though she still had a daughter to raise.

One day her doctor told her, "You're going to die unless you do something about your mental state. You should learn how to meditate." The story is told that when she first went to practice meditation, she was so weak that she had to crawl up the temple stairs in order to get inside.

Eventually, Dipa Ma emerged from her grief with enormous wisdom and compassion, and in 1972, she became one of my central teachers.

One day in 1974, I went to say good-bye to her before leaving India for a brief trip to the United States. I was convinced I'd soon return and spend the rest of my life in India. She took my hand and said, "Well, when you go to America, you'll be teaching meditation."

"No, I won't," I replied. "I'm coming right back."

She said, "Yes, you will."

And I said, "No, I won't. I can't do that."

We went on this way, back and forth.

Finally, she held my gaze and said two crucial things. First, she said, "You really understand suffering, that's why you should teach." This remark was an essential catalyst that enabled me to reframe my story: The years of upheaval and loss were not just something I had to get over but a potential source of wisdom and compassion that could be used to help me help others. My suffering might even be some kind of credential!

The second thing Dipa Ma said was this: "You can do anything you want to do. It's your thinking that you can't do it that's stopping you." What a different slant on my usual story of incapacity, incompleteness, and not being enough! I carried Dipa Ma's farewell message with me back to the States. It set the course for the rest of my life.

To say I am grateful for the things I went through in childhood is a bridge too far for me. But I know those experiences are what allow me to connect to people, heart to heart.

In a similar spirit, Zen teacher Roshi Joan Halifax cautions against trying to convince ourselves to regard childhood traumas as gifts. In a recent talk, she suggested, "Think of them as givens, not gifts." That way there's no pretense or pressure to reimagine painful experiences. If something is a given, we don't deny it or look the other way. We start by acknowledging it, then see how we can have absolutely the best life possible going forward.

TO TRULY LOVE OURSELVES

TO TRULY LOVE ourselves, we must treat our stories with respect, but not allow them to have a stranglehold on us, so that we free our mutable present and beckoning future from the past.

To truly love ourselves, we must open to our wholeness, rather than clinging to the slivers of ourselves represented by old stories. Living in a story of a limited self—to any degree—is not love.

To truly love ourselves, we must challenge our beliefs that we need to be different or inherently better in order to be worthy of love. When we contort ourselves, doggedly trying to find some way to become okay, our capacity to love shrinks, and our attempts to improve ourselves fill the space that could be filled with love.

Maybe we don't need to correct some terrible deficiency. Maybe what we really need is to change our relationship to what is, to see who we are with the strength of a generous spirit and a wise heart. St. Augustine said, "If you are looking for something that is everywhere, you don't need travel to get there; you need love."

$$2$$

THE STORIES OTHERS TELL
ABOUT US

✳

Ultimately . . . it's not the stories that determine
our choices,
but the stories that we continue to choose.

—SYLVIA BOORSTEIN

J UST AS THE STORIES WE tell ourselves shape our experiences, so do the stories others tell about us. They can come with
either a positive or a negative spin, undermine us or support us. And
sometimes they aren't even stories at all, but ideas conveyed by nonverbal signals, such as body language or facial expressions, or even
by a single word or phrase: *shy, withholding, generous, self-absorbed.*
It's a gift when these stories lift us up. They remind us that we matter,
and they reinforce real love for ourselves.

For Melody, the reminder came from a security guard at her high school. Melody had been fighting with her mother, who was on her back because her grades had been falling, and when Melody ended some old friendships to join a rougher crowd, it created even more friction between them. The security guard noticed Melody with her new friends while patrolling the edge of campus where they hung out. One day Melody was walking back to class when he quickened his steps to catch up with her. "*Mija*," he said, "don't you know you're better than that?"

This was pretty much what her mother had been trying to tell her, but her cutting, accusatory tone caused her message to fall into the widening chasm between them. But the security guard's voice was caring, and his words stayed with Melody all that day. Did she want to argue with the idea that she was better? No. In fact, before the guard spoke up, she'd been feeling that no one really saw her—how good she was and how hard she was trying—so why bother anymore? When the security guard showed her that people did see and expect good things from her, she was lifted up. Not long after, Melody pulled away from the rough crowd.

There are so many different ways we can interpret our experiences, based on the cues we internalize from others. Gus was the middle of five brothers and, almost from birth, seemed to have been born in the wrong place. His Montana family loved the outdoors, camping, hunting, and fishing. Gus loved reading and music and hated hiking and roughhousing. As the boys grew older, Gus was the odd kid out, and he could have had a very lonely childhood. But his uncle Don saw him clearly and admired the boy's sensitivity. If he heard someone put Gus down, Uncle Don would intervene: "Don't be so hard on Gus. Gus has a gift." The family came to view Gus as someone unique who should be celebrated for his difference, and Gus grew up seeing himself that way, too.

When our loved ones mirror our goodness and strengths, and

their stories cast us in a positive light, we naturally feel more love for ourselves.

THE WEB OF FAMILY

FAMILIES OFTEN ASSIGN us roles that shape our stories. We may not even remember how we acquired these labels or recall if we chose them for ourselves. And if you have had one bestowed on you, you know that even positive labels can become confining. Someone who has always been "the responsible one" can find herself in deep internal conflict when, on a particular occasion, she doesn't feel like being so responsible. Or "the funny one" who's having a bad day may feel he's letting humanity down because he's not up to fulfilling his role.

My friend Billie talks about the narrative she absorbed as she was growing up: "What is *wrong* with you?" her father often asked. Although Billie's home provided the opportunity for "a lot of wonderful disclosure," she describes it as a place where "a lot of bullying banter took place, as well." As a result, Billie developed her own brand of self-ridicule. She now refers to her dad's characteristic question ("What's wrong with you?") as her "first heartbreak, followed by deeper blows and losses" throughout her teens and young adulthood.

After internalizing this negative self-image, Billie resorted to substance abuse to relieve her pain. It was only after many years that she joined a recovery program where she found a new community— one that told a very different story about her. "One fortunate day, in my thirty-second year on earth, providence blew a blessing all the way across the universe, and it landed squarely on me," she recalls. "I fell in with some people who had found a better way to live; a community of recovering addicts who had experiences that reflected my own. The value of them sitting with me, day after day, was without parallel. They reached out, reached in, and helped me heal. They paid quiet, dedicated attention to me, and that taught me to pay the same kind of attention to myself."

In the group, Billie was a person with innate value, someone who could help others. She found that this new story helped strengthen her growing appreciation for herself. As with any new habit, adopting a revised view of oneself can be difficult and takes practice. But by committing to the group and the day in, day out work of recovery, Billie says, "I learned tenderness toward myself and was able to reach out tenderly to others who were suffering. I have been able to find contentment and gratitude in many things and for many years now."

Sometimes the story a family member tells about us reflects only a single aspect of our character, yet unconsciously, we embrace it as the whole truth. Kathy's mother started calling her a "tough old broad" when she was a teenager. It was true that the circumstances of their life together had been tough and that Kathy had responded with grit and discipline beyond her years. But the label always felt like an insult to Kathy—a limitation, not a compliment. How could she allow herself to be vulnerable or tender? How could she love herself? Who would want to love a "tough old broad"?

Yet there was another, equally true story that I could tell about Kathy's vulnerability and empathy. A single oft-repeated phrase ("tough old broad") had led Kathy to define herself with—or defend herself against—a very limited set of characteristics. Her identity had solidified around that story, even though the world did not always call on her to be tough—and even though she in fact did not respond to all situations with toughness.

At one time in Kathy's life, being a young "tough old broad" had been a brilliant adaptive mechanism, but it wasn't a healthy way for her to see herself forever. That's why we must repeatedly test the limits of our story, to prevent it from becoming solid, to create some give, some stretch, some room for revision. When our narrative is flexible, each and every moment offers a fresh opportunity to welcome all aspects of our being. Kathy came to appreciate that she had been tough when necessary—and she could be tough again if it was required—but that toughness was not the whole of her.

THE JUDGMENT OF FRIENDS

BEN TELLS THE story of a second-grade playdate that shattered his confidence and changed his narrative about his family. "At recess, I was friendly with a kid named Justin, so my mother suggested inviting him over one day after school," Ben recounts. "I didn't know much about his family background—when you're seven, you don't really pay attention to such things. But it turned out that Justin came from a very wealthy family and lived in a big house in a fancy neighborhood. The day he came over, he just stood outside our modest rented brick duplex and said, with a look of horror on his face, 'Ugh, *this* is where you live?'

"I'll never forget it," Ben says now. "I was devastated. Until that moment, I believed my home and family were perfect. We were happy. We had plenty of food on the table. My father worked for the post office, and my mother taught kindergarten. But after Justin's remark, doubt and shame crept in. I felt as if there was something fundamentally wrong with us, especially me, which took years to get over."

When we believe a wounding story, our whole world is diminished. It's as though someone suddenly turns off all the lights, and we lose faith in our dreams, as well as in our capacity to love and be loved. If we accept it as true, that one story can plant seeds of jealousy, resentment, anxiety, and depression that we struggle with for years to come.

Sometimes, though, the perspective of a friend can help us see our behavior more clearly and restores our foundering faith in ourselves. One of my students, Julia, feels profound gratitude for her friend's caring but honest assessment of Julia's relationships with men.

"One of my female friends has been honest with me in how she perceives I behave romantically," Julia explains. "She wants me to treat myself better. Seeing her insight and pain on my behalf has pushed me to regard myself differently. She's not trying to guilt-trip me. She just wants me to care for myself in the way she thinks I deserve. Seeing how deeply she loves me and wants to protect me makes me want to love and protect myself more."

Taking in another's criticism, even when it's offered out of love, requires courage. Had Julia reacted to her friend's comments defensively, not only would the friendship have likely suffered, she might have continued to relate to men in ways that were disrespectful to herself.

Today, with social media as a primary tool of communication, there's more opportunity than ever before to learn what others think of us. Sometimes what we hear is positive and affirming, but too often it's not. Internet bullying and smear campaigns spread like wildfire and can do irreparable harm: 52 percent of kids report having been bullied online, while about 20 percent of those who've been targeted contemplate suicide, and one in ten attempt it. Given the proliferation of cell phones and social media usage among young people (the average age for obtaining a mobile phone is between eleven and twelve), the viral spread of damaging rumors and accusations has become a disturbing social phenomenon. And of course many adults are flamed and shamed, too.

If we truly love ourselves, do we avoid sharing anything that is deeply personal, or do we publicly stand up for who we are and what we believe? What approach best reflects your care and concern for yourself?

OUR RACE, RELIGION, social class, ethnicity, or gender and sexual identity are all constructs that imply different things about us to others, depending on their conditioning. That's why it's so meaningful—and essential for the growth of our society—when limiting, negative stories undergo revision on a mass scale.

Sometimes a dramatic shift in a society's projections can confer a sense of legitimacy and belonging that once seemed unimaginable. Such was the case with the Supreme Court's landmark 2015 ruling on same-sex marriage, which has liberated gay men and women in ways that far surpass the freedom to walk down the aisle and legally say "I do." *New York Times* columnist Frank Bruni movingly described his own response, at age fifty, to the ruling:

> Following a few extraordinary years during which one state after another legalized same-sex marriage, the Supreme Court rules that all states must do so, that the Constitution demands it, that it's a matter of "equal dignity in the eyes of the law," as Justice Anthony Kennedy writes.
>
> I can speak for a 50-year-old man who expected this to happen but still can't quite believe it, because it seemed impossible when he was young, because it seemed implausible even when he was a bit older, and because everything is different now, or will be. . . .
>
> And that's because the Supreme Court's decision wasn't simply about weddings. It was about worth. From the highest of this nation's perches, in the most authoritative of this nation's voices, a majority of justices told a minority of Americans that they're normal and that they belong—fully, joyously and with cake.

Around the same time that the Supreme Court issued its ruling, Paul Brandeis Raushenbush, a gay clergyman who had already been with his partner for thirteen years and married for almost two, commented on the ambivalence of religious authorities who had inched toward support, only to later withdraw it. "The idea that some random people are debating my life and my love now seems strange and insulting," he wrote in *The Huffington Post*. "While I will continue to pay professional attention to these debates, as a member of the media and a person who cares about justice for all people, on a personal level I couldn't give a shit what these people think about my life. I'm not going to give them that power . . . I know I was beautifully made by God and that my relationship . . . is blessed."

Still, whether gay marriage is denounced by religious leaders or upheld by the Supreme Court, the conversation never would have taken place without decades of prior struggle by members of the LGBT community—often at great risk to their safety—to openly identify as gay. Only then could the issue of marriage equality be put forth.

For any marginalized group to change the story that society tells about them takes courage and perseverance. I've seen low-wage workers in the United States bravely face the possibility of losing the only jobs they have (however poorly compensated), standing up to their bosses and telling them, "We're human beings with innate worth who deserve to be treated as such and paid a living wage." For many of these workers, it has been both frightening and empowering to take action.

Sometimes the stories we internalize originate not just in our family, our community, or the wider social sphere but a combination of all three. When the messages are negative, they can result in an emotional pileup of pain and suffering that requires time, awareness, and an intentional practice of self-love to disentangle.

Trudy Mitchell-Gilkey, an African American Buddhist lay disciple and mindfulness-based psychotherapist in Takoma Park,

Maryland, grew up the youngest of thirteen children in a relatively poor household in rural Arkansas. Early in life, Trudy says she absorbed the message from her early childhood suffering: "I had little worth compared to those from better homes and gardens," she explains. Although within her family Trudy says she felt plenty invisible at times, when she entered first grade at her town's newly integrated elementary school, she was too visible—in a bad way. Trudy suffered from blatant discrimination and physical assault, and after being cast in a role in the school play, she was told she wouldn't be allowed to participate. She knew it was because she was black. "The first story I was told when I ventured out into the world was, 'You're not really a whole person,'" she reflects.

It wasn't until she got an A+ on a writing assignment in tenth grade that she caught a glimpse of her inherent worth. "My teacher wrote in bright red pen, 'I love the way you write!'" Trudy recalls. "That teacher was the first white person who gave me a lasting, positive reflection of myself, and those six words changed the course of my life." Yet she still needed to qualify her experience: "When you've had so much hatred festering in your heart from adventitious forces, it takes more than one person saying you matter to clear up all the darkness inside."

Trudy had other important mentors along the way, including a friend from church who helped her see that she "could confront all this suffering and get beyond it. Talking to her blew open the door," Trudy says, "and I saw that I had the capacity to be somewhat present with suffering—my own and the suffering of others—and to transform it." She earned a master's degree in social work a few years later and, soon after, began practicing psychotherapy.

Still, early in her psychotherapy career and without a refuge that was yet secure, one year, in the throes of loss and grief, she felt suicidal. In a moment of grace, when she was sitting in her car in a garage with the motor running, she received a phone call from a caring therapist. Trudy turned off the engine so she could hear what the woman had to say. Later on, another moment of grace occurred when Trudy was writing a suicide note. She says, "I had given myself about thirty days off work to finish the suicide note, which somehow went from lines to paragraphs to chapters in a book that I decided I needed to write in order to adequately explain my death to my very young daughter. Oddly enough, by the time I had finished the first draft, I felt a deep sense of peace and calm, as if my life suddenly had become just a little more workable. I was fortunate that a good friend had introduced me to yoga, and while in the corpse pose, I had felt a similar sense of peace and calm unlike I'd ever experienced before in this life. And so, having gone from feeling suicidal to writing the suicide note that saved my life, I was ready to find a way to live again."

Seeking the same sense of peace she'd felt during yoga, Trudy found a meditation class and began practicing in earnest. "Going to the class is what lit the match. The Buddha's teachings were the fuel," she says. In time, a teacher—Tara Brach—invited Trudy to train to become a meditation teacher herself.

She adds that her sense of "little worth" was further transformed through the skillful means of working with therapy clients. "By seeing the universal suffering in others and reaching in deep to help them love themselves better, I was healed by the same meditation on lovingkindness that I was offering them."

It's not easy to know who we are underneath the stories others tell about us and the labels society heaps upon us. To do so implies a willingness to take risks, to step into the unknown and choose courage over fear. When we do, as Trudy discovered, a door blows wide open. We can free ourselves from the old stories that have reduced us and allow real love for ourselves to blossom.

REFLECTION

TRY RETELLING YOUR story as a hero's journey, where you survived hard times and failures to become the stronger and wiser person you are now. Try telling it as a series of random events over which you had no control. Then rewrite the story. How did your choices shape who you are now?

Are you living someone else's story? What would happen if you declared independence? Are you fighting someone else's fight? Does loyalty to that person keep you from choosing happiness now?

Does the situation bring up parts of your story? Does your story help you in the present, or does it make things harder?

WELCOMING OUR EMOTIONS

*

REAL LOVE FOR OURSELVES BY definition includes every aspect of our lives—the good, the bad, the difficult, the challenging past, the uncertain future, as well as all the shameful, upsetting experiences and encounters we'd just as soon forget. This doesn't mean we have to celebrate everything that's ever happened to us or write thank-you notes to people who have hurt us. But, like it or not, the emotional residue of our experiences is part of who we are.

If we resist any aspect of it, we feel like impostors, unreal and split off from ourselves.

If we neglect our authentic selves, we risk being dominated by others, instead of being in loving relationships with them. But when we open our hearts to the breadth of our experiences, we learn to tune into our needs, unique perceptions, thoughts, and feelings in the present moment, without being trapped by judgments based on the expectations of others. That is how we eventually sense our own worthiness.

This kind of integration arises from intimacy with our emotions and our bodies, as well as with our thoughts. It arises from holding all that we know and want and fear and feel in a space of awareness and self-compassion. If we reject or resent our feelings, we won't have access to that kind of intimacy and integration. And if we define ourselves by each of the ever-changing feelings that cascade through us, how will we ever feel at home in our own bodies and minds?

When I first began my meditation practice, I was only eighteen years old, and although I knew I was deeply unhappy, I wasn't aware of the separate threads of grief, anger, and fear at play inside me. Then, through meditation, I began to look within more clearly and to detect the various components of my sorrow. What I saw unsettled me so much that at one point I marched up to my teacher, S. N. Goenka, and said accusingly, "I never used to be an angry person before I began meditating!"

Of course I was hugely angry; my mother had died, I barely knew my father, I felt wrenchingly abandoned. Meditation had allowed me to uncover the strands of that pain. When I blamed Mr. Goenka and meditation itself as the causes of my pain, he simply laughed—then reminded me of the tools I now had to deal with the difficult feelings I used to keep hidden, even from myself. I could begin to forge a new relationship with my emotions—to find the middle place between denying them and being overwhelmed by them.

TAKING REFUGE INSIDE

MINDFULNESS MEDITATION CAN be a refuge, but it is not a practice in which real life is ever excluded. The strength of mindfulness is that it enables us to hold difficult thoughts and feelings in a different way—with awareness, balance, and love. This, rather than trying to annihilate painful feelings or eradicate negative patterns of thinking, is what heals us. Actress Daphne Zuniga came to a realization similar to mine during a ten-day silent retreat.

Before arriving at the retreat center, Daphne had been meditating on her own and experiencing, in her words, "a very heightened state of happiness and openheartedness." But by day four, she recalls:

"I was sure something was going wrong. Reeling with insecurity and loneliness, I thought maybe our esteemed teachers were not so talented. I remember sitting in the room where we put on our shoes; jackets hung on the walls, shoes in cubbies below, water bottles and hat-filled shelves above. All of a sudden, I had a flashback to being a little girl in elementary school, at those same cubbies, and I was overwhelmed with shame. My parents had divorced when I was six, so Dad left, and it made sense to me then that I was not good enough to have both a mommy and a daddy, because there were many things wrong with me.

"Tears came to my eyes. My body felt just like it did back then, a rock of immovable shame in my stomach. I looked around with my head lowered at people's feet, legs, and jackets. I wondered if they felt what I was feeling? Then I thought, what if all along it was true? I wasn't worthy of what others had. What if I will always be alone because I'm not worthy of more? I left the meditation hall feeling the dread that the retreat couldn't help me with my faulty-at-the-core self.

"I went to bed crying, facing the wall with the blanket pulled around me tightly, the way I had in my bunk bed when my mom and dad were fighting in the other room."

The next day, Daphne asked to see me. "How are you?" I asked. Daphne was only too ready to let me hear it!

"I have never been so lonely in my life! This is crazy. All these loving, trusting people around me, we all came here trusting you, and I just keep having painful negative feelings about myself! I am a happy person! Before I came here, I was waking up smiling! I was in a state of real joy and love for everyone." She was crying now, letting it all pour out of her. "I mean, you can't just take all these people and make us feel this way. It really hurts."

I gently pushed the box of Kleenex across the table toward her. "You're right on course," I said.

Daphne was incredulous. "What do you mean? I was meditating every day and feeling this flow of ecstasy, like I've never felt before. I had so much love for all of life."

So I told her, "If you think of meditation practice as building a house, you began in the attic. Now you're starting at the foundation."

Daphne wasn't too sure, but I encouraged her to just keep going.

She stayed at the retreat. She stayed with the feelings and kept bringing her attention back to her breathing and to her feet as she walked, one step in front of the other. Daphne told me, "And I began to notice something remarkable. The quality with which I noticed my thoughts and feelings arise and disappear became very gentle and compassionate, like a mother watching her beloved child. A mother interested in each barely perceivable breath, a mother who wasn't going anywhere. Apparently, I *was* enough, I was worthy of attention by just breathing. That presence became stronger as the loneliness faded. Even when memories or sensations of a familiar loneliness would come, they were just memories. I lovingly noticed them come, then pass.

"*I'm going to protect you, precious one*, I thought. *I'm going to protect you.*"

OPENING THE DOOR TO FEELINGS

IF WE TRY to block off or deny a big part of what we experience, our wakeful, connected relationship to ourselves gets sharply whittled down. How then can we possibly feel alive?

Awareness and love are qualities we can rely on moment to moment. They help us find ourselves when we've lost our way. They protect us during whatever storms or blowouts we undergo. And they help us let go of our preconceived notions of what we should feel or how life should be at any given time.

In June 2015, shortly after the massacre of African American churchgoers in Charleston, South Carolina, I co-led a retreat for people of color. One evening in a question-and-answer session, a woman named Erika spoke to the group about her experience during meditation. "I imagined I was having a dinner party and decided to invite all the different parts of myself that I usually try to avoid," she said. "It was hard, but I just had to let profound sadness sit at that table and fully acknowledge it was there, not just try to get on with my life." As she spoke, a chorus of soft weeping rippled through the meditation hall.

When, like Erika, we welcome every emotion with mindfulness, we can live with our feelings as they move through us, without getting defined by them.

Interestingly, a recent study underscores the importance of letting ourselves feel *all* of our emotions, including those we usually consider "negative," such as anger and sadness. Using the biodiversity of ecosystems in the natural world as a model, the researchers found evidence for the notion that *emodiversity*—their word for the whole spectrum of human emotions—plays a key role in our overall health and well-being.

This idea was beautifully rendered in the Pixar animated film *Inside Out*, in which the emotions of an eleven-year-old girl named Riley are personified by avatars who live in the girl's mind and reflect her moods. They are: Joy, Fear, Anger, Disgust, and Sadness. At the start of the movie, Joy dominates the action. But when Riley's family moves across the country and she must adapt to a new school, as well as the loss of her best friend, the other emotions start to jockey for power, especially Sadness. It isn't until Riley allows Sadness— who trudges around in a blue dress—a chance to express herself that she begins to heal and enjoy the promise of her new life.

Many years ago, during an intensive retreat at the Insight Meditation Society (IMS), I had my own experience of waking up to the importance of welcoming all emotions as they arise. A few months earlier, a close friend had committed suicide, and I was filled with sadness and grief. Still, I was reluctant to let myself experience the full force of my feelings or share them with the Burmese monk leading the retreat, Sayadaw U Pandita. In my mind, I saw him as an ascetic who had left the world of messy emotions behind. I believed I should be stoic, too, the way I imagined him to be, and tried to refrain from feeling the depth of my sorrow.

One day during an interview, after I shyly told him about my sadness, Sayadaw U Pandita asked me if I'd been crying.

I tried to contour my response to what I thought he'd want to hear. "Just a little bit," I said.

His reply shocked me: "Every time you cry, you should cry your heart out. That way you'll get the best release."

After that conversation, I let myself cry fully. Eventually, the sadness moved through me. Once I allowed it in, I was no longer held captive by it.

HEALING IS AN INSIDE JOB

WHEN EMOTIONS ARE long held and extremely complex, it sometimes takes years for them to enter fully into awareness. Until then, they cannot be released and healed.

This was true for my friend Barbara Graham, whose memoir, *Camp Paradox*, describes coming to terms with an experience that had taken place decades earlier.

"It took me thirty years to understand that what took place between my camp counselor and me the summer I was fourteen—and she was twenty-eight—was sexual abuse. It took another decade for me to forgive her for touching me and—hardest of all—to stop blaming myself," Barbara told me.

"When at last I understood what had happened, I was stricken by a grief that had been there all along but which I never knew I carried," she added. "I wept uncontrollably. After a time, grief gave way to rage that had also gone undetected. Before then, I had felt only great shame, believing there was something intrinsically wrong with me. The shame was accompanied by a kind of numbness whenever I thought about that summer at camp, but mostly I tried not to think about it.

"It's clear to me now that both the grief and the rage were necessary. I needed to experience the internal hurricane that had been bound up inside me for so long."

As Barbara later discovered, experiencing the raw power of her emotions was a critical step toward realizing love for herself. Sometimes, we find that we must go further—by speaking the truth not only to ourselves but to others, as well. We may feel the need to take action, pursue justice, or seek to make amends of some kind. But even when opening to our emotions is just the first step, it is the foundation of real love and happiness.

CHAPTER 3 PRACTICES

RAIN: An exercise for welcoming your emotions

Most people who come to meditation are looking for respite from what is sometimes called the "monkey mind"—the perpetual, hyperactive (and often self-destructive) whirl of thoughts and feelings everyone undergoes. But the truth is that meditation does not eradicate mental and emotional turmoil. Rather, it cultivates the space and gentleness that allow us intimacy with our experiences so that we can relate quite differently to our cascade of emotions and thoughts. That different relationship is where freedom lies.

RAIN is an acronym for a practice specifically geared to ease emotional confusion and suffering. When a negative or thorny feeling comes up, we pause, remember the four steps cued by the letters, and begin to pay attention in a new way.

R: RECOGNIZE. It is impossible to deal with an emotion—to be resilient in the face of difficulty—unless we acknowledge that we're experiencing it. So the first step is simply to notice what is coming up. Suppose you've had a conversation with a friend that leaves you feeling queasy or agitated. You don't try to push away or ignore your discomfort. Instead, you look more closely. *Oh*, you might say to yourself, *this feels like anger*. Then this might be followed quickly by another thought: *And I notice I am judging myself for being angry*.

A: ACKNOWLEDGE. The second step is an extension of the first—you accept the feeling and allow it to be there. Put another way, you give yourself permission to feel it. You remind yourself that you don't have the power to successfully declare, "I shouldn't have such hateful feelings about a friend," or "I've got to be less sensitive." Sometimes I ask students to imagine each thought and emotion as a visitor knocking at the door of their house. The thoughts don't live there; you can greet them, acknowledge them, and watch them go. Rather than trying to dismiss anger and self-judgment as "bad" or "wrong," simply rename them as "painful." This is the entry into self-compassion—you can see your thoughts and emotions arise and create space for them even if they are uncomfortable. You don't take hold of your anger and fixate on it, nor do you treat it as an enemy to be suppressed. It can simply be.

I: INVESTIGATE. Now you begin to ask questions and explore your emotions with a sense of openness and curiosity. This feels quite different from when we are fueled by obsessiveness or by a desire for answers or blame. When we're caught up in a reaction, it's easy to fixate on the trigger and say to ourselves, "I'm so mad at so-and-so that I'm going to tell everyone what he did and destroy him!" rather than examining the emotion itself. There is so much freedom in allowing ourselves to cultivate curiosity and move closer to a feeling, rather than away from it. We might explore how the feeling manifests itself in our bodies and also look at what the feeling contains. Many strong emotions are actually intricate tapestries woven of various strands. Anger, for example, commonly includes moments of sadness, helplessness, and fear. As we get closer to it, an uncomfortable emotion becomes less opaque and solid. We focus less on labeling the discomfort and more on gaining insight. Again, we do not wallow, nor do we repress. Remember that progress doesn't mean that the negative emotions don't come up. It's that instead of feeling hard as steel, they become gauzy, transparent, and available for investigation.

N: NON-IDENTIFY. In the final step of RAIN, we consciously avoid being defined by (identified with) a particular feeling, even as we may engage with it. Feeling angry with a particular person, in a particular conversation, about a particular situation is very different from telling yourself, "I am an angry person and always will be." You permit yourself to see your own anger, your own fear, your own resentment—whatever is there—and instead of spiraling down into judgment ("I'm such a terrible person"), you make a gentle observation, something like, "Oh. This is a state of suffering." This opens the door to a compassionate relationship with yourself, which is the real foundation of a compassionate relationship with others.

We cannot will what thoughts and feelings arise in us. But we *can* recognize them as they are—sometimes recurring, sometimes frustrating, sometimes filled with fantasy, many times painful, always changing. By allowing ourselves this simple recognition, we begin to accept that we will never be able to control our experiences, but that we can transform our relationship to them. This changes everything.

MEETING THE INNER CRITIC

✳

AN ARTIST NAMED JOSEPHINE DESCRIBED a recent rendezvous with her inner critic this way: "Some mornings when I look in the mirror, I feel my inner critic standing on my shoulder pointing out my many physical flaws and how poorly I am aging. And my appearance is just the starting point. I picture her holding a great long list written in thick calligraphy on ancient parchment, a list so comprehensive that it includes my moral lapses, blown opportunities, weaknesses, and embarrassing moments stretching back to grade school. The recitation of flaws is an oral tradition in my family, passed down across the generations like family heirlooms."

The inner voices that tell us, "You aren't good enough," are a huge obstacle to connecting fully to ourselves and feeling fully loved. We may sometimes argue with those inner voices, but when we feel disconnected from ourselves or suffering from loneliness, it's easy to fall prey to them. What's more, resisting their hurtful messages can be especially challenging in a culture that emphasizes individualism, ambition, competition, striving, greed, and perfectionism. But regardless of whether we believe or resist these messages, our in-house critic can keep us imprisoned by our own limiting thoughts.

Josephine hasn't banished her inner critic, but practicing mindfulness has loosened the critic's hold on her. Mindfulness has opened up the space between her authentic self and her critic, enabling her to give less credit to the critic's incessant negativity. Like Josephine, we can change our relationship to our experiences and feelings simply by becoming aware of them. We can begin to let go.

Lilah likes to think of working with the critic as a kind of ongoing experiment. "When I meditate regularly," she says, "I'm better at noticing when self-deprecating or critical thoughts come. Then I ask myself, 'Would I talk like that to a friend?' Or, 'What would I say if a friend was being so self-critical?' Or, 'How would I treat a younger version of myself?'" In each case, Lilah's investigation of her habitual negative thinking helps her to identify and disengage from her inner critic.

RECOGNIZING THE CRITIC

THIS PRACTICE IS really about communicating with the inner critic, and, as for Lilah, the first step is to catch that voice when it appears. We notice that the critic lives in a world of absolutes, with little room for nuance or gray areas. Her favorite words are *should*, *always*, and *never*, and blame is her operating system. "You've blown it, you *always* do." "You *should* just give up." "You're so different, no one will *ever* love you." "You're so flawed, you'll *never* be able to help yourself, let alone anybody else." Instead of creating a wide and open space for embracing our lives, the inner critic causes us to question our worth and collapse in on ourselves.

For some, the inner critic is a specific voice from the past—your mother, your aunt, a child, the boss who fired you. My friend Joseph Goldstein still remembers the first-grade teacher who gave him a big red F in cutting and pasting. (This was in the days when you mixed flour and water to make paste, and Joseph's work was apparently very messy.)

A friend or stranger may make an offhand remark that we take so deeply into our bodies and minds that they become part of our identities. And if, as in Josephine's case, the critical voices have been passed down "like family heirlooms," the identification goes even deeper. I have a friend who hears the scornful voice of her long-dead mother—a woman who revered thinness above all human attributes—when she gains even a few pounds. Paradoxically, at times, such critical voices may even comfort us by linking us to our past and to the most important people in our lives. The judgments of those we loved or admired are part of our story, and, if we don't spot them when they arise, they become the judgments we project on others, as well as ourselves.

Mindfulness helps us see the addictive aspect of self-criticism—a repetitive cycle of flaying ourselves again and again, feeling the pain anew. The inner critic may become a kind of companion in our suffering and isolation. As long as we judge ourselves harshly, it can feel as if we're making progress against our many flaws. But in reality, we're only reinforcing our sense of unworthiness.

Yet when we start to pay attention, we notice how quickly the critic jumps in, even when something good happens. If people befriend us, our critic may whisper that if they only knew how insecure and defective we are, they wouldn't stick around for long. Or say you've just run a marathon. Are you celebrating the fact that you trained, ran, and finished? Or are you upbraiding yourself for being the last person to cross the finish line?

One student told me that shortly after the birth of her second child she went into a tailspin of self-judgment because her house was messy and she wasn't keeping up her appearance or getting to the ironing. The noise of her self-abuse was so loud that it was more than a week before she realized she was comparing herself to her mother, a woman who always looked put together and kept a spotless home despite having two children—but she also happened to have a housekeeper who came in every day. Comparison is one of the critic's favorite weapons. Luckily, mindfulness is so much wiser and more robust than our inner critic.

THE POWER OF STARTING OVER

STILL, WHILE UNDER the tyranny of the critic, we believe that self-love depends on constant striving, success, and the love and admiration of others. In other words, we'll be lovable only when we get that promotion, master public speaking, drop fifteen pounds, and never lose our temper, exhibit fear, or cry in front of our children.

Burdened by such impossible standards, learning to treat ourselves lovingly may at first feel like a dangerous experiment. Students ask me, "If I constantly practice self-acceptance, aren't I just allowing myself to be lazy?" The key here is to recognize the difference between self-preoccupation and love. Often when we believe we are practicing self-control or self-discipline, we're actually confining ourselves inside an overly analytical, self-conscious mental chamber. This precludes us from giving and receiving love both from others and ourselves.

Though it may seem productive to cling to the voice of the inner critic in a culture that extols self-discipline and control, it turns out that the reverse is true. Studies show that just as stress causes our cortisol levels to rise, catalyzing our fight-or-flight response, self-criticism initially can make us feel revved up and motivated. But we're not energized sustainably, not connected to our creativity and self-trust. Over time, the critic's voice saps our energy, leaving us depleted, frozen, and afraid.

I remember a daylong class on lovingkindness I taught shortly after the recession hit in 2008. Many of the students attending had lost their jobs, and their worlds had been shattered. But it was hard for them to see this as anything but a personal defeat brought on by some failing of their own. One man's sense of humiliation was so overwhelming that it was as if there was no such thing as a world-wide recession.

This is not to say that he, or any of us, could not learn or do things differently. But self-blame and humiliation lead to passivity, not intelligent awareness and resolve. Taking responsibility for ourselves doesn't mean ignoring the circumstances of our lives. Instead, it inspires us to recognize a situation for what it is, then plot a new course of action.

The highly competitive world of sports models the difference between punishing blame and the wise use of energy. Although many coaches have famously berated their players to get them to perform, that approach simply doesn't work: in his book, *The Mindful Athlete*, mindfulness teacher George Mumford writes, "I came to realize that you couldn't solve problems with the same consciousness that you created them . . . It's only in changing your consciousness that you can solve problems and transform your game, whatever it is and wherever you're playing it." Mumford has taught mindfulness to the championship Chicago Bulls and Los Angeles Lakers, and now teaches the New York Knicks in addition to individual athletes. He recalls a golfer who "would lose it every time he made a mistake, his performance going from bad to worse because of his own internal negative self-talk." Fortunately, mindfulness taught him to relax on and off the golf course.

Mindfulness allows us to shift the angle on our story and to remember that we have the capacity to learn and change in ways that are productive, not self-defeating.

MANAGING YOUR INNER CRITIC

WHEN I TALK about the inner critic, people often say their goal is to silence it or knock it out of their heads. Although this is natural, it's not the most realistic or skillful approach. It sounds so violent, as if the only way to handle criticism is to tape the critic's mouth shut or banish him or her to solitary confinement. Yet when we direct a lot of hostile energy toward the inner critic, we enter into a losing battle.

My colleague Mark Coleman, meditation teacher and author of the book *Make Peace with Your Mind*, recounts, "Sometimes in my work with meditation students I find they need remarkably little nudging to make a radical shift in relation to their critic. One student comes to mind, a successful attorney in her forties. She was in a healthy relationship, financially stable, and living a relatively balanced and engaged life. Yet she felt deeply troubled. She lived with the nagging feeling of dissatisfaction, as if she wasn't doing enough, trying enough, succeeding enough.

"As the weeks went by, it became clear that she'd never really identified the fact that there was an insistent critical voice in her head. Although she was flourishing in her personal and work life, she was still living with an unacknowledged inner judge. No wonder something was casting a gray cloud over all her achievements! When I brought this to her attention, it was as if a lightbulb had suddenly switched on. The woman behind the curtain was revealed and she realized she could bring discernment to her constant inner criticism, and not be so caught in it. The voice had become so familiar it was like white noise, except that drone had a detrimental impact on her well-being.

"I suggested she could use her mindfulness training to identify the critic and see her remarks for what they were: just thoughts, unconnected to the reality of her life. Several months later, she reported that the critic still twittered away at times, but the volume was much lower, and she had ceased to care about what he had to say. She had found some genuine freedom and was able to enjoy the blessings in her life.

"When students ask me how to handle their inner critic, I often suggest, 'Make her a nice cup of tea and suggest she take a nap. She's tired, and it's been a long day. Going over and over those negative thoughts must be exhausting. She's beginning to repeat herself, a sure sign she needs a rest.'"

This gentle approach to the critic immediately diminishes her power. Does this mean that you are going to forever silence your negative thoughts? No, that's not likely. But you are going to be able to deal with them differently.

When you lull the inner critic into taking a nap, you're in charge—not her. You might still feel some anxiety arising and be stung by her critical voice, but you won't be tensing for a fight. You will strengthen your trust that you can learn from your mistakes and start over. This helps to convey a sense of peace or wholeness despite imperfection.

Another useful technique is to give the inner critic a persona—a name and perhaps a wardrobe. (Josephine gave her critic a "stern, black, schoolmarmish dress.") I named my own inner critic Lucy, after a *Peanuts* cartoon I saw years ago. In it, Lucy was telling Charlie Brown, "The problem with you is that you're you." Ah, yes.

That Lucy-dominant voice had been so strong in my early life. Through meditation practice I've learned to respond with, "Hi,

Lucy," or, "Chill out, Lucy." This way I avoid overreacting ("You're right, Lucy, I'm worthless," or, "Oh my God, I've been meditating for so long, I've spent so much money on therapy—how appalling that she's still here!") Instead, I give Lucy a nice cup of tea and she just sits there calmly.

I told that story to a group I was teaching, and a man responded that he'd adopted a similar technique through work in Al-Anon. He'd personified his inner critic as a punk rocker, a character he wouldn't take so seriously. Another man told me his inner critic was a forbidding judge in full regalia. Have some fun with this! See your inner critic as a crabby old relative coming for a visit. Sigh at his antics, or settle her down with tea, and spend a moment wishing that they themselves were more able to enjoy their lives.

REFLECTION

THE NEXT TIME your inner critic starts on you, take a step back to inquire:

–Does your critic have a voice or face? Whose?

–What happens if you thank your critic for worrying about you, but say you're just fine for now?

–Is your critic keeping you from trying something you might enjoy?

CHAPTER 4 PRACTICES

Remembering your goodness

If you find yourself ruminating on the things you regret and the mistakes you've made, try this exercise. It will help you redirect your attention and remember goodness within. The point is not to deny your mistakes, but if you keep rehearsing them, analyzing them, creating stories around them, you're simply reinforcing the pain and alienation they've already caused you. When you recognize and reflect on even one good thing about yourself, you are building a bridge to a place of kindness and caring. Standing in that place increases your ability to look honestly and directly at whatever is difficult and gives you the energy and courage to move forward.

Sit comfortably in a relaxed, easy posture and close your eyes. Now bring to mind one thing you have done or said recently that you feel was kind or good.

It does not have to be newsworthy! Maybe you smiled at someone or listened to their story, maybe you let go of your annoyance at a slow checkout clerk, maybe you were generous, maybe you sat down to meditate, maybe you thanked a bus driver. It's not conceit or arrogance to consider these things. It's nourishing and replenishing to take delight in the good that moves through us.

Or you might think of a quality or skill in yourself that you like or appreciate: perhaps you are enthused about helping others learn or committed to practicing patience toward your irascible neighbor.

If you still find yourself caught up in self-criticism, turn your attention to the mere fact that you have an urge toward happiness. There is kindness and beauty in that. Or simply recall that all beings everywhere want to be happy, everybody wants to be happy.

Never feel ashamed of your longing for happiness. Recall that this is your birthright. Seeking happiness is not the problem. The problem is that we often do not know where and how to find genuine happiness and so make the mistakes that cause suffering for ourselves and others. But that urge toward happiness itself is correct, and when we support it with mindfulness, it can become like a homing instinct or a compass pointing us toward freedom.

If any impatience or judgments emerge during this meditation, don't feel as though you have failed. This is entirely natural. Simply allow the negative reaction to ebb as a wave on the beach, and see if you can return to the positive contemplation without self-criticism.

LETTING GO OF PERFECTION

✳

If you don't love yourself, that's just weird.
—CALISSA GRACE PARROTT, AGE SIX

How do we relate to perfection? With caution. We tend to handle things we think of as "perfect" with reluctance— gingerly keeping our distance. Perfection is fragile; interacting with something that seems perfect puts it in peril.

Think of a perfect arrangement of flowers in a vase. As soon as they were cut, the flowers started to wilt. Or slice into a perfect cherry pie hot from the oven, and watch the lattice crust crumble. Then you take the first bite, and it is perfect. Three bites later, its sweetness may already be starting to cloy. Moment to moment, perfect passes into imperfect.

This is why clinging to our ideas of perfection isolates us from life and is a barrier to real love for ourselves. Perfection is a brittle state that generates a lot of anxiety, because achieving and maintaining unwavering standards—whether they're internal or external—means we're always under threat. We become focused on avoiding failure, and love for the self cannot be a refuge because it has become too conditional, too dependent on performance. As Oscar Wilde said in his play *An Ideal Husband*, "It is not the perfect, but the imperfect, who have need of love." And that means every last one of us.

The illusion that supports perfectionism is the notion that, with superior self-control, we can sustain a perfect life. But of course this is impossible. We may believe self-criticism will help make us "better," or more lovable, or even liberate us from suffering. But this is a displaced—and unproductive—use of our energy and attention.

As an internationally renowned yoga teacher, Kathryn Budig deals with the pressure of perfection on a daily basis. In a recent conversation, she explained to me, "It's common for people to start their day with the habitual negative narrative—to be unhappy with what you see—focusing on what needs to change about yourself." In order to not only survive but also thrive in her work, Budig has had to totally reframe what it means to be perfect. "Perfection is just a societal norm," she says. "During meditation, I constantly tell myself, 'I am perfect . . . I am not my body.'" By disconnecting the idea of perfection from her body (which the media tells her must match some fashionable ideal), she has been able to reach a place of self-acceptance and self-love. Like meditation, reframing our perspective in this way can become a practice.

Loving ourselves calls us to give up the illusion that we can control everything and instead focuses us on building our inner resource of resilience. When we learn to respond to disappointments with acceptance, we give ourselves the space to realize that all our experiences—good and bad alike—are opportunities to learn and grow. This itself is an act of love.

Elaine, a student of mine, actually defines self-love as the opposite of perfectionism. "Finding love for myself is letting go of the need to find the culprit for something that's wrong, in myself and with others," she says. And, she adds, "constantly assessing things in terms of success and failure means that *someone* must be at fault." But Elaine says she's learned to "change the channel" on this way of being, moving from a stifling and fundamentally noisy state of mind to one that is more expansive and forgiving.

THE FREEDOM OF IMPERFECTION

WHEN I FIRST started to co-lead meditation retreats, my perfectionism caused me a lot of suffering. Our retreats included an intensive day of meditation, with time for instruction and meetings with a teacher, followed by a formal discourse in the evening. I was thriving on interaction with the students, and I had much I wanted to say, but I was terrified of giving that evening discourse. I worried that I would lose my train of thought or state something so ineptly that my mind would freeze. The image of me sitting there speechless was so vivid that I refused to teach. I was silenced by my own perfectionism. One of my colleagues would just have to speak instead.

Months went by like that. Eventually, I decided I could try to give a talk on lovingkindness and lovingkindness only. I figured that if my mind went totally blank, I could launch into the traditional lovingkindness meditation, and maybe no one would notice my imperfect performance.

Then one day I realized that all our talks were basically about lovingkindness. The point wasn't to give a perfect performance, it was to connect with the people gathered to listen and to extend a sense of inclusivity and care to them. My ability to share my insights with more freedom came about when I started to connect to myself and to that space of care from within. I shifted my attention away from self-protection and needing to be perfect and focused instead on giving what I had to offer. It was a big shift in intention, a move away from the lonely self to a space of connection. And when I came to this recognition, I found my voice.

Many years later, I was one of the Western meditation teachers invited to speak at a weeklong event where the Dalai Lama was teaching about patience. It was the largest crowd I'd ever addressed, and my fears about getting it right resurfaced. Fortunately, the Dalai Lama gave us all a profound teaching about "getting it right." He was seated on his throne before about 1,200 people, explicating an eighth-century text. Following the usual format for such talks, he would read a passage in the original Tibetan and give his commentary, and while it was being translated, he'd flip ahead to the next passage he was going to discuss. At one point, something in the English translation caught his attention. He looked up from his manuscript and told the translator, "That's not what I said."

"Yes, it is," the translator replied. They argued back and forth for a while, until the Dalai Lama went back to the passage in dispute. He looked at it and burst into peals of laughter. "Oh, I made a mistake!" he exclaimed, as though he'd made a delightful discovery. The Dalai Lama's laughter amplified the love in the room. I'd guess many of us in the audience imagined that if we were as evolved as the Dalai Lama, we would never make a mistake. His comfort with himself, his easy admission of error, drew us all into the openness and light of the love available when we accept life as it is.

Though it may seem counterintuitive to our inner perfectionist, recognizing our mistakes as valuable lessons (not failures) helps us lay the groundwork for later success. In an interview with David Letterman reported in *The New York Times*, filmmaker Spike Jonze said, "I made a lot of bad stuff and each time I learned from mistakes and got a little better." And in a study of students in a neurosurgery program, a sociologist found that those who ultimately failed claimed that they rarely made mistakes, while those who succeeded not only admitted their mistakes but also revealed what steps they would take to avoid repeating those mistakes in the future.

PAY ATTENTION TO WHAT YOU LOVE

IF WE STOP setting impossibly high standards and punishing ourselves for failure—or what we perceive as failure—how will our lives improve? Getting curious about the origin of these standards is the first step to achieving more freedom from them.

First, ask yourself whose standards you're trying to meet. My student Charlotte talks about how her habitually critical father had instilled in her a pattern of profound self-criticism. But once she recognized this dynamic with her dad, she felt much more empowered and was able to make changes in their relationship and in her relationship with herself.

Often it's our peers who set the standard. Raina, a young meditator I know, was determined to create the perfect birth experience for herself and her baby. She planned to give birth exactly the way her best friend, Laura, did: in a deep Jacuzzi tub at a birthing center staffed by midwives and accompanied by a doula, with celestial music playing in the background. Everything was going according to plan the day Raina went into labor—that is, until the baby's fetal heartbeat began to drop dangerously low and the midwife had Raina rushed to the hospital for an emergency C-section. At first, she felt like a complete failure, having let down everyone important to her: her husband, the midwife, the doula, Laura, and especially her baby and herself. But as distraught as she was at first, the moment Raina cradled her infant daughter in her arms, she was able to let go of her disappointment. "It was a huge teaching moment for me," she recalls. "I learned once again that life calls the shots, not me or my plans for the way life should be."

If you can't put a name to the source of your perfectionism, try examining the social messages that surround you. Have you somehow bought into the notion that you should be the perfect (select all that apply): hostess, mother, son or daughter, partner, boss, employee, meditator, athlete, fashion plate? As soon as you begin to notice the messages you've internalized as distinct from *you*, you can begin to set healthy boundaries.

Next, get even more curious: Do you agree with the expectations you've identified? Do they reflect your innermost values? Mindfulness allows us to balance our drive for self-improvement with a healthy skepticism about external standards. Do you really want to maintain a spotless home just like your late grandmother, or are you willing to let that go to spend more relaxed, enjoyable time with your children? Loosening the grip of other people's goals lets you focus on what you love.

The wholesome pursuit of excellence feels quite different from perfectionism. Think of something you've made an effort to master, whether it's lap swimming, getting higher grades, or gardening, and then try to remember when you started feeling a strong inner push to do it. Did you take pleasure in making progress, even when it was incremental? Did you feel a strong desire to do it well, even when you knew no one else would notice? When we approach the journey acknowledging what we do not know and what we can't control, we maintain our energy for the quest.

I've heard this again and again from writers and artists. I have one author friend who compares writing his books to climbing Mt. Everest. "I always start out with a vision of making it to the top or, in my case, creating my perfect dream of a book. Sometimes I get pretty close and I feel like, maybe if I kept tinkering forever, my manuscript would indeed achieve perfection, only it never quite does. Still, at a certain point I have to decide it's good enough, say *Basta!*, and move on. Otherwise I'll go nuts." But, my friend adds, "Actually, I think this is a good thing. If one of my books was perfect, what would be the point of writing another? It's the gap between my aspiration and what I've actually created that gives me energy and fuels the next project. Which, of course, will be *perfect*." He laughs.

My friend has the wisdom to realize that perfectionism is the enemy of creativity. It is unforgiving and rife with fear. When we cling to unrealistic standards, we undermine our abilities and obsess unnecessarily over disapproval and rejection.

Yet it's also important to remember that pursuing excellence is not a problem. In fact, focusing on what we most care about, whether it's our work, our relationships, or collecting butterflies, can be a genuine act of self-love, but only if we're not fixated on the outcome of our efforts or on perfecting *ourselves*.

Fortunately, when we relate to ourselves with lovingkindness, perfectionism naturally drops away. We may realize we'll never sing an aria at the Met, but we can continue to love opera, follow our favorite singers, and perhaps join a local chorus. There's no frustration, bitterness, or self-criticism in this kind of loving acceptance. It doesn't mean we're complacent, but rather we stop resisting the way things actually are. Wholehearted acceptance is a basic element of love, starting with love for ourselves, and a gateway to joy. Through the practices of lovingkindness and self-compassion, we can learn to love our flawed and imperfect selves. And in those moments of vulnerability, we open our hearts to connect with each other, as well. We are not perfect, but we are enough.

CHAPTER 5 PRACTICES

Self-acceptance

1. Bring something you did or said that you regret very clearly into your mind and get in touch with your feelings about it.

2. Now imagine you are listening to a friend whom you care about deeply express regret, guilt, and self-blame to you in conversation. What would you say to console your friend?

3. Begin to look at yourself through the eyes of a caring, supportive ally.

4. Recognize that imperfection is a part of all human experience. We are no worse than anyone else because we have made particular mistakes. We can be complete in this moment just as we are.

REFLECTION

Step back to inquire: Are there particular areas of your life where perfectionism emerges most often? Appearance? Personality? Job performance? Social life? Parenting? What would "just okay" look like in these areas?

Try to catch yourself in the moment: When the anxiety of control arises, take time to breathe and repeat, "Let go, let go."

Follow the Dalai Lama's example: If you make a trivial but embarrassing mistake, admit it cheerfully and move on.

6

BECOMING EMBODIED

✳

I N HIS SHORT STORY "A Painful Case," James Joyce introduces
us to a Mr. Duffy, who "lived at a little distance from his body."
So, too, do most of us, and at times we may even feel we're dragging
a hostile stranger around. There is something profoundly healing
about reengaging with our bodies, remembering and rejoining who
we are. Just as we need to integrate our emotions in order to love
ourselves more fully, so, too, do we need to be reunited with our bodies.
The Ben Harper song "You Found Another Lover (I Lost Another

Friend)" talks about how the heart never lies to us. I often think about how, for so many of us, the body never lies. Our stomachs are called our second brains for a reason, and there is a growing amount of research on the mind-body connection. How can we feel a genuine connection to the world if we do not feel our own bodies?

The journey to loving ourselves doesn't mean we like everything about our bodies (or our personalities, for that matter). But it does mean stepping away from conventional obsessions about everything we have been told is wrong with us by parents, partners, our social group, the media, or the mean girls in high school. If we can feel and appreciate our bodies from within, we are not in bondage to the messages coming from without. When we contemplate the miracle of embodied life, we begin to partner with our bodies in a kinder way.

REFLECTION

Appreciating your aliveness

This reflection is adapted from the teaching of one of my colleagues, Kate Lila Wheeler.

We get only one body in this life, the one we are each endowed with right this moment. Please begin by giving yours the respect it deserves. Did you realize every atom in it is 14.5 billion years old? All bodies are part of matter, created at the big bang, 10 billion years before the earth appeared. Yes, your overall body is composed of about 7 octillion venerable atoms (that's a 7 with twenty-seven zeros after it), mostly produced by exploding stars. You are literally stardust; so is everything around you.

The water in this body seems to flow into your mouth from a fountain or a glass, then out again through pores and orifices. But like all the waters of the earth, no one knows where it came from. Perhaps a comet's tail, it's said. And if you have gold fillings, your teeth carry a share of all the gold that exists in the universe, for the number of gold molecules is finite.

Your body is not just mineral and elemental. No, it's vividly alive, as anyone knows who's ever danced, had a sore throat, made love, or stubbed a toe.

Try to sense the skin around your body. Feel how alive it is! For this, you can thank a single-celled creature. All the baroque variety of life on earth is considered to come from a common tiny ancestor who appeared about 4 billion years ago (again, no one knows quite how). And still today, on a cellular level, basic functions like respiration look similar in plants and animals. So does our DNA—we humans share about half our genetic information with plants. We truly aren't very far away from anything.

Our salty blood remembers oceanic origins; the structure of our spines and ribs was first developed by fish. Population geneticists agree that all of us are literally one human family. What would our world be like if everyone acted on this truth?

Yet as connected as we are, there is astonishing diversity even within being human. Each person is utterly distinct. Our fingerprints, toeprints, and tongueprints will never be reproduced.

But surely it is the brain that is our most fabulous body part. Scientists believe the human brain is the most complex object in the universe, capable of making one hundred trillion neural connections. Lay all your neurons end to end, and they'll reach to the moon and back. Awake, asleep, or dreaming, your brain is active night and day, a magic lantern. Its neurons interact in constantly shifting patterns of electrical energy and are deeply attuned to others and the outside world. Not only that, but your brain is capable of self-awareness.

Brain and body are inseparable collaborators, producing the symphony that fully absorbs us. This is the wonder of a life. How amazing that we can even be amazed.

CHAPTER 6 PRACTICES

Meditation: Lovingkindness for your body

I learned this meditation from a Sri Lankan monk who came to visit us at the Insight Meditation Society in the early 1990s. At age ninety-four, the Venerable Ananda Maitreya seemed to have more energy than the rest of us put together, and he was learning to use a computer, something I was struggling with at the time. How much of his vigor came from his repeatedly offering love to his body?

Focusing on different parts of the body in sequence, he had us repeat silently, "May my head be happy. May it be peaceful," or "May my eyes be happy. May they be peaceful." And on through the whole body.

We repeated this with our shoulders, our backs, our stomachs, parts we might normally term "bad," as in the case of a sore knee we call a "bad" knee, those parts we would love to hide more than anything if clothing manufacturers could only get more inventive, those parts we are usually neatly distanced from. Ending with, "May my toes be happy. May they be peaceful." Try it.

I met Phil at a daylong seminar I was teaching in the Midwest. At one of the breaks, he approached me, eager to describe how he had recently started to practice meditation when a friend gave him a book that offered a guided meditation on the body, moving attention from the top of your head slowly down to your toes.

Phil told me that the guided meditation was not calming him down. The focus on the body made him restless, and his inner critic filled up the space with abuse. When he felt a twinge in his ankle, he lectured himself that this would not be a problem if he'd just get off his ass once in a while and take a walk, just down the street. He had to start somewhere. He was wasting his life. When he dwelled on his knees, he noticed some tenderness there. Hadn't Grandma had both of her knees replaced when she was about his age? That would be terrible if he was laid up for weeks. When he focused his attention on his body with judgment, he wanted to jump out of his skin!

We can let go of the judgments or at least put them to one side as we continue to awaken awareness of our bodies, and we can also actively work with offering lovingkindness to whatever we discover.

Since Ananda Maitreya's visit, I have taught this meditation to many with serious diseases, with scars or injuries, with chronic pain, and with deep-seated hatred toward their bodies. It has been wonderful to see how feeling badly betrayed by one's body, and the alienation and humiliation born of that, can transform into a sense of alliance. A newly minted friendship with our bodies brings genuine peace to us, laced through with love.

┌─────┐
│ 7 │
└─────┘

MOVING BEYOND SHAME

✳

T HE STIMULUS FOR SHAME IS something we did, or failed to do, and all too often about things over which we had no control—like a parent's behavior or our family's economic status. Wherever the responsibility lies, shame creates a solid and terrible feeling of unworthiness that resides in our bodies: the storehouse of the memories of our acts, real or imagined, and the secrets we keep about them.

The heart contracts when our bodies are overcome by shame. In its powerful grip, our ability to feel love for ourselves shrivels, too.

Clara writes, "When I'm ashamed, my stomach gets tight, queasy, and cold, but the rest of my body burns. I'm told my cheeks flame with a brighter intensity than a blush. Of the fight, flight, and freeze options, many times I just get frozen. I hope against hope no one notices, but just in case, I start looking for the exit. I want to disappear, but in a moment of deep shame it can be difficult for me to move at all."

The root meaning of the word *shame* is "to cover," which suggests our longing to hide—even from ourselves. To avoid the excruciating feeling of shame, we may start acting in compulsive and harmful ways. Shame can make us eat too much, shop to excess, drink or use drugs inappropriately, often in a deliberate effort to quiet the turmoil within. Shame is usually out of proportion to the thing we're ashamed of. Small defects and minor lapses, barely noticeable by others, can generate overwhelming feelings of shame.

A difference becomes us. An illness becomes us. A blemish becomes us. A mistake becomes us. Our mentally ill parent becomes us.

Maria writes: "When my father thought that I had a weak teacher, he would go to the school and make such a fuss that I would always be moved. I was embarrassed, of course, and didn't feel that I deserved the place in the better class. When I wanted to get a summer job—maybe scooping ice cream like all the other kids—my father insisted it was beneath me. I was a great painter, he said, and I should spend my time painting and selling my paintings. I was a kid trying to fit in and learn kid things, like how to make a living. I have always been unrealistic in my choices of livelihood, and I blame (yes, blame) this on my father's unwillingness to let me be ordinary.

"I understand better now why he aspired to be larger than life, important, successful, rich, and always right. By most people's definition, he *was* handsome, wealthy, and successful, but in his own mind he was a failure and never good enough.

"I remember:

—my father screaming at my mother and hitting her in front of my brother and me

—my father driving head-on into another car because it was in his way

—my father stepping on a parking attendant's hands so that he would release a key

—my father having lovers and not really trying to hide them

—my father telling me, 'Don't fall in love. Just have sex.'

—my father on a trip with me, being delighted that people thought we were a couple and continuing to laugh about it no matter how enraged I became."

There is much glib celebration in pop culture of those who go their own paths: the dreamers, the mavericks. For many, feeling so distinct from those around them is not a comfortable place to rest. And if this sense of distinction arises from a parent we cannot govern or subdue, there is a huge potential for shame to fortify the walls of isolation.

Many children raised in dysfunctional homes carry with them the feeling that if they had been better people, their parents would have been better parents. Patty says, "I was raised by drunks and believed if others knew, they would shun me or bully me. I didn't invite schoolmates home because I was frightened that those friends would see how we really lived and spread that shameful secret to others at school. My secret became the most alive thing about me. Everything else went into a kind of death spiral.

"While I was a good student and loyal friend, I absorbed my parents' shame, as well as my own feeling of worthlessness, as central to my identity."

Shame weakens us. It can make us frightened to take on something new. We start to withdraw from whatever might give us pleasure, self-esteem, or a sense of our value. Comedian and activist Margaret Cho describes its effect: "When you don't have self-esteem you will hesitate before you do anything in your life. You will hesitate to go for the job you really wanna go for, you will hesitate to ask for a raise . . . you will hesitate to report a rape, you will hesitate to defend yourself when you are discriminated against . . . You will hesitate to vote, you will hesitate to dream. For us to have self-esteem is truly an act of revolution and our revolution is long overdue."

Lost in shame, we withdraw from the world and those who might love and support us. If we want to hide, we cannot easily feel or receive love. And it is increasingly hard to remember that we deserve to.

SHAME ABOUT ILLNESS

I WORRY ABOUT friends and students who seem to take on responsibility for absolutely everything, as though their thoughts could control the universe. I've known people who even feel ashamed that they have cancer or an autoimmune disease because they believe they brought it upon themselves by not living a sufficiently pure life.

While I think we're right to acknowledge the power of our minds to affect our bodies, it's an illusion to imagine we have total control. To imagine the way we think is the singular causative agent of all we go through is to practice cruelty toward ourselves. If you get cancer and all you can think of is that your thoughts caused it, it's your entire fault, you are to blame, I would first check out if you live near a toxic waste dump or maybe had a genetic predisposition.

Or perhaps a clear, direct cause might remain unknown. Not everyone with lung cancer smoked, for example, and not everyone who feels stressed has a heart attack. Can we acknowledge and nurture the power of our minds without turning that into a cudgel to beat ourselves up with? There may well be lessons to be learned in an illness; maybe we should consider that last spare rib we ate to be the last for this lifetime or recognize we'd do better physically if we learned to manage our anger better. But if we think we will be able to dominate the streaming rapids of life through our efforts at control, we are destined to fail, and we will be ashamed at our failure. If we add shame to what is already massively challenging, we can become cut off and isolated when we most need to feel connected, and when we most need to deepen our love for ourselves, just as we are.

SHAME ABOUT SUFFERING

IN MY BOOK *Faith: Trusting Your Own Deepest Experience*, I wrote about the suffering of my own childhood and my years of feeling isolated and unhappy. When he read it, my friend Bob Thurman said to me, "You should never be ashamed of the suffering you've been through." His comment really surprised me. In that moment, I realized how much subtle shame I had been carrying without realizing it.

Bob was passing along a message he'd received many years earlier, after he lost his left eye in an accident. His teacher at the time, a Mongolian monk named Geshe Wangyal, had told him, "Never be ashamed of what happened to you. You have lost one eye but gained a thousand eyes of wisdom."

I do think it's too simplistic to say that such awful experiences should be considered gifts. But acknowledging that a gift can emerge from pain does not mock the pain itself. It's affirming that we can look at any experience from the fullness of our being and that we can get past the shame we carry. Bob still lost an eye. I still had a really unhappy childhood. Patty's parents were still alcoholics, and Maria's father was still disconnected and hurtful. But if we use our experiences to care for and love ourselves more, and if we use them to connect more deeply with others, then losing an eye can indeed lead to a thousand eyes of wisdom.

REFLECTION

Exploring shame with RAIN

Once you acknowledge a difficult emotion, inquire whether shame is one of the feelings that is appearing. Explore what happens in your body when you are caught up in feelings of shame.

Embracing what is

We're conditioned to believe that painful feelings are "bad" and that pleasurable ones are "good." It's often easier—though not healthier— for us to avoid grief and sorrow, while only embracing sensations like happiness, confidence, and love.

But by accepting and learning to embrace the inevitable sorrows of life, we realize that we can experience a more enduring sense of happiness.

Of course this is difficult and requires practice. The following meditation is an invitation to experiment with what it feels like to meditate with an uncomfortable feeling or experience as the object of your attention, rather than just your breath, an anchoring phrase, or a mantra. So often we assume meditation is exclusively meant to be a tool for relaxation, stress relief, clearing the mind. And it often is. But this exercise shows that we can actually use meditation as a way to experiment with new ways of relating to ourselves, even our uncomfortable thoughts:

1. Sit comfortably with your back straight but not strained. You may choose to close your eyes or settle a soft gaze on the floor in front of you.

2. Bring to mind a painful conversation, situation, experience, or distinct feeling you have experienced. Call to mind what the emotion felt like in your body. As you tap into a more visceral experience of the discomfort, begin to deepen your natural inhales and exhales.

3. With each inhale, envision opening up to all of the discomfort and pain associated with the experience you've brought to mind.

4. With each exhale, release any pressure you may feel to react to the pain in a particular way.

5. Other thoughts, memories, and experiences may come up, drawing you away from the original anchor of your meditation. As different thoughts emerge, take the opportunity to be mindful of each one. This is a practice of embracing what is in each moment.

TAKING A STAND ON
HAPPINESS

*

GEORGIA IS A FREELANCE WRITER who works at home in a two-story loft space with tall windows that let in beautiful light. Some time ago, she was under tremendous financial pressure and took on too much work to compensate. With deadlines for projects following one right after the other, she started to slump.

Georgia is a good cook, but when the pressure hit, she began eating only junk. She didn't feel like exercising, so her life became confined to her four walls, where her dark mood closed in. Her housekeeping fell off, and of course, so did her meditation practice. She'd pledge to meditate forty-five minutes under the covers while in bed, but would then promptly fall asleep. And she began drinking more than she had at any other time in her life.

Georgia was devoting all her waking hours (and much of her sleep time) to the goals and demands of others. Her motivation was partially self-protective, as she needed the money. But the way she acted on it was not, and she burned out. She felt disconnected from her body and from everything that nourished her. And the way she spoke to herself became quite self-punishing.

For a while, Georgia couldn't see a way out of this downward spiral. And then, in a moment of awareness, she did. "I wasn't taking a stand on my right to be happy," she told me later. "I realized I had to do that in order to find a way back to self-love."

As a first step, Georgia drove to the supermarket to replenish her kitchen with healthy food. The store was brightly lit, music was playing, and as she wandered down an unfamiliar aisle, she came across a display of tall Mexican votive candles dedicated to the saints. Georgia is not Christian, but she loves candles, and her hand reached out to pull one off the shelf. On the front was the image of San Judas Tadeo, the patron saint of difficult and desperate cases. On the back was a traditional prayer in Spanish and English: "Pray for me. I am so helpless and alone." That summed up how Georgia had been feeling, so she brought the candle home. She showered and lit the candle.

Then she felt a bit silly, because she was not really such a difficult or desperate case. She reminded herself that she was healthy, enjoyed her work, and had many strong, close relationships. She just hadn't been acknowledging those things. *I need to remember my blessings*, she thought.

So Georgia took a walk down to the riverfront, and upon arriving home, she pulled up the blinds to let the light in and put on some music. Step by step, Georgia gradually reentered the world. She returned to her meditation practice, and with it as a foundation, she regained a kind of balance.

In order to restore love to her life, Georgia had to start with forgiveness: with forgiving herself for falling so low, and compassion for the pain that had kept her there. Lovingkindness, too, for the part of her that sought to be happy but chose the wrong tools when she reached for the wine bottle or the junk food, and then seemed to forget that she had a right to be happy at all.

It is fascinating to me that she phrased her turnaround insight as "I wasn't taking a stand on my right to be happy," because the particular form of meditation she found most helpful to her recovery was standing meditation.

She later wrote me: "As I stood at the top of the loft, I closed my eyes and imagined the strong connection I had to the world through my vulnerability, the desire to be happy, to be free from mental or physical suffering, and to live a life of ease, which we all share. How could I have felt so alone?

"I felt the earth supporting me. I felt my legs making those micro-adjustments to help me stay upright in a constantly moving, changing world. I thought, *My body knows how to do this*."

As Georgia continued her meditation, she says she felt herself freeing her heart from a cage.

She concluded, "Breathe in the connection to all things, to the beautiful world that is just beyond the window, to the birds I saw in the marshes by the river, to my neighbors and to myself. Breathe out to spread that awareness, to share it, with the little cities nearby and the big ones out in the distance, and all the places in between and beyond. Light pouring into me and light pouring out from me in a grateful relationship with the world."

Standing meditation remains the mainstay of Georgia's meditation practice. When she puts her body in a posture that expresses innate dignity, when she feels the support of the earth, when her chest opens with the breath, Georgia takes a stand on the rightness of her being and on her connection to all others.

CHAPTER 8 PRACTICES

Standing meditation

Georgia did this meditation barefoot, which is a good way to engage all of your muscles and experience fully how you maintain your balance in space. But feel free to wear socks if you'll be more comfortable.

Standing upright, close your eyes and feel the earth supporting you. Spread your toes wide, feeling the solidity of the floor under your feet or noting how the fibers of the carpet press into your soles. Start making micro-movements to distribute your weight broadly, testing the arch of the foot as you slowly roll the pad of your foot back and forth to loosen your ankles.

Now begin to experiment with restacking your skeleton bone by bone to form the foundation of a more solid and confident posture. Standing with your knees a little bent, let your ankles adjust to a straighter line, like a column. Then slowly straighten your knees without locking them, a movement of about an inch.

As your legs extend fully, feel how your pelvis lifts your spine as your shoulders pull back. This takes a lot of pressure off the small of your back and allows your lower back to elongate. Pause there for a while playing with this minor adjustment at the knees, enjoying how the more you straighten your legs, the taller you stand and the deeper you breathe.

The pelvis is the next place for investigation. Tip your tailbone down an inch, and the shoulders pull farther back. Moving your tailbone back and forth, feel how your ribs spread slightly with each tip.

Without forcing the movement of your ribs, feel your lungs rising and falling as you take each breath. Try breathing into the bottom of your lungs, where they press against the diaphragm. Then explore how they expand sideways. Then feel the breath moving into your back, under your shoulder blades. Visualize yourself freeing your heart from a cage. Continue to enjoy the rhythm of the breath and the expansion of your bones, taking a stand on your right to be happy.

9

FOLLOWING YOUR ETHICAL
COMPASS

✳

W HAT DO ETHICS HAVE TO do with loving yourself? After all, ethics is a Big Topic, while self-love seems more individualized, more intimate. We tend to equate being free and happy with doing as we please. But if we really look at our actions with eyes of love, we see that our lives can be more straightforward, simpler, less sculpted by regret and fear, more in alignment with our deepest values.

Paying attention to the ethical implications of our choices has never been more pressing—or more complicated—than it is today. Our options, many of them unimaginable one hundred years ago, have nearly spiraled out of control in today's global, digital world. Is it okay to eat meat, or should we be vegan? Why commit to one person when you can experience the rush of meeting someone new every day just by swiping on Tinder? To what lengths should we—can we, as individuals—go to protect our troubled planet?

How *do* we make choices when the possibilities appear limitless?

The Buddha offered this: "If you truly loved yourself, you'd never harm another." This is not a sanctimonious or repressive frame for morality, nor is it an invitation to deny our desires or judge them. It's not even a frame that focuses solely on compassion for another—refraining from stealing or lying because we don't want to cause someone else pain.

Causing harm is never just a one-way street. If we harm someone else, we're inevitably also hurting ourselves. Some quality of sensitivity and awareness has to shut down for us to be able to objectify others, to deny them as living, feeling beings—those who want to be happy, just as we do. We don't relate to kicking a table as a moral issue. For a person or animal to, in effect, become a table in our minds takes a lot of numbing (hard to shake off), a significant set of blinders (hard to see around later), and a lot of armoring (hard to remove at will). We grow a skin of indifference.

Yet even when we do our best to treat others with kindness, it's often a struggle to determine which actions best express our love and care for ourselves. We may, for instance, believe fervently that eating animals is ethically wrong. But what choice do we make when our physician diagnoses us with anemia and tells us we should eat red meat for our health? I have a friend in drought-stricken California who tries to monitor every drop of water she uses and worries over whether to let her daughter go to school in her favorite—but stained—dress, or run the washing machine when she doesn't have a full load. How do we know what's right for us when there are so many gray areas, so many imperfect answers?

LISTEN TO YOUR BODY

WHEN WE FEEL conflicted about a particular decision or action, our bodies often hold the answer—if we take the time to stop and tune in. Our minds tend to race ahead into the future or replay the past, but our bodies are always in the present moment. A tightness in the chest or a squeamish sensation in the gut may signal harm—even when reason may suggest that a given choice is perfectly ethical. A feeling of calm or a sense of expansiveness throughout the body sends us a very different message.

My student Sarah wasn't much of a drinker, but she enjoyed the occasional glass of wine at social gatherings. The problem was that once in a while—unpredictably—she'd get a raging migraine from just a single glass. Sarah knew from the constriction she felt in her throat when she even contemplated taking a drink that she'd be causing herself harm if she went ahead. Still, sometimes she chose to ignore her body's SOS. But recently, after years of playing Russian roulette with her health, Sarah decided to stop drinking wine altogether—and is now migraine-free. As she said to me, "Not drinking feels like a profound act of self-love."

RELY ON GUIDING PRECEPTS

WHEN WE CAN'T slow down enough to hear the body's message or when that message is unclear, we can protect ourselves by following a few essential precepts that are remarkably similar across the world's wisdom traditions.

My colleague JoAnna Harper derived the following precepts from Buddhist teachings. They are both simple and accessible, while also elegantly covering the basics:

Knowing how deeply our lives intertwine, I undertake the precept to protect life.

Knowing how deeply our lives intertwine, I undertake the precept to be generous.

Knowing how deeply our lives intertwine, I undertake the precept to protect the sexuality of myself and others.

Knowing how deeply our lives intertwine, I undertake the precept to be careful with my speech.

Knowing how deeply our lives intertwine, I undertake the precept to be free of intoxicants for a clear mind and heart.

These precepts demand that we pay attention to what we're feeling and what we most deeply want. They ask us to learn how to let go of desires gracefully, without judging ourselves. They also require that we recognize when we do or say something not in the spirit of the precepts, and resolve to begin again.

I've had students and friends who have worked hard to replace the harsh moral strictures imposed during childhood with their own set of values. One friend, describing her new understanding of strength and freedom gained through meditation, said, "If you really want to be a rebel, practice kindness." Or you might put it this way: "If you want to live on your own terms, breaking free from old habits and stories that no longer have any meaning, be different—practice love."

NOTICE YOUR SECRETS

I OFTEN USE secret-keeping as a kind of personal moral compass. I've seen it take a toll on the keeper of the secret, on the person left out of the knowing, and on all who are enlisted to isolate that person from knowledge of what is actually going on. We may pursue it blithely, but that doesn't mean it isn't consequential. As architect Christopher Alexander said, "Making wholeness heals the maker." In other words, the environment we create can help heal us or fracture us. This is true not just for buildings and landscapes but also for interactions and relationships. What does adding to fragmentation rather than wholeness yield? What happens within us when we increase division and isolation?

I think of my childhood, laden with secrets. When I was eleven, I was told that my father had been hospitalized after an "accidental" dose of sleeping pills. He lived in psychiatric hospitals from that time on, but it wasn't until five years later, when I was already in college, that I put the pieces together and realized that the overdose was not an accident. All those years, that vital, aware part of me lived in emotional and physical lockdown because my inner knowing didn't harmonize with the version of reality offered to me. Of course, my family was motivated by wanting to spare me pain, but even so, keeping secrets is a consequential act for all involved.

The more we practice mindfulness, the more alert we become to the cost of keeping secrets. John told me this story: "I was offered an apartment in New York City at a reasonable rent, in my desired neighborhood. It seemed too good to be true—and in fact it was. According to the rules of the co-op board that governed the building, the owner wasn't allowed to rent it out.

"I was hugely tempted. This wasn't contravening the laws of God or even the state! Who were these people on the co-op board, anyway? Probably an officious, power-hungry bunch. Talk about a victimless crime! I really wanted that apartment! My friends urged me on: 'Do you know how many people violate co-op laws every day! Go for it!'

"But then I imagined walking into that lobby every day, feeling furtive, hoping the 'right' doorman was on duty, the less observant one, the one less likely to ask after my supposed 'cousin,' the owner of the apartment. I knew I would start to worry that someone was calculating how long I'd been there, that I'd plan on staying away at times so I'd look more like a visitor than a resident. I saw my future:

paying rent for an apartment where I could never live in peace and happiness."

Even if we're never found out, as the old adage warns, "It's not the crime, it's the cover-up that will get you." The costs of keeping secrets include our growing isolation due to fear of detection and the ways we shut down inside to avoid feeling the effects of our behavior. We can never afford to be truly seen and known—even by ourselves.

The price of keeping secrets can literally weigh people down, according to research conducted by Columbia University professor Michael Slepian. In one study, he asked gay men to help him move some boxes. The result? Those whose sexual preference was locked in the closet moved fewer boxes. Another study revealed that people who had recently had affairs felt more burdened by daily tasks, such as carrying groceries upstairs. In an interview in *The Atlantic*, Slepian commented, "The more preoccupied people were with their secrets, the more effort they thought was required to keep their secrets, and so other things seemed more challenging."

I don't mean to imply that we need to disclose everything about ourselves to everyone. There is such a thing as discretion or lifestyle choices that aren't really anyone's business. But the fear of getting found out can start permeating our days and even our dreams. To me, that's a big clue that we're creating more suffering than wholeness.

MONITOR YOUR SELF-RESPECT

ANOTHER KEY BAROMETER to help us weigh the rightness of our actions is self-respect. I have found that my ability to accept whatever challenges life sends my way is largely connected to my degree of self-respect. When my self-respect has been strong, I've been able to go through difficult times without being disheartened— that is, difficulties did not reflect a lack of basic self-worth, and I could enjoy good times without trying to get a death grip on them, for fear that they would end and leave me feeling bad about myself. For me, self-respect definitely seemed to be key to maintaining happiness. And it became clear that my level of self-respect was rooted in how I behaved.

When we have that kind of self-regard, we're not grabbing onto experiences or relationships to make us feel better. We don't feel a deep hollowness inside that needs to be filled. Self-respect enables us to love ourselves more fully. And the self-respect that comes from loving ourselves enhances our ability to love more broadly.

Psychologist Barbara Fredrickson, a professor at the University of North Carolina–Chapel Hill, a leading scholar in the field of social psychology, and author of *Love 2.0*, developed the "broaden and build" theory of positive emotions. The idea is that cultivation of positive emotions, including self-love and self-respect, strengthens our inner resources and opens us to a broader range of thoughts and actions. In turn, we gain trust in our resilience and the ability to face whatever surprises life may throw our way. Indeed, life can be stressful, with periods of peril, but we can have confidence in our capacity to meet it, instead of being torn apart by it.

Following our ethical compass helps to support this new, more nimble response. Increasingly, we trust ourselves to behave ethically, speak thoughtfully, and act responsibly. We're not burdened by carrying a shameful secret that, if exposed, would ruin our reputation. In everyday life, we pay attention to how our actions line up with our values. This is another piece of the confidence that allows us to expand love.

HONORING OURSELVES

"IF YOU TRULY loved yourself, you'd never harm another." These words from the Buddha suggest that we're capable of much more than mediocrity, much more than merely getting by in this world.

As human beings, we're actually capable of greatness of spirit, an ability to go beyond the circumstances we find ourselves in, to experience a vast sense of connection to all of life. To settle for walling ourselves off through indifference, or the temporary high of getting what we want by whatever means, or the petty excitement of besting someone however we can is actually quite sad.

If we recognized all that we could be and honored ourselves for that, we wouldn't compromise our integrity and wholeness for the superficial sense of power that can come from lying to someone ("I know something you don't") or the fleeting rush and more enduring objectification and distance that come from exploitation. If we thought we were capable of much more than mediocrity, we'd envision more for ourselves than skulking though a building's lobby, hoping the doorman won't ask us what we're doing there.

If we truly loved ourselves, we'd never harm another. That is a truly revolutionary, celebratory mode of self-care.

REFLECTION

IS THERE ANYONE in your life whom you think of as a model of integrity in some area? Do you identify with that person, or do they seem too rigid to you?

Do you have disagreements with friends or colleagues about right and wrong behavior? Who would you talk with if you were trying to solve a moral dilemma? How do you decide what is right for you?

If you have a secret about an important area of your life, how is that affecting your relationship with others? With yourself?

SECTION 2

INTRODUCTION

*

Love as a Verb

I HAD A DREAM ONCE, and in it, someone asked me, "Why do we love people?"

Still dreaming, I responded, "Because they see us." I woke up thinking, *That's a really good answer.*

To see and be seen—this very notion might fill us with an expansive sense of satisfaction and ease. We might feel joy at the prospect of being affirmed because of who we are, rather than as a result of any achievement or effort on our part. Too, the thought of seeing and accepting another person for who he or she is might also make us happy. Such mutual recognition feels good, solid, balanced, authentic, and real.

Take Ellen and Gil, who recently celebrated their twenty-fifth wedding anniversary. "I work in an office with a lot of young people who come to me for dating advice," Ellen wrote to me. "I always tell them to look for unconditional love. They ask me how they'll know when it is present. Here's the story I tell that always gets a lot of 'Ohhhh . . . I get it now!' responses.

"When Gil and I were first dating, I was living in Brooklyn, and he'd pick me up at the train when I went out to Long Island to see him. One time, he was driving when I started telling him about my parents' divorce when I was seventeen—and all the before, during, and after of that. He slowed the car down and pulled over to the side of the road. When I asked him what was wrong, he said, 'You are telling me something important, and I want to listen and give it my full attention.'

"That was the big IT for me. He still listens to me . . . amazing!"

He sees her; she sees him. It's clear and it's real. If our close relationships actually felt like this day to day, we'd have a wonderful life.

The skills available to us through mindfulness make it absolutely possible to bring this kind of love to our connections with others. What we learn in meditation, we can apply to all other realms of our lives. A friend of mine suggested that the title for this book be *Real Love: Simple, but Not Easy*. That's a great description of the challenges we face.

UNLOADING OUR CULTURAL BAGGAGE

THE FIRST CHALLENGE is to slough off some limiting notions of love perpetuated by our culture. For example:

Love is an object or state to be attained, some kind of fixed ideal.

In reality, love is fluid; it's a verb, not a noun. Love is a living capacity within us that is always present, even when we don't sense it. And there are many kinds of love. Sanskrit has different words to describe love for a brother or sister, love for a teacher, love for a partner, love for one's friends, love of nature, and so on. English has only one word, which leads to never-ending confusion.

The height of love is romantic love—ecstasy and torment.

As playwright Oscar Wilde wrote in *The Importance of Being Earnest*, "The very essence of romance is uncertainty." It's a journey filled with peril; we're at the mercy of outside forces. We're shot through with arrows. We fall hopelessly. We lose ourselves. We're struck by lightning. We ask flower petals to reveal whether he or she "loves us or loves us not." In reality, when our eyes are fixed on romance, we can miss the deep, sustainable love right before us. I'll always remember overhearing a young woman tell a friend, "You know, I was telling my brother that I love my fiancé, but I miss how intense my last relationship was. And he said to me, 'Yeah, and all you're missing is the aggravation.'"

Love will rescue us and complete us.

This dictum tells us that without the love of another, we're insufficient, unable to live fully on our own. This kind of magical thinking fills old-fashioned bodice-ripper novels and Hollywood movies, the land of achy breaky hearts and blue eyes crying in the rain. But it doesn't have to shape our lives.

In a conversation we had, Linda Carroll explained to me that if we don't question these messages, we may unconsciously accept two extreme visions of love: "There's stage one, where everything is perfect, and stage three, where everything's horrible, rather than good-enough love or quiet love or we-had-a-good-day-and-sat-peacefully-and-supported-each-other (but-not-too-much) love. That's not a hot song. Who would buy it? It's the drama of love that we're hooked into in our culture, not the peacefulness of love."

Or as Molly, a woman I met at a meditation center, told me, "When I was younger, the only topic that interested me was heart-break. I was constantly heartbroken and fed off of it. I was always trying to capture that feeling of just being scraped out, raw, and desperate."

I'm not knocking passion or fireworks, but when our focus is on seeking, perfecting, or clinging to romance, the charge is often generated by instability, rather than by an authentic connection with another person. Then, as novelist Zadie Smith has written in her novel *White Teeth*, "The object of the passion is just an accessory to the passion itself."

RECOGNIZING REAL LOVE

REAL LOVE MAY run on a lower voltage, but it's also more grounded and sustainable. From our first breath to our last, we're presented again and again with the opportunity to experience deep, lasting, and transformative connection with other beings: to love them and be loved by them; to show them our true natures and to recognize theirs. In concert with them, we open our hearts to give and receive. We share joy and compassion, struggles and sorrows, gains and losses. And we learn in our bones what it means to be part of something bigger than ourselves.

Centuries ago, the Chinese philosopher Lao Tzu described a profound and empowering love: "Being deeply loved by someone gives you strength, while loving someone deeply gives you courage." And though the earth has spun on its axis countless times since then, we can still hear that truth if we listen for it. As a character in Toni Morrison's novel *Jazz* says, "Don't ever think I fell for you, or fell over you. I didn't fall in love, I rose in it."

My student Samantha wrote to me about the expansive, rever-berating love she witnessed in her own family. "This past year, my father had heart surgery," she said. "During his stint in the hospital, he pressed the call light for the nurse multiple times, which went unheeded. He ended up wetting the bed. My mother and I found him soaked and embarrassed when we returned from having lunch in the hospital cafeteria. My mother, who's a former nurse, went to work immediately—removing his soiled clothing, taking him to the bathroom to clean him, and changing the bed.

"As I watched her work with such determination and humility, I thought, *Now, that's what love is.* We are bombarded with media images of weddings, engagement rings, parties, and flowers, but this is not love. Love is defined by difficult acts of human compassion and generosity. I felt so proud of both of them that day (and always) for what they accomplished. They would be embarrassed by the telling of this story, but they are my heroes."

In Samantha's account, we see not only the depth of love between her parents but also how its power radiates outward to all who witness it. People often speak to me about feeling enlarged by their regard for another, stirred by mutual generosity and devotion. When I ask them to describe their experience of being loved, they talk about feeling at home in the world, cherished and recognized, affirmed and encouraged.

No connection is always easy or free of strife, no matter how many minutes a day we meditate. It's how we relate to conflict, as well as to our differing needs and expectations, that makes our relationships sustainable. Even when we do our very best to treat those close to us with utmost respect and understanding, conflict happens. That's life. That's human nature.

But what's also human nature, and what keeps us coming back to each other, is the fundamental desire to connect. "Human beings are social creatures," wrote author and surgeon Atul Gawande in *The New Yorker*. "We are social not just in the trivial sense that we like company, and not just in the obvious sense that we each depend on others. We are social in a more elemental way: simply to exist as a normal human being requires interaction with other people."

THE ATTACHMENT PARADOX

THAT URGE TO connect persists from the cradle to the grave, according to the late British psychoanalyst John Bowlby. Bowlby is the architect of attachment theory, which credits our early connections, especially with our mothers, as shaping our relationships throughout our lives. If our caregivers were able to meet our most important emotional needs, we gradually learn emotional regulation and self-care. We also develop the ability to form secure connections with others. If not, our attachment orientation will likely tend toward anxiety or avoidance.

I see both expressions of attachment difficulties in students all the time. For example, Nick's mother lost a baby a year before Nick was born, and she was still drowning in grief during his infancy. Today, Nick tends to worry obsessively that the people who matter most to him will suddenly abandon him. On the other hand, Elaine, whose mother was hospitalized for several months soon after Elaine was born, tends to withdraw as soon as a potential partner gets close. During the course of psychotherapy and meditation retreats, both Nick and Elaine identified these early disruptions in attachment as a source of their challenges in relationships.

But are strong attachments really a good thing?

Those who are familiar with the language of Buddhist teachings are often puzzled by our human need for close connections and worry that such relationships represent an unhealthy form of clinging. *Aren't I supposed to practice just the opposite?* they wonder. *Isn't non-attachment the preferred, more enlightened state?* As one perplexed meditator said to me, "I want to be like the Dalai Lama, but I also want to love my husband."

In reality, there is no conflict between loving others deeply and living mindfully.

There are particular people with whom we have strong connections, and this is a good thing: Our babies. Our beloveds. Our parents, siblings, and other family members. Our teachers. Our BFFs. In fact, the Dalai Lama often mentions special relationships in his life, notably with his mother, whom he credits with instilling in him the seeds of kindness and compassion.

The Dalai Lama has also said that we can live without religion and meditation, but cannot survive without affection. At the same time, the Buddhist teachings discourage us from clinging and grasping to those we hold dear, and from trying to control the people or the relationship. What's more, we're encouraged to accept the impermanence of all things: the flower that blooms today will be gone tomorrow, the objects we possess will break or fade or lose their utility, our relationships will change, life will end.

When we look closely at how the word *attachment* is used in both psychology and Buddhist thought, what we discover is more paradox than contradiction. As Baljinder Sahdra and Phillip Shaver, a psychology professor emeritus at the University of California–Davis, have pointed out in *The International Journal for the Psychology of Religion*, the terms may confuse, but the underlying intentions are quite similar: "Both systems highlight the importance of giving and receiving love and of minimizing anxious clinging or avoidant aloofness and suppression of unwanted mental experiences."

In my own teaching, I find it helpful to describe the parallels this way: the secure attachment of Western psychology is actually akin to Buddhist non-attachment; avoidant attachment is the inverse of being mindful and present; and anxious attachment aligns with Buddhist notions of clinging and grasping.

A WHOLE-BODY EXPERIENCE

WHATEVER LANGUAGE WE use to describe healthy relationships, when we're in them, we feel nourished by them, in body as well as mind. Roger, one of my students, writes: "I have love for my wife, my daughter, myself, my experiences, my friends. But what's the commonality? For me, it's a physical sensation that arises when I'm in a loving state. It's not a lustful state or a friendship state. It's that warm quality we know from practicing lovingkindness and compassion. For me, real love occurs when I'm experiencing that physical sensation."

In fact, scientists have begun to document the far-reaching physical implications of connectedness, which range from relieving pain to enhancing the function of our nervous systems.

Richard Davidson, a neuropsychologist at the University of Wisconsin–Madison, investigated the effects of touch and companionship during stressful experiences. In a 2006 study, he and his colleagues used magnetic resonance imaging (MRI) to monitor the levels of fear and pain experienced by women when they were given mild electric shocks. When left completely alone, the women felt both fear and pain, and the areas of their brains responsible for emotion were particularly active.

However, if a member of the lab team held their hands, the women's brains showed less fear, even though the physical pain remained. And when the women's husbands held their hands during the shocks, their brain activity calmed down markedly at every level. It turned out that the calming effect was directly proportional to the connection they felt with their comforter.

Science tells us that love not only diminishes the experience of physical pain but can make us—and our beloveds—healthier. Barbara Fredrickson has studied what she terms *micro-moments of connection*. "It's when you share a genuine positive feeling with another living being," she explained to the audience at a talk in New York.

"It could be laughing with a friend, or hugging your neighbor with compassion, or it could be smiling at a baby. It doesn't even need to be your baby. It could be the baby on the plane."

Fredrickson shared that science suggests these micro-moments may be more powerful than we think. Research found that when one person's smiles, gestures, and postures began to be mirrored by the other person, the synchronization was more than skin deep.

"When you're really connecting with somebody else," Fredrickson said, "your heart rhythms come into sync; your biochemistries come into sync. Even your neural firings come into sync." What's more, that biological resonance of good feeling and goodwill has lasting effects. Increasing the quantity of micro-moments supports the function of the vagus nerve, the long cranial nerve that wends its way from the brain to the abdomen, enhancing the body's ability to slow a racing heart and regulate inflammation and glucose levels.

"This isn't just about your health," Fredrickson said, "because when you're really connecting with someone else, your heart is getting a mini-tune-up and so is theirs. The more you connect, the more you fortify this wiring to connect, and the more you lower your odds of having a heart attack and increase your odds of living a long, happy, and healthy life."

Fredrickson says it gives her goose bumps to realize that merely smiling at someone can have significant health consequences. In her own life, she now sees every interaction as an opportunity to make those micro-moments happen, whether it's through playing with her cats and two sons or smiling at the toddler on the plane. "It's all part of a magic that keeps our bonds strong and our hearts healthy," she said. "So stop waiting for the cupid's arrow or the lightning bolt to choose you. Choose love. Choose to connect with the people in your midst."

In this part, we'll explore real love with our partners, our children, our parents and siblings, as well as our dear friends, close colleagues, and spiritual teachers. How do we love another skillfully? How do we take our beautiful and pure intentions and find expression for them? How do we contend with loss, disappointment, and hurt? And how do we stay vulnerable enough to experience real love, knowing that it's impermanent?

In a nutshell: one moment at a time. But of course there's more to it than that: simple, but not easy.

10

BARRIERS TO FINDING REAL LOVE

*

Love does not begin and end the way we seem to
think it does.

—JAMES BALDWIN

"PULL THE THORNS FROM YOUR heart. Then you will see the rose gardens within you," wrote Rumi, the thirteenth-century Sufi poet and mystic.

Why focus on the "thorns"—all of those barriers to love we may feel within—instead of cultivating it directly? And what are these thorns, anyway?

Though it may sound paradoxical, identifying our thoughts, emotions, and habitual patterns of behavior is the key to freedom and transformation. If we don't acknowledge the places where we're stuck, we inevitably twist ourselves into knots to bypass certain feelings and perceptions, and the love that would otherwise be available to us also becomes tied up in knots. But when we set an intention to explore our emotional hot spots, we create a pathway to real love.

For example, no matter what we think we *should* do, I don't think you can coerce yourself into loving your neighbor—or your boss—when you can't stand him. But if you try to understand your feelings of dislike with mindfulness and compassion, being sure not to forget *self*-compassion, you create the possibility for change. Your neighbor or your boss may still do things that annoy you, but the anger and tightness you feel in your chest whenever you see him is bound to diminish, leaving you freer and more available for love.

Instead of exclusively searching outside of ourselves for the source of our difficulties with others, we also look within. This is true for all relationships. Our longing for closeness brings us face-to-face with those inner blocks. And so we begin at home.

THE GREAT BALANCING ACT

YOU DON'T HAVE to love yourself unconditionally before you can give or receive real love. This turns the quest for self-love into yet another self-improvement project—an additional barrier to feeling whole and deserving of love.

The good news is that opportunities for love enter our lives unpredictably, whether or not we've perfected self-compassion or befriended our inner critic. When we develop our ability to love in one realm, we simultaneously nourish our ability in others, as long as we remain open to the flow of insight and compassion.

Just as a prism refracts light differently when you change its angle, each experience of love illuminates love in new ways, drawing from an infinite palette of patterns and hues. We gaze at an infant and feel our hearts swell, and when we notice it's not the result of anything the baby has done, we can begin to imagine regarding ourselves the same way. We learn from any relationship in which we've made a heartfelt connection.

Yet this balancing act between self-regard and love for others is delicate; we suffer when our sense of worthiness relies too heavily on what we give or receive. Some of us give away too much of ourselves and call it love. Perhaps we've been told that if we love others enough and sacrifice more, we will ultimately be fulfilled. Some of us try to possess others in order to feel whole. Perhaps we've been told that if we feel control in our relationships, we are more empowered. But when we come from a place of inner impoverishment, love becomes merely hunger: hunger for reassurance, for acclaim, for affirmation of our being.

For my student Emma, love was a lofty vision of idealism and self-sacrifice. The pattern began the summer after her freshman year of college, when she went to Italy to study Dante. "The professor focused on St. Francis as he's shown in Dante, and we visited Assisi," Emma recalls. "Francis was a hero of the *Divine Comedy* because of his ideal vision of love. He humbles himself completely, puts his face in the dirt, and renounces everything. The image our professor emphasized was that St. Francis emptied himself out like a cup— that he became an empty vessel to be filled with God.

"My idea of love was just being a steady, reassuring, utterly forgiving, and kind background, in front of which my brilliant significant other could play out his brilliance. I wanted to be selfless." What's more, she says, "I was drawn to men I perceived as deeply troubled genius types. I was an English major, and historic literary relationships, like that of Véra and Vladimir Nabokov, seemed to justify my notion of love, though my friends were horrified by how much autonomy I was willing to give up. Still, giving in entirely to another felt holy, pure, and essential.

"I remember once going on what seemed like a perfectly normal date to Boston's Museum of Fine Arts with my first serious boyfriend. It was springtime, and we went on a walk after, and he just kept repeating, 'I can't do this . . . I can't . . . I can't . . .' I panicked," Emma says in retrospect. "I couldn't figure out what he was so upset about. Finally, he said, 'I can't tell what you want, what you're thinking . . .'" Suddenly, Emma realized they were in actuality two separate people rather than her idealized vision of how a relationship must be: never two, only as one.

So often we operate from ideas of love that don't fit our reality. It was only after Emma unpacked her assumptions about intimate relationships that she was able to start treating herself with the kind of care and respect she'd bestowed on others—and her relationships gradually became more mutual and satisfying.

Ultimately, as Jungian psychologist James Hollis writes in *The Eden Project*, "The best thing we can do for our relationship with others . . . is to render our relationship to ourselves more conscious."

UNPACKING OUR ASSUMPTIONS

I ONCE GAVE a talk about equanimity, and afterward, a woman approached me. At first she mentioned the beauty of the church where the lecture took place; then she thanked me for coming. But the whole time, she seemed to be squirming inside her skin, her eyes darting around, not looking at me. "What would you say to someone you knew was being physically abused?" she asked finally, her gaze directed up at the ceiling. I didn't challenge whether her question was hypothetical or autobiographical, and I thought carefully about how to answer, sensing that a lot might be at stake.

"Well," I replied, "it's really important to have lovingkindness for oneself. When we talk about equanimity in the context of abuse, we're talking about boundaries. Sometimes people in abusive situations think they're responsible for the other person's happiness or that they're going to fix them and make them feel better. The practice of equanimity teaches that it's not all up to you to make someone else happy." She seemed to thoughtfully consider what I was saying, we looked deeply into each other's eyes, and she thanked me and left.

In fact, the practice of equanimity also makes us realize that it's *never* up to someone else to make *us* happy either. This can be a bitter pill to swallow, especially when you're lonely. Singer Janis Joplin famously said, "Onstage I make love to 25,000 different people, then I go home alone." It's not bad to go home alone if you feel whole. But if you go home alone thinking you're not enough without another person next to you, that can be a source of great pain.

My student Dan, who is vulnerable to depression, used to dream that once he became a parent, his demons would somehow magically disappear. "Maybe because I always felt so harshly judged by my own father, I believed that the only way for me to heal was to have a child of my own," he says now. "After my son was born, my most cherished hopes were realized. Being a stay-at-home dad gave my life meaning. My kid needed me and I was there, unlike my own dad. As Jake got older, we went to baseball and basketball games and on all sorts of father-son outings. I mean, we were a *team*, even after he started elementary school."

But once Jake hit third grade and became more interested in playing LEGOs with his friends than spending all his free time with his dad, Dan sank into a deep depression. "It was very painful, but the only way to climb out of that dark place was to really see the burden I'd laid on this little kid for my own happiness," Dan reflects. "For his sake as well as mine, I had to let go and let him develop into his own person." A combination of psychotherapy and mindfulness, with a strong emphasis on self-compassion, lifted Dan out of his codependent and depressive state, and ultimately saved Dan's relationship with his son.

In order to free ourselves from our assumptions about love, we must ask ourselves what those long-held, often buried assumptions are and then face them, which takes courage, humility, and kindness. Do we believe, as Dan once did, that someone else is responsible for our happiness? Or that we're responsible for someone else's happiness?

Our unconscious expectations take many forms. Kathryn explained what she learned when a significant relationship ended: "I realized that one of the underlying assumptions of this relationship that I had not communicated with him was this transaction: I'm going to take care of him and try to heal him, and then he was going to take care of me. When I went to therapy, I recognized that I, like my ex-partner, was also suffering from my own acute trauma. My father is an alcoholic. He was a difficult person and abusive in various ways. But what I wanted from my ex-partner was to fix him and then fall apart and have him fix me. We invest in these relationships with so much of our own personal pain and hopes. But this is deeply unfair to oneself and to the other person."

Perhaps we've believed that if we loved a friend or child or sibling or spouse enough, our love would cure all ills. We'd suffer fewer painful setbacks, as would our loved ones. No more desperate midnight phone calls or interventions. Do we believe that we're at fault because someone we care for is suffering deeply? Do we expect another person to complete us or fix us?

MAKING PEACE WITH FEAR

WHEN WE PAY attention to sensations in our bodies, we can feel that love is the energetic opposite of fear. Love seems to open and expand us right down to the cellular level, while fear causes us to contract and withdraw into ourselves. Yet so often, fear keeps us from being able to say *yes* to love—perhaps our greatest challenge as human beings.

Close relationships ask us to open our hearts and expose our innermost thoughts and feelings. Yet if you felt unseen or unappreciated in childhood, the risk of self-disclosure can seem almost life-threatening. Or if you were valued only as a "good kid" and not encouraged to express your individuality, intimacy may feel suffocating. How we felt in relation to our caregivers in childhood is the (often unconscious) prototype for our connections later in life. Becoming more conscious of those early feelings can make us less fearful of dropping our protective masks.

This fear of loss is natural, especially if you've had a big loss early in life. But it can also keep you from savoring the love that's available to you right now.

WORKING WITH THE BARRIERS

AS WE EXPLORE new ways of loving and being loved by others, we need to equip ourselves with open, pliant minds; we need to be willing to investigate, experiment, and evaluate as we approach a topic we thought we knew so much about.

I imagine an internal version of a position taught in tai chi, in which the knees are always slightly bent. Sometimes called the Horse Stance, it is thought to increase the flow of energy throughout the body. It also lowers the center of gravity, increasing stability in the event of an unexpected blow.

In the practice of mindfulness, the counterpart to the Horse Stance might be called the Stance of Inquiry. We attend to the present moment. We gather in our attention, again and again, and open to whatever comes, humbly accepting it. In doing so, we begin to peel back the layers of conditioning and unconscious expectations. We can't judge whether they're realistic or not until we know we have them. We start to discern what, in actuality, is available to us, both in terms of what we can give and what we can receive. And at a deeper level, we realize that love simply, perpetually exists and that it's a matter of psychic housekeeping to make room for it.

As psychoanalyst and philosopher Erich Fromm said in his book *The Art of Loving*: "Love is not a relationship to a specific person; it is an attitude, an orientation of character which determines the relatedness of a person to the world as a whole . . ."

CHAPTER 10 PRACTICES

Loss and gain meditation

This practice is one of neutralizing our fears when it comes to love for others. We can recognize that all of life's conditions are constantly changing, which naturally includes our relationships. In any moment, we may encounter some element of change, which can be triggering for some, particularly those who have developed certain fears around intimacy.

1. With our inhalations, we allow ourselves to engage with the pain of fear, especially surrounding the potential for change in any moment. Rather than pushing the feeling away, we welcome it with each breath.

2. With our exhalations, we recognize the capacity we have in each moment to gain perspective, even amid discomfort. We recognize the space we have for acceptance and gratitude, and see the constant changes of our relationships with curiosity and flexibility.

This practice is one of dis-identifying with our self-preoccupations around love for another, and empowering our fears into growth.

Inner abundance practice

In this exercise, we'll examine the feelings of deficiency and self-contraction that often get confused with love for others—when we become lost in feeling like we are responsible for the happiness of others, and lose sight of our inner abundance in the process.

1. Throughout the day, notice moments when you become overwhelmed with feelings of responsibility for others— be it a parent, significant other, child, student, or friend. You may be convinced that it's your job to give more of yourself to this person, or perhaps you feel a sense of resentment—that this person should feel the same way and doesn't.

2. Try connecting to the weight of this feeling with more spaciousness, and explore what happens both in your body and to your mood as you relax.

3. Take as long as you need to describe your experience of relating to the feeling in different ways—with self-judgment, resentment, fear of permanence, and/or fear of loss versus that state of adopting a "big mind" perspective. Look for moments of:

   - *Anger*
   - *Desire*
   - *Judgment and/or self-judgment*
   - *Restlessness/impatience/frustration*
   - *Uncertainty*

This practice is completely portable, meaning you can try it out during any experiences of overwhelm. It particularly helps strip away those confusing and restrictive assumptions about love for others—such as the all-too-common notion that love is about recognizing our responsibility to fix others or be fixed by others in return. It is a practice of cultivating open awareness, which makes us become more curious and creative in the ways we relate to others and ourselves. Through recognizing the space we have within ourselves, and the availability of the feeling that we are enough, we make room for real love.

CULTIVATE CURIOSITY
AND AWE

✳

ONE FOUNDATION OF LOVING RELATIONSHIPS is curiosity, keeping open to the idea that we have much to learn even about those we have been close to for decades. I think of the night when an old friend of mine stood up at a dinner party and launched into a rousing German drinking song. I looked at her in wonder as her hands swept the air. She had most of the table singing along with her by the second refrain. And this from a shy and soft-spoken woman who had always run from the spotlight. All these years, and she could still surprise me.

Who knows what capacities lie dormant in those we hold dear? We have a history together that has set a tone between us, and we've bonded through common interests and shared experiences. We may even say to mutual friends that there's nothing about him or her that would surprise us.

But think for a minute. Do your children, your spouse, your closest friend know everything about you?

Jenny was a high-powered corporate lawyer. She'd never found a partner she thought was a "fit," even though she'd dated with deliberation for months at a time. She had never wanted children. She was brilliant, funny, generous, a great friend and traveling companion who, as she neared middle age, didn't seem to have a shred of a nurturing instinct.

When a mutual friend was diagnosed with Stage 4 ovarian cancer, Jenny used her formidable advocacy skills to get our friend into a promising clinical trial. That was impressive—and just the kind of skillful effort that Jenny was famous for.

But as our friend was hit by the side effects of multiple powerful drugs, I saw a new side of Jenny. She went to our friend's house every day, anticipating provisions or gear that would give her some comfort, smoothed communications with her doctors, and stayed close as her cancer gradually went into remission.

One day I thanked Jenny for her tender caregiving and said I was amazed at how she'd stepped into this role. Jenny then told me something I hadn't known: right after high school, she'd spent three years as a volunteer at the hospice where her beloved grandmother had died.

Suddenly I understood: this part of Jenny had been set aside as she focused on work, but it was there when she (and our friend) needed it. After our twenty-two years of friendship, Jenny had caught me by surprise, I was in awe of her and in awe of all the things about her I might yet discover.

What makes awe such a powerful call to love is that it's disruptive. It sneaks up on us. It doesn't ask our permission to wow us; it just does. Awe can arise from a single glance, a sound, a gesture.

Say you're sitting with a relative and you tell him something that makes him laugh. He has a great laugh, loud and long and free. That laugh is an aspect of his generosity in its most outward manifestation. And because you're paying attention, even though you've heard this laugh countless times before, now you hear it with awe.

SEEING WHAT'S RIGHT IN FRONT OF US

FRITZ PERLS, THE co-founder of Gestalt therapy, said, "Boredom is lack of attention." Our tendency, of course, is to seek out intense experiences in order to feel alive. If our attention is not trained to notice routine or subtlety, we simply wait for the next big hit and switch off until then. It often requires a conscious effort to take an interest in the person before us, to look past our assumptions about them, but it's an effort that keeps us open to connection.

I've met many people who have tremendous power and resources in conventional terms, people who seem to have it all, who elicit envy from almost everyone they meet. It is only by not buying into some projected persona (it could be my projection or theirs, or sometimes both) that I've been able to see them more deeply and to discover their vulnerability. It's only by being fully present that I've been emotionally available to hear about their alcoholic brother or troubled teen, their immense frustration and anxiety, and the beauty of their undying love for their family member.

I've also met many people with very few resources, who are really broke or depressed, but who reveal surprising strengths. They are buoyed up by helping their disabled neighbor or the troubled kid down the block or other people in their community who are hurting. It's all too easy to slot someone into the category of "needing help" and not to recognize the tremendous help they are offering to others.

THE POWER OF AWE

IT'S TOUGH TO have an authentic relationship with awe in the age of "awesome," a word that has become so overused as to be drained of its meaning. These days when someone says that something is "awesome," they usually mean it ironically: "I had to wait for three and a half hours at the DMV. That was awesome." Or perhaps they're just complimenting us on the appetizer we order: "Awesome choice." But genuine awe connects us with the world in a new way.

A student of mine comes from a family that prizes self-sufficiency. She was brought up to be able to do things for herself; asking favors was frowned upon. When she met her husband, self-sufficiency was something they had in common. They were drawn to each other's competence. "We've been married a dozen years now," she says, "and we definitely get stuck in routines, but there are aspects of him that still blow me away. Whenever I come home from a trip, he just assumes he'll pick me up at the airport or train station. I don't even have to ask." She's reminded each time of his generosity, made even sweeter because both of them know she could easily make her way home on her own. "Each time I'm a little surprised. It always feels as if I've stumbled upon this tender gift."

LETTING GO OF FANTASY

WHEN IT COMES to finding a partner or even a close friend, most of us carry within us an idealized image of "the one." We search for that perfect person, often projecting our fantasy ideal onto others.

And when, inevitably, the people on the receiving end of our personal Hollywood movie don't measure up, we're left feeling lonely, frustrated, and pessimistic about our chances of ever finding our match.

Whatever the source of our imagined ideal—whether we've conjured it from books, songs, movies, real-life role models, or all of the above—it's essential that we bring our notions into the light of awareness. It's only when we start to distinguish reality from fantasy that we can humbly, with eyes wide open, forge loving and sustainable connections with others.

In the past, Yvonne had always fallen for tall, handsome, and powerful but withholding men. Alejandro, on the other hand, was shortish, pudgy, nurturing, and playful. And though his interest in her was keen, Yvonne had long delayed getting involved with him because he didn't fit her "type." Then one day she got lost—literally.

Yvonne had a terrible sense of direction, and getting lost had always been a problem. This brain glitch of hers was so severe that she got lost even when using her GPS. Her previous boyfriends had been critical and insulting when she called them from the road, so she was afraid to telephone Alejandro, whom she had started dating despite her initial resistance. Since she'd been driving around in an increasing frenzy for more than half an hour trying to find his house, she finally broke down and called.

"Pull over as soon as you can," Alejandro advised. Even after she stopped the car, she was still agitated, waiting for a negative putdown. "I love you," Alejandro assured her. "Just tell me where you are." He found Yvonne's location and guided her turn by turn, staying on the line the whole time. When she arrived at his house, he greeted her with a loving embrace and dinner on the table.

Being welcomed this way came as a shock to Yvonne, who was used to being with men who regarded her vulnerability with disgust.

But Alejandro made her feel cherished and safe. He loved her for the person she was, not for some idea of the person he thought she should be. And Yvonne, too, came to love him for the person he was, leaving behind her romantic ideal.

When we identify the thoughts that keep us from seeing others as they truly are, instead of hoping they'll magically live up to some idealized image, we prepare the ground for real love.

SET AN INTENTION

IN RECENT YEARS, many teachers and therapists have been talking about relationship as a path of awakening. This vision of love is not confined to achieving psychological wholeness; looked at in this way, personal connection becomes a spiritual practice.

In *Embracing the Beloved*, authors Stephen and Ondrea Levine wrote: "If another person is the most important thing in your life, then you're in trouble and they're in trouble because they become responsible for your suffering. But if consciousness is the most important thing in our lives and relationship is a means toward that end . . . Ah! then we are approaching paradise. We are approaching the possibility of actually becoming a human being before we die."

The place to begin is with intention, say the Levines: "When one commits to practices that clear the mind and expose the heart—such as mindfulness, forgiveness and loving kindness—what once seemed unworkable may well become the very center of the relationship . . . Our intention itself has considerable healing potential."

And so we begin with an intention: to stay open to the present, available to curiosity and awe, and to pay attention to the beings the universe sends our way, knowing that we might come to deeply cherish them.

CHAPTER 11 PRACTICES

Attention

Feelings of apathy as they relate to our relationships often stem from insufficiently paying attention to those around us. Remember: everyone we interact with has the capacity to surprise us in an infinite number of ways. What can first open us up to each of our innate capacities for love is merely to recognize that.

But how?

This exercise is about finding creative ways to pay attention to our relationships with greater intention—to open up, to cultivate curiosity, to recognize the infinite potential to feel awe in our lives.

1. Start by paying attention to each of your interactions with more focus. Notice if the intentions you bring to different interactions vary depending on who it is you are engaging with. Are you more closed off to some? Carrying certain assumptions with others? Try to notice any urges, expectations, yearnings, and judgments you may have as they come up. You don't have to push them away, but recognize how they might be affecting your perspective.

2. Within each interaction you have, try to notice something surprising, or to try a new mode of interacting. Maybe you had never made such deliberate eye contact with a given person before—and doing so makes you see them in a new way. Perhaps you tend toward steering conversations with friends; maybe you commit to practicing more restraint, allowing your friend to take the lead. You may find you see your friend in a new light.

3. Consider the following open-ended questions to ask friends, family members, significant others, and acquaintances. Surely there are some situations that may not be

ideal for these questions, but even considering in your own head how different individuals may answer them can help us sustain a sense of curiosity.

Questions:
- *What's one of your most poignant memories from childhood?*
- *Is there a certain poem, piece of music, or work of art you've encountered that has moved you in a memorable way?*
- *What experiences do you associate with each of the seasons?*
- *Have you ever had a job you don't often think about?*
- *What's your favorite time of day?*
- *Who was the person you felt closest to during your early childhood? Adolescence?*
- *Where in the world do you feel warmest and safest?*
- *How do you relax?*

Asking questions is an opportunity for creativity and personal expression, both for the person asking and the person answering. Feel free to come up with some of your own questions to help bring more attention and curiosity to your interactions, but make sure to recognize your intentions consistently. Resolve to bring more mindfulness to the connection between your larger aspiration to find deeper connection and awe in your relationships at large, and the small gestures that comprise your everyday encounters.

Meditation: Lovingkindness toward a benefactor and friends

We start with offering lovingkindness to someone who has been of help to us. This person is known as a benefactor—maybe it's someone who's been directly generous to us or kind to us, or maybe they've inspired us even though we've never met them. They symbolize the power of love for us. The benefactor is the one who when we think of them, we smile. It could be an adult, a child, a pet.

As you call to mind a benefactor, you can get an image of them, say their name, and begin to offer the phrases of lovingkindness to them. "May you be safe, be happy, be healthy, live with ease."

Then, after some time, move on to offering lovingkindness to a friend. You can start with a friend who's doing well right now. They're enjoying success or good fortune in some aspect of life. You can get an image of them, say their name to yourself, and offer the phrases of lovingkindness to them: "May you be safe, be happy, be healthy, live with ease."

And then a friend who's having difficulty right now, they're experiencing some kind of loss, or pain, or fear; bring them to mind. Get a feeling for their presence, as though they were right in front of you, and offer the phrases of lovingkindness to them.

You can end the sitting with a spontaneous offering of lovingkindness to whoever comes to mind.

AUTHENTIC COMMUNICATION

✳

PLAYWRIGHT LILLIAN HELLMAN FAMOUSLY SAID, "People change and forget to tell each other." Though I'm guessing she made that comment with tongue pressed firmly against cheek, it contains a priceless nugget of truth. When we don't tell those we love about what's really going on or listen carefully to what they have to say, we tend to fill in the blanks with stories. For example, we might conclude that a friend who appears sullen or distracted is angry with us, when in fact she's depressed or overwhelmed. Or we might worry that our partner doesn't love us anymore when he seems to snap at us for no reason, only to discover that he's terrified of being downsized from his job and is afraid to tell us.

Very often in close relationships, the subject being discussed is not the subject at all. As psychologist Virginia Satir put it, "The problem is not the problem; coping is the problem."

So how do we identify what's really going on between us and those we love? How do we train ourselves to communicate the truth of our experiences and listen without judgment to theirs? How do we avoid falling into the trap of repetitive, predictable, and frustrating patterns of communication and behavior?

From both a Buddhist and Western psychological perspective, the place to start is with kindness. This may sound simplistic, but studies conducted at the Gottman Institute in Washington State confirm kindness as the key predictor of successful marriages. Although many people regard kindness as a nice general quality, it's not generally perceived as the cornerstone of healthy relationships.

But setting the intention to practice kindness toward one's partner or family members or friends does *not* preclude getting angry or upset. It doesn't mean sugarcoating the truth. Practicing kindness is about getting real, but in ways that are constructive and support the growth of the relationship. As Julie Gottman, co-founder of the Gottman Institute, said in an interview with *The Atlantic*, "Kindness doesn't mean that we don't express our anger, but the kindness informs how we choose to express the anger. You can throw spears at your partner. Or you can explain why you're hurt and angry, and that's the kinder path."

My friend Carolyn recently reminded me that she and her partner consulted a therapist early in their relationship to deal with conflicts arising from the frequent presence of Carolyn's ex, with whom she shared custody of her son. At the end of the first session, the therapist remarked that she believed the couple would be successful in resolving their difficulties because they exhibited such "goodwill" toward one another. In other words: kindness. That was thirty-five years ago.

Kindness is not a fixed trait that we either have or lack, but more like a muscle that can be developed and strengthened. We exercise kindness in any moment when we recognize our shared humanity— with all the hopes, dreams, joys, disappointments, vulnerability, and suffering that implies. Such simple but profound awareness levels the playing field. We are all humans doing the best we can.

SELF-DISCLOSURE AND NON-JUDGMENTAL LISTENING

IN CONSCIOUS RELATIONSHIPS, we set the intention to investigate the old stories we tell ourselves and our habits of thinking and behavior. Practically speaking, this means that we take responsibility for our actions and reactions, as well as for defensive strategies such as withdrawing, keeping secrets, or blaming someone else for our suffering.

"People thrive in a climate of 100% accountability, where nobody blames or claims victim status," explain relationship experts Kathlyn and Gay Hendricks in a blog post for *The Huffington Post*. "From this empowered position, problems can be solved quickly, because time and energy are not squandered in a fruitless attempt to find fault."

Taking responsibility for oneself is by definition an act of kindness. Yet, though 100 percent accountability is a worthy ideal, we're imperfect beings, and at times, it may take some struggle to get there. My friend Jonah, a committed meditator, told me about an experience he had with his best friend, Peter. Ever since they met in college, the two men have been like brothers, sharing just about everything. In fact, most people who meet them for the first time assume that Jonah and Peter *are* brothers. They even look alike.

What's more, their birthdays are two days apart, and they always celebrate together. Last year, however, when Jonah phoned Peter to make a plan, Peter dodged the subject, claiming he was too busy to think about it, and promised to get back to Jonah the next day. But after not hearing from Peter for a week, Jonah called him and was shocked and hurt to learn that Peter's new boyfriend had invited him to go skiing the week of their birthdays—and that Peter had accepted, without telling Jonah.

Jonah's mindfulness went right out the window. He flew into a rage, accusing Peter of deliberately deceiving him, then slammed down the phone. Peter, aware that he'd behaved thoughtlessly, called Jonah several times to make amends, but Jonah refused to pick up or return Peter's calls. Finally, Peter waited outside Jonah's building for his friend to get home from work and followed him inside.

He apologized profusely, admitting that he'd been afraid to share his plans with Jonah for fear of upsetting him. Instead of telling the truth, Peter had avoided confrontation and disappeared—a strategy he'd adopted as a kid when his alcoholic father went on one of his rampages. For his part, Jonah acknowledged that Peter's behavior triggered old feelings of being unseen and unimportant in his large family. Though painful, the conversation proved healing for both men. Not only did they come up with an alternative plan to celebrate their birthdays, they agreed that a conflict that could have destroyed the friendship ended up deepening their bond.

"As tough as it was at first to open up, being vulnerable and saying what was true made all the difference," reflects Jonah. "Peter and I both came through trusting that if we can be honest and keep it real, even when it's hard, our friendship will survive just about anything."

In their book *And Baby Makes Three*, psychotherapists and Gottman Institute co-founders John and Julie Gottman describe good communication between partners when issues arise—which I think applies to dear friends, as well: "They ask, 'Is there a story behind this for you, maybe some childhood history that makes this so crucial for you?' They want to uncover not just the topmost feelings, but the deeper layers as well."

LIVING WITH YOUR TEACHER

WHEN WE LIVE together in a committed relationship, we live with our teacher, says George Taylor, a therapist who specializes in working with couples. "We're tested daily, and every day we have the opportunity to meet our own resistance and reactivity. Moment to moment, what's going on inside us is reflected in our body language and our response to our partner, and vice versa. We're incredible mirrors for each other."

The good news, Taylor adds, is that we're highly trainable. "In my own marriage as well as in my work with couples, I've seen how paying attention to our often unconscious reactions and judgments enables us to choose to respond differently. Even small moments of mindfulness can be powerfully transformational."

When we are willing to explore our own experiences, we open the doorway to deeper connection and intimacy, he explains. We grow to love and appreciate our partner for who she or he truly is, and he or she loves and appreciates us for who we are, unmasked and whole. In the light of one another's gaze, we are *seen*.

Daniella and Rayne fell in love and married on a California beach in 2010. After the Supreme Court upheld same-sex marriage legislation in 2015, the couple held a second ceremony to legalize their union. But by then, their relationship had been tested nearly to the breaking point.

That happened after they decided to open a café together. Although both women had previously run businesses, only Daniella had restaurant experience. Still, the early dreaming phases in which the couple experimented with recipes and envisioned their café inspired them both and brought them closer. It wasn't until they signed a lease that they began to fight over every decision. Daniella is wildly creative but has difficulty limiting her options, while Rayne has ADHD and gets flustered when things don't happen quickly. They reached a crossroads when it became clear that either they could continue to be enraged by each other's quirks and deficiencies, or they could embrace them and help each other grow. They consciously opted for the latter path.

Now, says Rayne, "We reflect on how much we've accomplished together."

Adds Daniella, "If there are any struggles, we try to do better. We're constantly trying to learn more about ourselves. Our life together has been a complete eye-opening rebirth."

Although much of the work we do in committed relationships we do with our partners, sometimes it's necessary to start with ourselves.

Clara learned this during a difficult passage in the seventh year of her marriage to James, when their two children were young. She'd left her job to care for them, and most days she was content. But often, by the end of the day when she was feeling tired and the children were cranky, she resented her husband, especially his TV habit.

Every night when he got home from work, he'd grab the dinner she'd made for him and plant himself in front of the TV. Clara felt angry and frustrated by his lack of interest in her. She worried that their marriage had reached an unhappy stalemate, and it was clear that James felt it, too. One night when she greeted him after work with her usual scowl, he remarked, "Just once I'd like to come home to someone who was happy to see me."

That statement went straight to Clara's heart. She didn't want to hurt James, yet she wasn't sure how to handle her distress. Then she remembered the practice for working with difficult emotions that we reviewed in section 1: RAIN—Recognition, Acknowledgment,

Investigation, and Non-Identification. (Detailed instructions are on page 52.)

Clara began with Step 1, Recognize, and let herself fully experience her feelings. She stood in the doorway looking on as James watched TV. She noticed that her arms were tightly crossed, with one hip pressed against the doorjamb in a closed, angry posture. Staring at her husband, she thought, *He doesn't give a damn about me.* Before they had kids, things were different. Sometimes Clara would put on music and dance with James; sometimes they'd sit and talk. Usually these thoughts raced through her mind, unnoticed and unchallenged. But when she stopped to recognize them, as well as the bitterness and self-pity wrapped up in them, she experienced a startling moment of awareness.

Sitting in the kitchen, Clara moved on to Step 2, Acknowledge. She acknowledged how sad she was to have such negative, unloving thoughts about James, while also acknowledging how lonely and taken for granted she felt. She missed her job, too. She didn't regret her choice to stay home, but she allowed herself to feel how much she longed for aspects of her professional life that had given her joy.

Paradoxically, allowing her sadness was a relief for Clara, and she felt less defensive and angry. As she moved into Step 3 of RAIN, Investigate, she began to probe why she felt the way she did. She realized that at the core of her loneliness was a sense of abandonment that echoed her feelings when her parents divorced. After their breakup, life had become busier and harder for her mother, and Clara didn't want to be a bother, so she put a lid on her feelings— just as she'd done with James.

Clara came to see things from James's perspective, too: putting in long hours on the job, feeling the pressure of supporting the family. Her resentment softened. She realized that she and James had made choices together, and she no longer needed to identify herself as the injured party. She had arrived at Step 4 of RAIN, Non-Identify. This was simply a phase in their lives. In a few years, the kids would be in school, and both her marriage and work life would offer new possibilities.

By exploring the truth of her experience, Clara was able to reconnect with James. She chose quiet times for short talks, and her honesty created an opening for him to share his own feelings of missing Clara while also being frustrated by having so little time for himself. "We initiated a dialogue that is a work in progress," says Clara. "And that feels very good. Very alive, compared to the stuck place we were in before. We're much more loving, and trying our best to deal with my need for connection and his need for space. Now, when we get into tangles, we *talk* about what's going on."

"In the hothouse atmosphere of committed relationships, our defenses arise again and again," says George Taylor. "But the tools of mindfulness allow us to work with them and to fulfill our own vision of becoming a loving person, with all the care, forgiveness and generosity that suggests."

THE PRESSURE COOKER OF FAMILY

COMMUNICATION AMONG FAMILY members is often as volatile as it can be between couples. Adult siblings, children, parents, and other close relatives may harbor intense feelings like hurt and resentment—yet often these feelings become buried and then expressed in unskillful ways. Though partners and close friends may aspire to more honest dialogue, many families shut down around recognizing differences.

There are many good reasons for this: self-protection or the desire to protect others; the need to individuate and separate; rivalries; strong emotions, such as fear and shame; mental or physical illness; parental conflict and divorce; remarriage; economic instability; generational differences; the early death of a parent. The causes of familial discord and distance are countless, but the results are often the same: secrecy, blame, sadness, hurt, confusion, and feelings of loss and grief.

At some point in our adult lives, we may recognize the love that lingers beneath the pain, and yearn to heal. But even then, we can't assume that a family member will have a mindfulness practice or be comfortable with self-disclosure and non-judgmental listening. That doesn't matter: remarkable openings can occur when one person sets out to transform an old, unhappy dynamic.

In his book *It Didn't Start with You*, therapist Mark Wolynn recounts how he repaired his damaged relationships with both of his parents. After traveling to the far corners of the globe, he realized that the peace and spiritual healing he sought could be achieved only by reconnecting with his mother and father back home in Pittsburgh.

Wolynn started with his father. His parents had divorced when he was just thirteen years old. Wolynn and his father rarely got together after the divorce, even though his father didn't live terribly far away. But now Wolynn invited him to have a weekly lunch with him, and his father agreed.

"I had always craved a close relationship with my father, yet neither he nor I knew how to make it happen. This time, however, we kept talking. I told him that I loved him and that he was a good father. I shared the memories of things he did for me when I was small. I could feel him listening to what I was saying, even though his actions—shrugging his shoulders, changing the subject—indicated he was not. It took many weeks of talking and sharing memories. During one of our lunches together, he looked directly into my eyes and said, 'I didn't think you ever loved me.' I could barely breathe. It was clear that great pain welled in both of us. In that moment, something broke open. It was our hearts. Sometimes, the heart must break in order to open. Eventually, we began to express our love for each other."

Wolynn went on to find a new connection with his mother, as

well. "For the first time I could remember," he writes, "I was able to let myself receive my parents' love and care—not in the way I had once expected it, but in the way they could give it."

CHAPTER 12 PRACTICES

Experimentation with RAIN

Earlier in this chapter, we saw Clara use the RAIN method as a way of becoming less reactive and impetuous during a conflict with her husband. As explained more comprehensively in section 1, RAIN is an instructional acronym used to summarize a mindfulness practice geared toward helping us adopt a more expansive and flexible relationship with emotional suffering. Recognize. Acknowledge. Investigate. Non-Identify.

Now to review a more detailed explanation of the process once again . . .

When a thorny emotion comes up, we can simply remember RAIN. The first step, *Recognize*, is about noticing what is coming up. The next step is an extension of the first: we *Acknowledge* the feeling, allowing it to just be. Next, we *Investigate* the emotion by asking questions. We can find freedom in allowing ourselves to move closer toward the feeling with curiosity, rather than away from it.

The final step of RAIN—*Non-Identify*—means that we consciously don't allow ourselves to be defined by a given emotion, despite having explored it more deeply.

Now let's try it.

1. Recall a tough situation or conflict in which the intensity of your emotions kept you from communicating in a way that felt direct, authentic, and from a place of integrity.

2. Next, with the benefit of some perspective, comb through the emotions you felt during the conflict. This step

precedes the RAIN method and is meant to immerse you in the memory. Did you start out angry? Resentful? Did you say hurtful things out of guilt? Disappointment?

3. After determining some specific emotions that came up, think about an alternative situation in which you *could have* practiced RAIN. This is not an invitation to look back with regret but to feel the power of self-reflection. What happens when you simply *Recognize* how you were feeling? When you *Acknowledge* the situation for what it was? How does it feel to *Investigate* the situation and your emotions with curiosity? Does *Non-Identifying* help expose the places where we may become blinded by fear or anxiety?

4. Now that you've familiarized yourself a bit with the RAIN technique, feel free to write a short reflection about your reactions to the exercise. You may even want to try actually rewriting the story of the situation in question in the present tense, as though you are actually using the RAIN steps as a guide. This can be an empowering exercise for showing us how capable we are of communicating with greater mindfulness.

Lovingkindness for a family member

One of the reasons that authentic communication can be so difficult with family is that our family members are often the people we are both closest to and also those from whom we feel the greatest need to separate and individuate. These underlying dynamics create paradoxes and tensions that we may not always be conscious of, but that can contribute to the reactive communication style that mindfulness so powerfully helps to shift.

In this exercise, we practice a simple lovingkindness meditation on behalf of a particular family member. This person may be someone with whom you've had conflict, someone from whom you've received tremendous generosity, or someone with whom you have a more complicated and variable dynamic. Either way, the idea is the same—to open up to the possibility of transforming a relationship we often think of as set in stone.

1. Sit (or lie comfortably on your back) with your eyes closed or your gaze lowered.

2. Offer lovingkindness to a family member of your choice by silently saying, "May this person be safe. May she be happy. May she be healthy. May she live with ease."

3. Repeat the phrases at a pace that works for you, focusing your attention on one phrase at a time.

4. If your attention wanders, remember you can gently begin again.

5. As you end the session, consider whether or not you want to reach out in some way to that person.

Keeping it real

Recall the wisdom from psychotherapists and Gottman Institute co-founders John and Julie Gottman in their book *And Baby Makes Three*: "[Couples] ask, 'Is there a story behind this for you, maybe some childhood history that makes this so crucial for you?' They want to uncover not just the topmost feelings, but the deeper layers as well." In my mind, this kind of radical honesty is productive for our closest friends, as well.

In this exercise, reflect on difficulties you may face in a current relationship (romantic, professional, platonic, or any other type), perhaps one that has resurfaced as a pattern. Without overidentifying with these difficulties, take note of them and explore them.

1. Begin by asking yourself some questions. Here are a few to get you started: Do you have trouble voicing your needs? Are you afraid of expressing anger? How do you react when someone else expresses a need from you? Even if you identify certain things as personality traits, remember that you have the power to become more mindful of them, and communicate the difficulties you have in an effort to work on them.

2. The second step here is to explore *why* these patterns may have come to be. Perhaps there is no reason you can think of, but often we channel dynamics we are familiar with from childhood in our adult lives. This can be a very personal exercise that you do in your mind, simply by thinking. You may choose to write about it, or you may, as the Gottmans' quotation suggests, discuss it with a loved one. In all of these ways, this practice of becoming more conscious of ourselves opens us up to become more conscious of others.

PLAYING FAIR: A WIN-WIN PROPOSITION

＊

To love well is the task in all meaningful relationships, not just romantic bonds.

—bell hooks

WITH OUR CLOSE FRIENDS, FAMILY members, and lovers, we hope to create a special world, one in which we can expect to be treated fairly, with care, tenderness, and compassion. We hope to trust that the commitment we've made to each other is mutual and that we'll work actively to keep it alive.

B. Janet Hibbs, Ph.D., is a family psychologist whose clinical approach involves relational ethics—what we owe and deserve in family relationships. In her book, *Try to See It My Way: Being Fair in*

Love and Marriage, she describes a radical rethinking and thoughtful negotiation of the fundamental aspects of fairness at the center of good relationships. She writes about the challenges of fairness, even though she notes it's a lesson most of us feel we learned by kindergarten. "We all think we know what's fair, but we don't always agree—with a spouse, or a partner, or a child (growing or grown) . . . and then what? Fairness is a muddled mix of beliefs, traditions and multiple and sometimes opposing truths. Yet you need to learn how to be fair to keep your relationships healthy and make love last."

Her advice requires a willingness to let go of long-held positions and to approach issues from a fresh perspective. I call this a willingness to begin again, as we do in meditation. Stop keeping score, Hibbs suggests. Stop needing to be right. Stop doing things the way you used to just because that's what you know. Be open to the possibility that there are other paths available to you in relating to yourself and to another.

If we are really thinking about the "relational ethics" of our relationship, that means I'm sponsoring you to have the best life you can, and you're sponsoring me. We are co-sponsors. We regard our time together as a collaborative effort to make life better for each of us.

It also means that we don't keep a ledger. I've done three good things for you, so when are you going to do three good things for me? Real love doesn't keep score. We're aware that from time to time one person's needs will take precedence or another person can't contribute as much as before. A friend becomes ill and needs extra help for a month or two; a close colleague needs a place to stay after breaking up with his partner. Yet each person must feel seen and respected, with his or her needs taken into account. Mutuality is one of life's great balancing acts.

In the very first discussion group I held to help me explore the topic of real love, a man said, "Most people think of a good relationship as fifty-fifty. My dog and I, we're one hundred–one hundred." I've kept that story in mind looking at love between partners, parents and adult children, friends, and others.

Hibbs and I recently had an e-mail exchange about score-keeping. "Ideally in love relationships," she wrote, "reciprocity is a seesaw of turn-taking, which has a generous feel. People recount quid pro quo accountings of who owes what to whom when there is a felt (or real) violation of give-and-take. The trick of course is 'what counts' to whom, a largely unspoken deal which requires renegotiation when things go awry, and the seesaw gets stuck in a power play (you owe me and I'm in control, or I owe you but on what terms of repayment?)."

What might "count" as a gesture of kindness or generosity to one person in a relationship might be something that would go unrecognized by the other. There's nothing fundamentally wrong with having different emotional value systems. What does matter is establishing a secure and mutual vocabulary within the relationship, to know the kinds of things that "count" to you and that "count" to your loved ones—not in order to maintain a transactional system but to give authentically with the intention of merely giving, rather than, for instance, giving something *we think* counts.

REFLECTION

THINK OF A few relationships in your life, and simply note what counts for you in that dynamic, what is your strongest value in that circumstance. To the degree possible, see if you can discern (or, where appropriate, resolve to ask) what counts for the other person.

The idea of repayment is firmly rooted in a vocabulary of transaction and ultimately doesn't engender organic reciprocity. We can't give with the intention to be given back to, to be repaid; rather, we recognize the unpredictable ebb and flow of each person's emotional needs in any relationship, and don't seek to control it by establishing a rigid currency for emotional availability. We trust the other person, and the other person trusts us.

MUTUALITY IS CRUCIAL

I RECENTLY GOT to know a young woman named Jackie who broke off her engagement after an incident with her fiancé. The day I met her, she was sobbing in the living room of a friend's house. She'd just come from lunch with her fiancé at a restaurant where nothing on the menu had appealed to her. She asked the waiter if it was possible for the chef to make her a simple pasta dish that would be easy to prepare but wasn't on offer. With that, her fiancé lit into her with fury.

"You are so demanding. You are such a bitch!" he snapped.

After she'd caught her breath, she said, "You know what I want? I want a partner who will look at the waiter and say, 'She's really special. Could you see if it's possible to get her what she wants?'"

As Jackie understood intuitively, we each deserve to be cherished and seen as special in the eyes of our beloved. "To love and to cherish" is part of traditional wedding vows. I thought Jackie was very clear-sighted to grasp the significance of her fiancé's reaction to her request. It wasn't just that her wishes were trivial to him. The very fact that she had asked had triggered his hostility. I admired her healthy sense of her own value, something that's not easy to hold on to when we're under attack. She didn't try to soothe her fiancé or worry that she was embarrassing and demanding. Instead, she looked down the long arc of years that lay before them, and didn't like what she saw. She didn't like that her simple needs and requests for a little extra something would be shouted down. She didn't like that she might end up suppressing her needs just to keep the peace.

A psychologist friend of Jackie's happened to be sitting with us in the living room that afternoon. She said to her, "I'm going to offer you one word to guide your future relationships—*mutuality*."

FAMILY OBLIGATIONS

IF YOU HAD siblings, you probably remember protesting to your parents, "That's not fair!" And unless you're lucky, those old fairness wars can reignite when elderly parents start to require care and support.

Gone are the days when Nana lived around the corner, Mom and Dad didn't hightail it to Florida, Arizona, or a cute little village in Mexico, and all the adult children in the family stayed put.

Today's sandwich generation juggles multiple pressures, from finances and demanding jobs to child-rearing. Adding to the pot, many older adults who need help suffer from a mixture of shame and anger at their loss of independence. And when old unresolved feelings of hurt, anger, and injustice get provoked, you've got a sure-fire recipe for bringing tensions to a boil.

I hear so many stories: the sister who, whether by choice or by simple geographic proximity, becomes the primary caregiver for aging parents—and feels burdened and angry; the brother who foots the bill for assisted living and smarts with resentment; the siblings who go to the mat over every detail related to their parents' care and, later, the disposition of money and family heirlooms; and parents who rage against any interference by their adult children.

Happily, I've also known many families who've worked things through successfully. The key is usually a willingness to view the situation from each family member's perspective, ultimately arriving at a common understanding that takes into account each person's skills, resources, and life circumstances. In other words: awareness, flexibility, and generosity. Even if just one family member initiates open, mindful dialogue, it often turns out to be wonderfully contagious.

About a year ago, my student Max hit a wall of exhaustion. Between caring for his ailing mother, his busy pediatric practice, and home life with his wife and two kids, he knew something had to give. But he wasn't sure what, since his younger brother and only sibling, Tim, lived halfway across the country with his family. Tim kept in touch and came to visit once or twice a year, but only for a few days at a time. The more stressed Max became, the more fury he felt toward Tim. Yet he knew that trying to shame Tim into stepping up over the phone would backfire. So he waited until Tim's next visit to have *the talk*.

"I knew Tim would get defensive and shut down if I blamed him for not being more involved," reflects Max. "So when we got together, I simply told him how alone I felt, how physically and emotionally drained. Up until that moment, I don't think Tim fully grasped the situation. That was partly my fault, because I'm so good at playing the silent suffering martyr. As a doc, it's part of my job description. But I think because he didn't feel attacked, he really heard me. He promised to spell me one week out of every month, which, luckily, he can do because he's able to work remotely. He's kept his promise, and I trust that if at some point we need him more, he'll show up. Most important, his presence hasn't been just a relief for me; it's been a great gift to my mom—and to Tim, as well. Of course, it's true," Max adds, "that our involvement with our mother isn't exactly quid pro quo, and it never will be. But that's okay. In this scenario, we all win."

THE DANCE OF CARING

RECENTLY, A WOMAN wrote to me about the love she shares with her adult children. "When I see my children, my whole body feels joy," she said. "I want to touch them. I want to hug them because they are so precious to me. I feel relaxed and at ease because they know all the different ways I behave. They have seen me in more situations than anyone else. Now that they're adults, I don't have to hide anything from them. I'm no longer the ambassador for the way one is supposed to behave. They're old enough to make their own choices, and I can be more candid about mine; also I can admit more weaknesses, be more vulnerable. We've been through some big crises together and come out the other side. My children are protective of me now. I feel the mutuality. I feel fluidity, meaning the power between us is shifting in their direction as I get older. Last year, I borrowed money from my son. My daughter sat at my side and read to me when I woke up from surgery. More and more in the future, they will be caring for me. But I feel safe because there is a central core than has been tested. I feel free."

Clearly, this woman hadn't cared for her children with a payoff in mind. She did so because she loved them, and she wanted their home to feel safe and happy. The flow of giving and receiving nurtures them all.

CHAPTER 13 PRACTICES

What is fairness?

Hibbs defines fairness as a "muddled mix of beliefs, traditions and multiple and sometimes opposing truths." And of course, the idea of "playing fair" in our relationship is complicated by the fact that we all have our own definition of what it means to be fair. When we are clinging to our own definition of fairness during a conflict with a loved one, it's not that we are not being fair, but we may not be as open as we could be to the notion of this "muddled mix of beliefs"— essentially a compromise.

In a notebook, consider the qualities of fairness you value in relationships. You may find that certain qualities are more important than others—or even that a particular behavior or lack thereof might be non-negotiable. Here are some questions to get started:

–What does fairness mean to you?

–What behaviors or ways of communicating do you value in others?

–Did you experience any issues with trust or notions of "fairness" in your childhood or in certain past relationships?

–What has been your experience with generosity in relationships? Do you feel that you tend to give more than you get? Do you keep track of these dynamics or find yourself drawn to people who keep score?

Too often, we believe certain things about ourselves and our relationships without assessing whether or not we are focusing on the presence of certain long-held assumptions, judgments, or reactions to past wounds. This exercise is one of gaining clarity—in creating a vocabulary for your own value system of fairness. That way, when the time comes for you to talk about fairness in a conflict, you can use "I statements" and speak from *your* experiences and belief systems, rather than assuming what you think is a universal truth.

Letting go of right and wrong

Hibbs's related belief of "relational ethics" in a relationship refers to the creation of a world in which we can expect to be treated with care, tenderness, and compassion. We may have different beliefs about fairness than those with whom we interact—but we are both fundamentally committed to supporting one another.

Being ethical—"fair"—in our relationships is really about being able to approach things from a new perspective—constantly. We don't cling to a set idea of what we think is "right versus wrong" or "virtuous versus unjust" or even "kind versus cruel"—but are open to co-creating a system with those we love to ensure we are both heard, seen, and recognized.

This practice is a basic meditation, but one that shows us the relationship between "beginning again" in meditation and seeing things with fresh eyes again and again in a relationship. The overarching practice of letting go is also one of gaining resilience and insight.

1. Sit comfortably, with your back straight. Close your eyes or not; if you feel sleepy, you can open your eyes and gaze softly downward to stay awake.

2. Bring your attention to your body. Notice any sensations you may feel in your hands (heat, cold, pressure). Notice where you are most conscious of your breath—at the nostrils, chest, or belly. Breathe naturally, noticing each inhalation and exhalation. Feel one breath, and then let it go.

3. Some may choose to make a mental note of *in, out* or *rising, falling* to support awareness of the breath. But let your awareness rest on the sensations, rather than the words that accompany them.

4. As images, thoughts, emotions, and concerns come up in your mind, notice them and let them pass. You will not clear your mind when you meditate—but rather develop the practice of noticing distraction and then beginning again and again (and again), each time without rumination or regret.

This process of noticing distraction and then letting go, and coming back to the breath, is often a catalyst for judgment and guilt among meditators, myself included (it's a practice!). But the moment when we notice ourselves veering away from the present moment is the most important. We see where we've become lost and begin again.

This is similar to how we can expand our perspective in relationships. Any time we find ourselves relying on the ideas of an absolute, frozen state of right and wrong—or fairness versus unfairness—that we are used to, we can compare the habit to distraction during meditation. We are relying on something that we are habitually conditioned to do; then we make the intentional choice to let go and begin again as much as we need to—each time without rumination or regret.

NAVIGATE THE SPACE
BETWEEN

✳

*Certainly there are very real differences between
us . . . But it is not those differences between us that
are separating us. It is rather our refusal to
recognize those differences . . .*

—AUDRE LORDE

WHEN SHE WAS IN HER early twenties, Diana believed that
the only way she would ever find her soul mate was to have
sex with prospective partners soon after they met and then to spend
every possible minute with them. In her mind, they would experience such an exquisite blending of body and soul that the man in
question would never want to leave her side.

"I wanted us to be so attuned to each other, we'd be like one
person in two skins," she says now. "I even remember saying to my

true love du jour that I couldn't tell where I stopped and he began. Needless to say, my designated soul mates were terrified of my dependency and headed for the hills. It took me years to unpack my neediness and see that I was trying to heal my lonely childhood by trying to merge with my lovers. Thankfully, I learned that in order to truly see and be seen by another person, there has to be differentiation and space between you. We *cannot* be one."

In every intimate relationship, there are three elements: us, our loved one, and the space between us. That space is rich with possibility, but it can also become a battleground or an inhospitable no-fly zone. How do we balance privacy and intimacy, self-protection and vulnerability, fear and longing? Can we love without trying to possess? If we're hurt or betrayed, can we trust in love again?

Mindfulness practice gives us a way to explore the space between and to discover safe ways of navigating it. When we meditate, we hope to create space—whether it's a step away from our chattering minds where we can gain perspective, or a new opening to tenderness and goodwill. We come to realize that we can fill that space between with generosity, respect, support, and fairness—or anxiety, resentment, anger, and silence. How we traverse the space between us is critical. How do we remain open when it makes us feel vulnerable?

We humans suffer from a porcupine problem, trying to live with bodies that combine a soft underbelly and a back bristling with spiky quills. The German philosopher Schopenhauer invented this metaphor to describe the dilemma of relationships. In the cold of winter, his porcupines tried to huddle together for warmth. But when they got too close, they stabbed one another, so they'd move off to a safe distance until they got cold again.

The psychotherapist Deborah Luepnitz investigated this tension in her book *Schopenhauer's Porcupines: Intimacy and Its Dilemmas.* "Definitions of love, aggression, intimacy, and privacy vary enormously, of course—by culture, historical moment, and social class," Luepnitz wrote. "Without making universal claims, we can assume that people in the contemporary West . . . live lives bedeviled by the porcupine dilemma. That is, we struggle on a daily basis to balance privacy and community, concern for self and others, sexual union and a room of our own."

HOW WE CONNECT

IF OUR TENDENCY is to be anxious and grasping, we might try to fill the space between with whatever we think will hold others to us. We try to become indispensable. We're determined to be the most helpful, the sexiest, the most perfect, the smartest, the kindest, the most interesting. Of course, not only are we being inauthentic but also we're often wrong about what the other person really wants from us. We're making assumptions based on our own needs, and we may even be trespassing on the other person's autonomy.

One of the most poignant ways that many people, historically women, try to bridge the gap between themselves and their loved ones is to disappear, to make their own needs and desires invisible. Gina told me about the awakening she had as she worked on healing from cancer: "I used to be the kind of woman who would be driving in the car with my husband, feeling boiling hot, and the most I could bring myself to say was 'Are you warm, dear?'"

We can also attempt to erase the space between by keeping the focus on our own needs. Another student, Bill, says that he found a "liberation of the heart" only when he stopped needing to be completely center stage in his wife's life. That realization came when she told him she wanted to leave home for a three-month trip with her sister following the death of their mother. His honest response: "That doesn't really suit me, but if it's what you really need, you should go." Her gratitude helped him see that honoring the difference in their needs was a way of strengthening their love. As Eleanor Roosevelt once said, "The giving of love is an education in itself." We learn as we go.

For both Bill and Gina, until they recognized within themselves the anxious desire to fuse, they were unable to grow as individuals or with their partners. Rainer Maria Rilke described the sacred space between people beautifully in his book *Letters to a Young Poet*:

"The point of marriage is not to create a quick commonality by tearing down all boundaries; on the contrary, a good marriage is one in which each partner appoints the other to be the guardian of his solitude, and thus they show each other the greatest possible trust . . . Then a marvelous living side-by-side can grow up for them, if they succeed in loving the expanse between them, which gives them the possibility of always seeing each other as a whole and before an immense sky."

MOVABLE BOUNDARIES

IN ALL LONG-STANDING, committed relationships, whether between partners, spouses, relatives, or friends, the space between will wax and wane over time, pushed and pulled by circumstance, changing as each person moves through life. Barbara writes about how she learned to tolerate the expansions and contractions in her lifelong relationship with her cousin Sue.

"Sue and I used to be such close friends," says Barbara, who is now in her fifties. "But we've grown and changed. When we were younger, I gave her these two hugging monkeys that were attached to one another with Velcro. But I think my idea of being best friends was smothering for her. Her way of being is different—she needs more space. She told me that best friends didn't have to mean 'Barb and Sue' on a plaque. That really stung me, and it still hurts to this day. But it was also a lesson that other people aren't always going to reciprocate love the way that I want them to."

Between parents and children, the boundaries are always moving; preparing children to become independent is the number-one job of parents and their greatest gift of love. But that doesn't mean it's easy to see your child walk to school for the first time, or get behind the wheel of a car and wave good-bye as he drives away, or head to college—in each instance, leaving you behind. Joyful and afraid for what may lie in store for their beloved children, parents cheer and cry and worry all at once.

I've always believed that a particularly difficult line to navigate is the one between fear and love, especially for parents, who want more than anything to protect their children from suffering.

Claudia, a longtime meditator, ran head-on into her fears during a vacation on a Caribbean island. Her nine-year-old was excited about hiking a famous trail that wound precipitously through the tropical forest down to the ocean below; Claudia's anxious mind filled with the guidebook's warnings about jagged rocks and scorpions, conjuring up images of broken ankles, venomous bites, and heat exhaustion. But she also loved her son's eagerness and wanted him to have the adventure he craved. And so they set out.

"He dashed ahead down the path like a baby mountain goat," she wrote me, "stumbling but staying upright. I lagged behind, calling out reminders to be careful, to slow down, to watch his step, to steer clear of wasps and webs." For Claudia, this was not fun, and she realized she was tipping into panic.

Claudia told herself what she'd said so often to anxious friends: Breathe. Relax. Soften into the moment. Exactly what might bring her into mindfulness. But she was breathing too hard to shift gears quickly. A few breaths passed. And then, as she recalls, "Up from the depths of my belly, I heard a voice whispering a Buddhist teaching: 'Rest the fearful mind in the cradle of lovingkindness.'"

Yes. Of course. I can do that! she thought. She began by silently offering lovingkindness toward herself, a mother filled with love but rocked by fear. "May I be safe and protected from harm," she whispered. "May I be peaceful and at ease." Next, she sent love and wishes for well-being to her son as he scrambled down the trail. Some hikers appeared, heading uphill. They looked tired and sweaty. Claudia sent goodwill their way. And by the time she and her son neared the trail's end, she felt so happy that she was wishing peace and safety to everything around them, the trees and the rocks and even the scary, scuttling creatures that had thankfully left them alone.

Without intending to, Claudia had worked her way through all of the traditional phases of the lovingkindness meditation, from herself, to her son, to strangers, and to all the beings she encountered. Most important, by managing to control her fear, she gave her son the space he needed to fulfill a dream and flourish. That was her gift of love.

THE DIFFERENCE IS THE BOND

HOW WE TRAVERSE the space between us when conflict arises has a profound effect on the health and longevity of our relationships. Over the past four decades, psychologists John and Julie Gottman have studied thousands of couples, sometimes focusing on how they discussed a current problem in their relationship, and at other times observing them during ordinary everyday interactions. They discovered that a few measurements, focused on what they call "emotional safety," enabled them to predict with more than 90 percent accuracy whether couples would be happy, together but unhappy, or broken up several years later.

Couples who responded to a conflict with contempt, criticism, defensiveness, or stonewalling were on the path to unhappiness. Not just their words but also their bodies told the story; when their physiological signs were recorded, they were in fight-or-flight mode. Even in less stressful moments, their physical tension was measurable, and they often ignored or cut short their partner's bids for attention.

The couples who remained together did not suppress their conflicts, but also took a specific approach to them. They found ways to express their needs clearly, without attacking or belittling each other. Each partner assumed that the other's overall intentions were good, even if their actions had been hurtful. And they created a background of safety by everyday small acts of kindness, attention, and generosity.

Candace told me a wonderful story about the day when she and her husband finally accepted their differences. As she recalls, she'd recently read an essay by the renowned Thai teacher Ajahn Chah in which he wrote, "If you want a chicken to be a duck, and a duck to be a chicken, you will suffer."

She thought about her last fight with her husband, and the metaphor clicked. So the next time conflict loomed, she said to him, "I really think when we get into these binds, it's because you're a duck and I'm a chicken, and we're trying to change each other." She continued, "We both liked that. A few days later, we got into an argument when he had a rash. I wanted him to go to a doctor, and he refused. So I said, 'How come whenever I want you to do something, you want to do the opposite?' And he said, 'Because I'm a duck.' Ever since that time, we've been working with that image."

In *No Man Is an Island*, Trappist monk Thomas Merton declared, "The beginning of love is the will to let those we love be perfectly themselves, the resolution not to twist them to fit our own image."

Bottom line: We have to know ourselves to know where we end and another person begins, and we have to develop the skills to navigate the space between us. Or else we will seek wholeness through false means that honor neither us nor those we love.

CHAPTER 14 PRACTICES

Balance is the answer

Whether we fear the existence of boundaries with others or crave more of them, there's no denying that individuation and separation are inevitable parts of loving relationships that become the site of tension. And of course, navigating these questions is an ever-changing process.

What is a key ingredient in this process of navigation is balance or equanimity. Equanimity can be hard to talk about, as the idea of "balance" doesn't feel that *rich* or *vibrant*, words we definitely think about when it comes to love (along with others like *passion*, *fervor*, *desire*). Some associate balance with a kind of apathy or withdrawal. The idea of feeling love for a person in a "balanced" way may even seem like an oxymoron. But the irony is that approaching love from this expansive state of wisdom and insight creates a more hospitable and sustainable environment within which real love can thrive.

Without equanimity, we might give love to others only in an effort to bridge the inevitable and healthy space that always exists between two people. Or we might give love to others because we think it's what they want—and end up feeling self-judging as a result. Equanimity is the ingredient that brings us clarity and calm in relationship to navigating the space between, as we are able to release the idea of rejection and clinging as the only two possible modes of engaging in a loving relationship.

In this equanimity practice, we begin by thinking about a relationship in which space has come up as an issue.

1. Bring this person to mind. Perhaps it is a teacher upon whom you've become dependent for affirmation, and any space leaves you feeling insecure or lost. Perhaps it's a lover who is far more interested in spending all of his

time with you, and you are at a loss for how to articulate your need for space kindly.

2. Begin repeating honest phrases to yourself silently about the person you have in mind. Possible phrases could be: Things are as they are. I care about you, yet I know we are two different people. We are both the owners of our actions, and we are each whole unto ourselves. Both of our happiness depends on our individual actions.

3. Feel free to experiment with phrases that resonate for the particular questions you are encountering in your relationship. Keep the phrases simple and oriented around the practice of equanimity—accepting things as they are.

$\boxed{15}$

LETTING GO

✳

Even as I hold you / I am letting go.

—ALICE WALKER

SOME YEARS AGO, A GOOD friend was in extreme psychological distress, punctuated by lengthy psychiatric hospitalizations. I wanted so badly to help him but felt powerless. I asked one of my Tibetan teachers for guidance. He advised me to "stop trying"—an extremely subtle teaching. He wasn't suggesting that I withdraw or stop caring, but was telling me to just "be with" my friend, without needing to fix him. And that's what I did.

I'd sit in his hospital room and see other friends offer advice.

Just take fifteen drops of this tincture and you won't be depressed anymore. Or see this healer or try that supplement and you'll be cured. Their advice was given out of love, but my sense was that my friend felt somewhat pressured by it. *What if I don't take their advice? What if it doesn't work?* I could imagine him wondering. *Will they stop showing up or caring about me?*

When Ram Dass had a stroke, it took focused intention for me to apply my Tibetan teacher's wisdom and simply *be with* my friend. We'd been close for decades, and I felt devastated. I could see the impulse to fix things arising in my mind; I wanted him to get better and recover fully. But then I'd visit and see his living room piled high with gifts from concerned friends. *Just take this tincture*—and so on.

It was genuinely beautiful that so many people cared, but I could tell that Ram Dass did feel pressured by it all. I wondered if he would be abandoned by those whose tinctures didn't have him walking and talking fluently again. One day a package arrived while I was there, containing a bottle of Ganges water with a note assuring him that if he drank it, he would walk again. "Don't drink that!" I said. "It will give you cholera!" That was one instance in which I couldn't help but put in my two cents.

I don't mean to suggest that we shouldn't offer our loved ones help in the spirit of generosity; of course we should—and it's most loving if our offerings are made freely, without strings attached. Letting go is the opposite of clinging to our hopes or ideas about how things should be and allowing them to be just as they are.

For me, it was invaluable to see the difference between wanting to help out of my own need to make things better and simply *being with*. I came to understand that healing has its own rhythm, as does any life transition. Of course, it's not easy to step back and let go; it's human nature to want to seize control when the people we love are suffering. But trying to impose our personal agenda on someone else's experience is the shadow side of love, while real love recognizes that life unfolds at its own pace.

THE ART OF RECEIVING

PARADOXICALLY, LETTING GO sometimes means allowing ourselves to receive the love and care of others. Our can-do culture has made many of us believe that we should always be self-sufficient. Somewhere along the way, we also got the message that asking for help is a sign of weakness. We often forget that we're interdependent creatures whose very existence depends on the kindness of others, including—with a bow to Tennessee Williams—strangers.

When Sebene was diagnosed with breast cancer at age thirty-four, she recalls that she was fortunate to be surrounded by many loving friends and family members who were ready to support her. But, she says, "I didn't think I needed much. I was already a meditator with a healthy self-care routine. Although friends played a big part in supporting me emotionally, there was a way in which I kept people (and myself) distant from my experience of fear, sadness, and despair. I spent a lot of my time with people showing them just how very together I was."

She adds that it wasn't until things started falling apart that she began to be able to take in the love that was offered to her. "No one knew exactly what was wrong with me, but I ended up extremely sick," she explains. "I was totally dependent on my friends for everything: walking the dog, doing my laundry, filling prescriptions, preparing food, drying my tears. And in a sense, that's when everything became easier. Letting go of control (or having it ripped away) helped me open to the love all around me. The late Zen teacher Charlotte Joko Beck said, 'Joy is exactly what's happening, minus our opinion of it.'

"When I ended up in the hospital with kidney failure, weak and in pain, with tubes down my nose, I got into a hysterical laughing fit with my dear friend Ahmad," she continues. "I dropped my opinion about the situation, which I disliked, and found a moment of pure laughter, of joy, in the absurdity of it all. I think love and joy come from the same place—the ability to be with what is happening with an open heart and mind. So if joy is whatever is happening minus our opinion of it, maybe love is whatever is happening minus our attempt to control it.

"I realize now how much I resisted opening to what was happening to me, mostly because I didn't want to feel the pain and fear or burden others with it," she reflects. "But in trying to control what was happening, I couldn't be in any moment wholeheartedly. I couldn't open to the joy and love that were already there, waiting to be received."

FREEING OURSELVES FROM THE
IMPOSSIBLE DREAM

SO MANY RELATIONSHIPS are built on the hope that the unconditional love of another will somehow, magically, heal our wounds and restore us to wholeness. Even when our rational selves recognize that this is a fantasy, we may continue to nurture it, if only in our unconscious. In his book *The Eden Project: In Search of the Magical Other*, Jungian psychologist James Hollis writes that the "great false idea that drives humankind is the fantasy of the Magical Other, the notion that there is one person out there who is right for us, will make our lives work, a soul mate who will repair the ravages of our personal history; one who will be there for us, who will read our minds, know what we want and meet those deepest needs; a good parent who will protect us from suffering and, if we are lucky, spare us the perilous journey of individuation." Hollis adds that the paradigm for our relationships is formed from our earliest experiences and is actually hardwired into our neurological and emotional network.

Although on the one hand we may be terribly disappointed to discover that the Magical Other we've been seeking is a phantom, this awareness can also usher in relief. By recognizing that each of us is in charge of our own wholeness, we pave the way for satisfying and reciprocal relationships. But that takes awareness and the intention to let go of our fantasies of the one who will set us free.

In a blog post on the Greater Good Web site, psychologist Christine Carter wrote: "I've found that releasing my fantasies around my relationship requires acknowledging a loss, and then grieving it. I really, really, really wanted to be with someone who was deeply romantic, in that poetry-writing and song-singing kind of way. But realizing that my romantic fantasies were created by the film industry (and perhaps the flower industry, and the greeting card industry—not to mention the diamond industry) and not by any actual needs of my own helped me release those fantasies. I felt saddened by the loss of my fairytale hopes for a little while. If you're sad, grieve," she advises, "but then move on."

For Julia and her husband, accepting that neither of them can give to the other what only they, as individuals, can give to themselves has been a central theme of their marriage.

"I'm married to a good and kind man," Julia says. "We love and care about one another. He's emotional and sensitive, and so am I. We're both wounded and we can acknowledge that." Yet, she adds, they each struggle with their own *shenpa*—a Tibetan word that literally means "attachment," but also suggests a state in which old triggers get activated and make people feel uneasy, then cause them to seek relief. In her relationship with her husband, Julia explains, "He wants so much to feel that I hold him in high regard so that he can feel good and confident about himself. I want so much to feel protected, that he has my back in the way I feel no one ever has. This is our edge."

However, in a recent couples therapy session, she reports, "Our counselor told us that my husband can give this regard to himself and doesn't need to wrest it from me on all occasions. He also told me that I no longer need to be protected because I can protect myself just fine."

Julia is clear that her longing for protection has its roots in her relationship with her father, an authoritarian man prone to violent outbursts. In particular, she recalls a night when he exploded, pinned her down, and hit her in the head. Yet even knowing this, she says she's still primed to be disappointed when her "sweet and caring husband fails to be protective in the way I long for, a way, in his world of experience, he doesn't even see or recognize."

As Julia learned, there are fissures and cracks in each of us, carved from our early experiences. And there may always be a gap between what we yearn to find in another and what's actually available. But when we let go of our hope that someone will come along to close the gap, we see that it's just waiting to be filled with love and compassion for ourselves.

TAKING REFUGE IN YOURSELF

JUSTIN, A SOCIAL worker, tells the story of making a pilgrimage to see a Hindu teacher whom many people view to be an incarnation of divine love. A number of Justin's friends had already visited the ashram where she teaches and described the experience of spending time with her as *ecstatic*, *life-changing*, and *profoundly healing*. Justin, who describes himself as wired for anxiety, had high hopes that when this teacher looked into his eyes and saw his pain, she would immediately relieve him of his suffering. He believed that his friends' transformations were genuine and prayed for the same for himself.

In fact, he became convinced this would happen the night before his first group meeting with her, when he had his worst recurring nightmare, of being suffocated to death. "I believed the nightmare, which left me feeling panicky, was an auspicious sign," Justin says now. "When I woke up, my terror was so raw and exposed, I was certain that she would recognize the depth of my pain and, with her infinite love, free me from my fears once and for all."

But when it was his turn to be with her, Justin felt absolutely nothing, and after the encounter, he experienced the same level of discomfort as before. He was devastated.

"I felt unseen, alone, rejected, and trapped inside my own pain," he says. "It was as if my suffering was too much even for this magnanimous and loving teacher. I was hurt beyond description."

It took time to unpack his experience, but a few years later, Justin realized that what at first he had perceived as abandonment was in fact a gift, a hard but essential lesson. "I see now that regardless of my friends' experiences, what I needed was to take refuge in myself and learn to trust my own capacity to heal. When I finally met my own fear with compassion, I was able to let go of the fantasy that some all-wise, all-knowing being would swoop down and save me."

Letting go of the belief that we're powerless to help relieve our own suffering not only enhances our ability to heal but also to genuinely love and receive the love of others, whether they're spiritual teachers or partners or beloved friends.

BETWEEN PARENTS AND CHILDREN

ALTHOUGH I'M NOT a parent, it's easy to see how the letting go that life asks of parents toward their children as they gain independence is profound, poignant, and one of the greatest movements of real love. As Barbara Kingsolver wrote in *Animal Dreams*: "It kills you to see them grow up. But I guess it would kill you quicker if they didn't."

The balancing act between taking charge and letting go starts early for parents, the day their toddler takes her first step away from them and out into the world. The path shoots off from there, through adolescence into young adulthood and beyond. Fortunately, in most families, the trajectory follows a fairly standard course. There are growing pains for both parents and children, followed by tender, bittersweet, but inevitable separations. Letting go—then more letting go.

But for parents whose children are diagnosed with mental or physical illness, the course is rockier and studded with unimagined twists and turns. For these parents, letting go of preconceived ideas about their child's health, behavior, or future can be immensely challenging and is often stymied by a hefty dose of self-blame.

Jack, a filmmaker I met through a friend, describes his journey after his son began hearing voices five years ago. "One night when he was thirty years old, Noah told me that he was hearing strange, angry voices," Jack says. "They were telling him what to do, and he was hearing them all the time." Over the next few weeks Noah, who was then in law school, became increasingly paranoid, anxious, and out of control. Though there were periods when he was better and the voices diminished, he was in and out of psychiatric units for the next two years.

"It was a living hell for me as well as for Noah," says Jack. In fact, he was so distraught he felt as if Noah's experience was happening to him, too. When Noah was confined, Jack visited him every day and felt as if he couldn't live his own life as long as his son was suffering. "I tried to reassure him, talk him down, just love him, but nothing helped," he says. "I kept thinking that if only I did this or that, he would get better. I felt so responsible, it literally made me sick."

Jack wound up with a blocked artery in his heart. "If I hadn't stopped trying to take on Noah's pain, it probably would have killed me," he says. "It was the biggest letting go I've ever had to do. I was too entangled, and I had to separate myself from him. I had to remind myself that this was happening to Noah, not to me. It wasn't doing him any good for me to be a wreck." Jack's strong bond with his wife, Cathy, helped him through, as did his meditation practice and the loving support of his Zen community.

Things have improved for Noah, too. As of this writing, he hasn't been hospitalized in three years and is living in a studio apartment on his parents' property. Working with his psychiatrist, after much trial and error he's found the right medication to help quiet the voices. What's more, he's been able to hold down a job for the past year. Noah may not be the human rights attorney he'd hoped to become, but he seems to have made peace with his "new normal." And though Jack and Cathy, too, have had to let go of their once-cherished dreams for their son's future, by meeting him where he is, they've been able to reclaim their own lives and help him reclaim his.

With mindfulness, lovingkindness, and self-compassion, we can begin to let go of our expectations about how life and those we love should be. Letting go is an inside job, something only we can do for ourselves. But at times, as we'll see in the next chapter, our commitment to living mindfully may also require us to take direct action in our relationships with others.

CHAPTER 15 PRACTICES

Looking back, letting go

In more ways than any of us can name, love is wrapped up with the idea of expectation. We expect things from the people we love, we expect them to expect things from us. We expect things from the feeling of love itself. And while these expectations differ from person to person, there is a sentiment common among most of us when it comes to love—letting go can feel scary.

The idea of letting go of control when a loved one is suffering feels unimaginable; letting go of our desire to appear okay to those who love us might make us feel weak; and letting go of our universal expectations around love can feel like a recipe for disappointment.

The key in letting go is practice. Each time we let go, we disentangle ourselves from our expectations and begin to experience things as they are. We can *be with*. We can show ourselves repeatedly that letting go is actually a healthy foundation upon which we can open up to real love—to giving, receiving, and experiencing it authentically and organically.

1. Bring to mind (or write down) a situation in which you felt afraid of letting go. Perhaps you wanted to help someone feel better and were frustrated by your inability to change certain circumstances. Perhaps you were afraid to let go of a certain self-image you sought to project. Perhaps you had an expectation in mind for a particular interaction or experience.

2. Based on the ideas about letting go in this chapter, try to ask yourself some new questions about this situation. Were you responding only to the incident, or were there other contributing factors that created more tension? What other factors might have influenced your feelings, thoughts, and behavior?

3. Now let's consider the other person in the dynamic. Were there consequences for you or the other person based on the difficulties you experienced? Did you try to offer help in a situation, and then express impatience or frustration when you were not able to fix it? Explore how the other person may have been responding to your behavior.

4. Now imagine yourself in the same situation with a sense of calmness, openness, and warmth, allowing yourself to

exist in the present moment with acceptance. How do you behave differently? Have you developed new insights about the situation? Feel free to write down any reflections you have.

For some, this practice is an internal dialogue; for others, a formal writing exercise. Others may want to think of this practice as a more abstract visualization or meditation about the situation they have called to mind—and an exploration of what "letting go" feels like in their bodies. Be creative!

$$16$$

HEALING, NOT VICTORY

✳

Nobody has ever measured, not even poets, how
much a heart can hold.

—ZELDA FITZGERALD

A FRIEND OF MINE HAS been seeing the same psychotherapist for more than two decades. In the face of divorce, remarriage, serious illness, and the death of a parent, her therapist has been so insightful that my friend refers to her as "the Rocket Scientist." "I have no intention of ever stopping," my friend says. "I plan to see her until one of us dies."

After so much time and so much support, my friend knows that when she introduces a new emotional entanglement or problem in her multigenerational family, the Rocket Scientist will listen carefully, pause thoughtfully, and then respond with the same opening phrase. Sometimes, my friend jumps in and says it for her:

"I know, I know—you're going to tell me that 'this is a fabulous opportunity!'" She and the therapist share a laugh, and then they get down to work.

To look at painful marital and parent-child conflicts, in-law dustups or friendships run aground as opportunities may seem counterintuitive. But when we can step back even briefly from our hurt, sorrow, and anger, when we put our faith in the possibility of change, we create the possibility for non-judgmental inquiry that aims for healing rather than victory.

This is the promise of mindfulness. Mindfulness won't ensure you'll win an argument with your sister. Mindfulness won't enable you to bypass your feelings of anger or hurt either. But it may help you see the conflict in a new way, one that allows you to break through old patterns.

DISMANTLING THE BARRICADES

SAM AND LUCY have been having the same argument for years. She gets angry at him for not doing more around the house. However, from Sam's perspective, Lucy is so critical of how he does things that he feels anxious about what her response will be whenever he completes a task. As a result, Sam often checks out and doesn't follow through on many projects he takes on. But his withdrawal only fuels Lucy's anger and frustration. Now, with the help of a therapist, Sam and Lucy recognize the repetitive nature of their conflict and are taking steps to address it in a more productive and caring way. Yet at times they still reach a heated standoff.

When things approach the boiling point, a time-out is in order, counsels couples therapist George Taylor. We may have told ourselves to be understanding, and we may aspire to speak more consciously, but sometimes we're simply flooded with emotion. "This flooding is usually a signal that some childhood issue has been triggered," he writes in his book, *A Path for Couples*. "Couples need a clear way to stop the escalation and to calm themselves down. It's hard to practice authentic communication when our biology is going haywire. Our bodies are saying to us, urgently, 'Flee or fight.'"

Taylor notes that many of us practice unconscious time-outs when our systems get overwhelmed with anger or anxiety, and like Sam, we withdraw into ourselves. But, he says, "This method of ending an argument works to de-escalate the feelings, but it doesn't bring any transformation. There is no closure, no understanding." Instead of changing a painful pattern, withdrawal may simply reinforce it.

In order to help couples shift the energy, Taylor recommends that they practice deliberate time-outs. At a time when they are not fighting (perhaps with their therapist's help), Sam and Lucy agree to pause when either of them gets triggered or defensive. (Maybe Lucy can identify when her voice is rising or she's going into attack mode. Maybe Sam can recognize when he wants to escape.) They also agree on a signal, verbal or nonverbal, to stop right away and, in a few words, decide when they will come back to their discussion. Range of time for the pause varies depending on the severity of the conflict. During the pause, they might do a practice like RAIN or any other technique that helps them get calm enough to explore their thoughts and physical reactions. Once they feel stabilized within and safe with each other, they are much more likely to find common ground—a solution that works for both.

Taylor says that he and his wife, Debra—"both passionate, outspoken people with our own histories of emotional turmoil"—have found taking time-outs extremely beneficial. "I often feel some level of shame, for example, when Debra says what she wants. Part of me thinks, *I should have read her mind and known that*," he writes. "In this moment of self-judgment, I can escalate into defensiveness.

Shame is one of the hardest feelings for me to know and describe. I have an internal conflict: I want to protect myself from feeling the shame, and I want to acknowledge her needs. This conflict is hard for me, so I get emotionally confused. This is a good time for me to time myself out, before I react angrily or withdraw."

Taylor adds that although at first time-outs may seem awkward and artificial—after all, we're adults, not four-year-olds who snuck more than our fair share of cookies—the practice helps to heal recurring, painful patterns of reactivity and eventually becomes second nature.

ENLARGING THE PICTURE

AT TIMES, HOWEVER, a relationship becomes so broken that it seems we have nothing to build on. Then it can help to view our suffering through a wider lens.

In a private meeting during a lovingkindness retreat, Megan told me that she couldn't stop thinking about her ex-husband. They'd had a contentious divorce following her husband's affair with a co-worker, a woman he was due to marry that week. Megan's daughter was the designated flower girl and her nine-year-old son was the best man. This had Megan so agitated that she'd signed up for the retreat to help her get through the week of the wedding.

Alas, neither the meditation nor the silence was having a soothing effect. As Megan sat on her cushion, her mind bombarded her with images. She envisioned her ex and his bride blissfully walking down the aisle accompanied by her children, which aroused her sense of betrayal, sorrow, and rage, along with a generous helping of revenge fantasies. She imagined her children crying every night because they wanted to be with her. In this context, she kept trying to offer lovingkindness to her ex-husband, but each time she silently invoked the phrase *May he be happy*, her next thought was, *Not while I'm miserable!*

When we met, she told me how unsettled she felt.

I asked, "But don't you want your children to be happy?"

"Of course I do," she replied. "What kind of mother would I be if I didn't want my children to be happy?"

When I saw Megan a few days later, her face was much more open and free of scowls. Despite her initial resistance to my question, it became the focus of her meditation. She'd switched her attention from trying to wish her ex happiness to affirming, without hesitation, that she wanted her children to be happy. Along the way, she realized that previously she'd wanted her children to be happy only when they were with her, a bitter and restricted wish for their happiness.

It became clear to her as she meditated that a truly loving wish would be broader and allow her children to be happy with all of the people in their lives, not just her. She wanted them to live in a world where their relationships were solid and sustaining, and the people they encountered were kind. Her question became, "Don't I want my children to be loved and accepted wherever they are?" She knew she did, which meant that she wished her ex to be happy in his new marriage, too.

Not deliriously happy, however. Just happy enough so that being with him would be good for her children. Deliriously happy would be asking too much, and concepts such as lovingkindness should never be used as weapons against our real feelings. For Megan, the challenge was to hold her own pain alongside the wish for her children to live a life as friction-free as possible. This did not come easily; expanding her focus and reframing her story took intention and practice. Yet because she wanted her children's lives to be graced by love, she recognized that as long as she did battle with her ex—either in reality or in her heart—her son and daughter would pay a steep price.

A PLACE FOR PLEASURE

WHEN I ASKED for stories for this book, a friend sent this one with the caveat that it might be *too* real:

"My husband and I married in our late thirties and rushed to have a baby right away. I was so proud to be pregnant that nothing fazed me for nine months. But once our son was born, my body seemed to feel its job was done. My husband was tender and patient, but the more he advanced, the more I pulled back. After work, it was all I could do to make dinner, get the baby to bed, and collapse myself.

"The pattern got more and more painful. I could tell when he wanted to have sex, and I would just shrink into myself, trying to make myself disappear. I hated feeling pursued. I knew he felt rejected, sad as much as angry, and that made me feel worse about myself. We got along pretty well on the surface, but he was going to bed drunk many nights, and there was an undertow of unhappiness in our lives.

"I think it was an article I read in a magazine—that some couples made dates to have sex. Maybe that could be us. If we could agree on one night a week, I'd have six nights a week to myself. I didn't have to feel turned on, I just had to be willing. The first surprise was that he was okay with that. The second was that once we started, I began to enjoy myself. Things relaxed between us.

"It was still a long haul to where we are now. His drinking didn't magically go away, and neither did my depression. But our bodies had made a deal to be together, to live skin to skin. Once a week, we acknowledged that we were at home with one another.

"I sometimes imagine how pathetic this might seem to a hot young couple. But we have gotten better through the years, past cancer, past joint replacements, more playful, more creative, more celebratory in how we give each other pleasure. There is a green shoot at the center of our marriage, and we are both grateful for it."

CHAPTER 16 PRACTICES

Time out!

We learn from conflicts only when we are willing to do so—if we can open ourselves up to recognize why certain emotions are coming up, and be willing to negotiate with someone else's feelings. After all, a relationship is the union of two psychological systems. While mindfulness may help you gain insight into your role in conflicts with others, it won't single-handedly help you resolve them.

This practice builds upon George Taylor's notion of a time-out. Of course, both people in a given relationship must agree to participate in the time-out system in order for it to work.

1. Get to know the indications that you've been triggered and are slipping into a mode of regression, self-defense, or resentment. Are you raising your voice? Are you being provocative for the mere sake of provoking the other person? This first step is a practice of mindful self-awareness—of thoughts, patterns of behavior, and bodily sensations. Getting to know these signals is the first step in developing a time-out system that works.

2. Get to know the other person's trigger points. Odds are, you know this person fairly well—and there is a certain dynamic at play during the conflict that contributes to your reactions. By getting to know your own behaviors in Step 1, it becomes easier to notice the signals in the other person that trigger you. You may even want to find a time to discuss these dynamics with the other person during a non-conflict time.

3. In the moment of a conflict, determine a mutually agreed upon signal, verbal or nonverbal, that indicates it's time for a time-out. Essentially, this step can be likened to

choosing to meditate or close your eyes and breathe during a time of stress. Rather than allowing the situation to
spin out of control, we take a step back to give ourselves
space for insight, reflection, openness, and healing.

4. Before taking the time-out, make a clear agreement on
   when the time-out will be over. Depending on the conflict at hand, perhaps it's only an hour. For other conflicts,
   maybe a few hours—or even an entire day. Be realistic,
   and know that the time-out isn't a gesture of withdrawal
   but actually one of opening up to seeing what is.

5. During the pause, take some time to reflect. You may want
   to practice the RAIN method (explained in chapter 3),
   to explore why you were set off or why your feelings became exacerbated in response to the other person. This is
   a time for real investigation (Step 3 of RAIN), so that
   you can eventually come back to the other person with a
   clearer sense of why things went the way they did and
   what you need and would be willing to give in order to
   avoid conflicts like that in the future.

Anger's kaleidoscope

While the previous exercise focused on really exploring the particulars of a given conflict, this practice is more about noticing the ways
in which our habits of mind can contribute to the way most of us
tend to relate to anger. In this practice, rather than investigating the
nuances of your feelings or the situation and how it unfolded, we
will explore the role of perspective in conflict—and how we can
release the grip of anger even in the midst of feeling it.

1. Bring to mind the person who you are angry at—during
   the height of your conflict. Really get in touch with your

feelings, as much as you may feel guilty or distasteful toward the negativity.

2. Now imagine that person sitting across from you, looking at you. Feel what it feels like to have that person mirror your feelings of anger, hurt, resentment. Look at yourself through these feelings.

3. Once you have felt the anger from both sides, you may find you feel angrier with the other person as a result of recognizing that they may feel angry with you. But part of the practice is recognizing the choice we have when it comes to perspective. We can see ourselves and others in a different way.

4. Next, try imagining how the other person's mother, father, sibling, or teacher sees them. You may even want to recall a time when you saw the other person with such joy and warmth. This may have been as recently as a few hours before the conflict!

In practicing these shifts in perspective, you may find that your feelings of anger are wrapped up with vulnerability—worries about being the object of the other person's anger or frustration.

You may try sending phrases of lovingkindness to the other person during this exercise or afterward for a short meditation. In this practice, you silently repeat phrases of lovingkindness ("May he be happy, be peaceful, be healthy . . .") to the other person, in an effort to recognize your oneness, despite the temporary feeling of separation and alienation. Or you may find that you're not quite ready to do that, and that's okay, too.

THE HEART IS A GENEROUS MUSCLE

✳

Thousands of candles can be lighted from a
single candle, and the life of the candle will
not be shortened. Happiness never decreases
by being shared.

—BUDDHA

A WOMAN I KNOW COMMITTED to a six-hundred-mile, seven-day bike ride to raise money in memory of a friend who had died of AIDS. The fund-raising scared her more than the physical demands of the trip, but as it turned out, raising money was effortless. So many other people had loved her friend that she became one of the top fund-raisers that year. When she crossed the finish line, glowing from the sun, her whole family and many of her donors were waiting to cheer for her. All had something to celebrate: her achievement in finishing the long ride; the months of training that preceded it; the generosity that brought them together; a chance to honor and remember their lost friend. My friend still draws on the joy generated on that day.

Buddhism has a term for the happiness we feel at someone else's success or good fortune. *Sympathetic joy*, as it is known, invites us to celebrate for others. We stand up and cheer when, after some struggle, a promising teenager graduates from high school. We dance late into the night at a dear friend's wedding. At other times, sympathetic joy can come as a gasp of relief. A friend is sick and waiting for some crucial test results and they come back fine! There may be complications ahead, but for this moment, we can share one of the flashes of connection that hold our lives together.

These are times when sympathetic joy comes naturally, but in a complex relationship, with all its unspoken comparisons and personal disappointments, the heart may not leap up so easily.

After a recent talk I gave on sympathetic joy, a woman I didn't know asked to meet with me privately. When we sat down, she confessed that although she felt terribly guilty, she was so upset that her best friend was getting married that she could hardly sleep at night. "I know I should be happy for my friend," she told me, her voice quivering, "but I haven't been in a relationship for three years, and every time I see her, it feels like pouring salt into a gaping wound. I know she really cares about me, but a big part of our bond has been being single together, each other's Saturday-night date. I know it's crazy and irrational, but somehow I think that because she's found someone, I never will. I'm supposed to be her maid of honor, only I can't imagine how I can make it down the aisle on her big day."

So often we react from feelings of scarcity, as if there were rations for things like love and success. Our individualistic society often leads us to believe we're alone in this world and must scramble for every morsel we can grab. When we believe there isn't enough to go around, we cling to what's ours and respond begrudgingly if someone close to us gets something that we, too, might like to have. Like the woman distressed by her friend's marriage, we may recognize that our feelings are irrational. We may even be able to trace them back to some source in childhood. But that doesn't necessarily free us to leap for joy on our friend's behalf.

DISCERNING THE BLOCKAGES

YEARS AGO, I used to spend winters in California to escape the harsh weather on the East Coast. One March, as I was about to return, New York was hit by a huge late-winter snowstorm. I decided to postpone my trip home, and I called my doctor's office to cancel an appointment I'd made. The assistant kept saying she could barely understand me—was the connection going down?

"Oh, I know what's happening," I said. "I'm walking on the beach in Malibu, and the waves are so loud they're drowning out my voice."

"You're on the beach at Malibu?" she said. "I hate you."

Of course, she was joking, but it was the kind of joke that felt like a little slap. She and I shared the same desire—to escape winter in New York, but now it seemed like a zero-sum game. I was up; she was down. My good fortune diminished her.

There is a word, originally in German, that refers to delight at the misfortune of others—schadenfreude. It's the companion of looking at someone's success and thinking, "Oooh, I would be happier if you had a little bit less going for you." Envy and jealousy are almost inevitable when we focus on what we lack—and on what others have.

A friend recently told me about her tendency to measure herself only against everyone else's best. If she thought of Amanda, she didn't think of Amanda's disastrous cooking; she thought of her perfect yoga poses. If she thought of Susan, she didn't think of Susan's chaotic household; she thought about her title at work. When we feel incomplete, when we don't notice what we have, and most especially when we feel less than fully loved, we need to be especially mindful to catch those tendencies.

I was once co-leading a retreat with my friend Krishna Das, who leads Hindu devotional chanting, plus a yoga teacher. We teachers got along wonderfully, but there was a small contingent of retreat participants who didn't like meditation and therefore didn't like me much. The yoga practice released long-held tensions in his body, one told me. The chanting brought him to a state of bliss. The meditation, in contrast, brought him face-to-face with his impatience, self-judgment, and wandering mind. Rather than thinking of it as a time to develop a more loving relationship to himself in the face of those very things, he was just annoyed and brought along his friends to complain.

One day, I was just worn out by this, so I took a nap after lunch. I was awakened by a loud knock. I opened the door to find a young staff person holding a beautiful bouquet of flowers. She handed it to me, and I thought, *Someone loves me after all.* Then she said, "You're Krishna Das, right?" Sighing, I handed the bouquet back and said, "No, he's in the next cabin."

Fertile ground for jealousy, for sure, but Krishna Das and I are very old, close friends. So I laughed when I told him the story, and I said I hoped he enjoyed his flowers. And when I traveled on to the next place I was teaching, the first thing I saw in my room was a dozen roses from him.

WHERE DOES YOUR HEART GET BLOCKED?

ARE WE MOST vulnerable around work? Relationships? Finances? Do we shut down when our partner gets promoted and starts bringing in more money than we do? When our best friend gets pregnant after years of trying? What thoughts, emotions, and body sensations accompany our resistance to feeling joy for someone else's happiness?

I know a number of writers and artists who admit to wrestling with difficult feelings when a friend wins a coveted award or gets a great book deal or a rave in *The New York Times*. "I know I should be happy for so-and-so," they might say. "But their success makes me feel insecure—like I don't measure up." They may also confess to secret relief when a friend gets a negative review or is turned down by the gallery of their dreams.

But, oh boy, can that ill will bubble up when we see them happy. Apparently, they eat at better restaurants than we do, have gym memberships they actually use, and have the most photogenic children on the planet. The comparing mind can soar into the stratosphere, stimulated by these announcements. *Why does she get to be so happy and adored, while I still live alone with my cat?* Without fail, other people's meticulously chosen images will surpass the entirety of our uncurated offline lives.

Or we can be in a bad mood when we log on and decide that whatever this "friend" is celebrating is so below our standards as to be laughable. Upon seeing images from a couple's twenty-fifth anniversary cruise to Alaska, we dismiss their enduring commitment, their spirit of adventure, and their success at accumulating the resources—time, money—that got them to this point. *Ach*, we think, *I would hate to be trapped on a cruise ship. I'd lose my mind.*

When we're caught up in our own suffering, sympathetic joy is a real stretch. But it's actually a practice that can make a difference even when you're going through difficult times. First, you need to be realistic about your own capacities and let go of any "should"—as in, "I should feel good about their good fortune"—that you hold as some impossible ideal. We need to start with compassion for ourselves and be very kind and patient with our actual internal experience.

Even as we recognize our resentment, bitterness, or jealousy, we can also honor our own wish to be happy, to feel free. When a friend of mine catches herself operating from a constricted, negative place, she can often release herself from it by announcing the resentment or envy and then proclaiming, "I'm embracing the petty within!" Laughing at your pettiness probably works better than scolding yourself for it.

The more we identify and acknowledge those moments when we're unable to genuinely share in someone else's pleasure and ask ourselves whether another person's happiness truly jeopardizes our own, the more we pave the way for experiencing sympathetic joy.

EXPERIMENTING WITH SYMPATHETIC JOY

WHEN BICYCLISTS (LIKE my friend who raised all that money) are riding together, they form a pack loosely shaped in a V. Cyclists take turns being at the front. It's a position of extra labor more than of prestige, as all the riders pedaling behind are drafting off the leader. Just so, when we open our hearts to sympathetic joy, we draft off the happiness of others, taking a little bit of benefit for ourselves. We know that, in the normal order of things, we will get our own turn at the front, but for now, as a member of the pack, we can relax and let the vibration from another's happiness be a sustaining undercurrent in our lives.

So often we are taught to arm ourselves with cynicism and irony, to cut ourselves off, dismissing displays of kindness or generosity as phony or self-serving. It takes a lot to say, "I am going to conduct an experiment to look at things another way."

That is why sympathetic joy is a practice. It takes time and effort to free ourselves of the scarcity story that most of us have learned along the way, the idea that happiness is a competition, and that someone else is grabbing all the joy. By experimenting with sympathetic joy, we break from the constricted world of individual struggle and see that joy exists in more places than we have yet imagined.

SHARING JOY AT HOME

MOST OF US make a real effort to support a friend or partner when bad news strikes, even if our attempts sometimes misfire. But some interesting research suggests that how we respond to good news is even more important.

Shelly Gable, professor of psychology at the University of California–Santa Barbara, has studied hundreds of couples to discover what goes right in relationships. In a 2006 study, she and her colleagues described a crucial moment when one partner tries to share his or her excitement over news like getting a promotion or being accepted to med school or winning an award.

Let's look at a situation my writer friends will appreciate. Imagine coming home elated and telling your partner, "I got an offer to publish my book today." How would you feel if the response was "That's nice—it's about time. How much are they paying you?" Or, "Well, I have some good news, too," signaling a 180-degree pivot away from you. Or a casual "That's great, babe," with eyes barely lifted from the cell phone. Gable and her colleagues have actually catalogued responses like these to show how many ways there are to shut down joy—and ultimately undermine the relationship itself.

The generous response, of course, is to give your complete attention to your partner and amplify the pleasure for both of you. "Wow—that's fantastic! Oh my God, you've worked so hard! When did you get the call? What did they say? Is that the person you told me about last week?" Gable calls this an "active constructive" response, where the partners join in savoring the good news—and in the process build their relationship.

In fact, when she followed up with the couples in her study, Gable found that partners' reactions to each other's good news were better predictors of whether the relationship would last than their reactions to bad news. Trust, intimacy, satisfaction—all were built on the everyday kindness and generosity of sympathetic joy.

THE CRITIC TAKES A VACATION

GEORGIA HAS KNOWN Dan since he first picked up the saxophone in high school. She remembers his slobbery bleats as he tried to get his mouth around the reed, and she also remembers how he put aside his rock-and-roll dreams when the girls didn't seem all that impressed. Then when Dan was in his thirties, after the breakup of a long relationship, he picked the saxophone up again and managed to get into a band. Georgia, who's a longtime jazz fan with a discerning ear, thought Dan's playing was not very good and sometimes downright bad, but she went to his gigs anyway. Being on stage made Dan happy, especially when people in the audience danced, and she loved seeing the boyish joy he radiated after a show.

"I wanted to be there to see Dan fulfill his dream," Georgia told me with a grin. "And when we're senior citizens, I'll be able to remind him how he got people dancing, and we'll share it all again." This may seem like a small gesture, but Georgia was filling the space between them with love and generosity. If she had chosen to make jokes about Dan's dream, or to give him advice about his playing, or to compare his band to one she liked better, that space would start to fill with judgment and perfectionism. Instead, Georgia took her own expertise out of the picture. She saw Dan clearly enough to know he needed a friend, not a coach.

To celebrate someone else's life, we need to find a way to look at it straight on, not from above with judgment or from below with envy. It isn't someone else's pleasure that causes our unhappiness; we make ourselves unhappy because our negativity isolates us. When we feel most satisfied with ourselves, when we look with compassion on the totality of other people's lives, we are most able to greet their triumphs with a sincere and robust cheer.

CHAPTER 17 PRACTICES

Roots of sympathetic joy

The practice of sympathetic joy is rooted in inner development. It's not a matter of learning techniques to "make friends and influence people." Instead, we build the foundations of our own happiness. When our own cup is full, we more easily share it with others.

Before we get into the practice itself, here are a few of the essential benefits:

1. We nurture our sense of connection with the larger whole, noticing that the whole is only as healthy as its smallest part. One day, I overheard a woman in my neighborhood talking with a street person who was usually on our corner. "I had a terrible winter," she said. "I was sick with pneumonia for a long time. But now spring is coming, and I feel so much better. So today I want to share the joy." And she put a roll of bills into the other woman's hand.

2. We develop awareness of our inner abundance. This is the foundation of generosity. When I studied in Burma, I saw that even the poorest people freely made small offerings of food to support meditators, and they seemed delighted to watch us eat. Giving enlarged them. If we have nothing material to give, we can offer our attention, our energy, our appreciation. The world needs us. It doesn't deplete us to give.

3. We learn to notice our moments of happiness and the happiness of others. When I was studying with the great

teacher Munindra in Burma, someone in our group asked him why he practiced mindfulness. His answer that day (for there were many others): "So that when I'm walking down the road, I won't miss the little purple flowers growing by the wayside."

The practice of sympathetic joy is something we can call upon in our everyday lives, although it can also be practiced more formally in meditation. The meditation on sympathetic joy is quite similar structurally to lovingkindness meditation, although the phrases are different. You may try something like, "May your happiness and good fortune increase further." We start the sequence with a particular person who is doing well in some area of their life—and it may be an area of our lives where we are seeking more success. We skip ourselves in the sequence, as the practice is about rejoicing in the happiness of others. We may decide to move on to others in our lives who are experiencing happiness or good fortune, or stay with one individual.

The more we practice sympathetic joy, the more we come to realize that the happiness we share with others is inseparable from our own happiness.

FORGIVENESS AND RECONCILIATION

✳

This is the world I want to live in.
The shared world.

—NAOMI SHIHAB NYE

CARLOS TOLD ME, "After two divorces and several painful breakups, I finally met the woman of my dreams. She was everything I had hoped for; nonetheless, I found myself cynical about relationships. I was carrying around so much resentment, anger, and blame toward my past partners that it was standing in the way of fully embracing this new relationship that I really wanted to be in.

"I decided to focus my meditation on a practice of forgiveness. I focused my sittings on seeing my past relations more clearly. At first it felt like nothing significant was happening. Until one day, while on a long airplane flight, I had a breakthrough. On the back pages of a book I was reading, I made a time line of my life. I included all the painful relationships and alongside them I chronicled the life events I considered successes.

"I saw the need to more honestly grieve the loss of a couple of those relationships before I could feel free. For another, I watched my resentment, fully acknowledged, transform to a feeling of gratitude for her contributions to my life. And for yet another, my biggest regret, and my resolve to let go, came from seeing just how much rent-free space she (long gone in real life) still occupied in my mind. It was considerable!

"Seeing the relationships and the successful life events side by side showed me how they might be interconnected, how each relationship and partner could have played some role in helping me get to where I was at that moment. That moment, the forgiveness, the gratitude for my life in total, opened my heart to fully embrace my new partner, whom I married and deeply love."

When we forgive someone, we don't pretend that the harm didn't happen or cause us pain. We see it clearly for what it was, but we also come to see that fixating on the memory of harm generates anger and sadness. Those feelings then prevent us from savoring the love and joy available to us right now. Forgiveness is the way we break the grip that long-held resentments have on our hearts.

But real forgiveness in close relationships is never easy. It can't be rushed or engineered. The spike of defensiveness we feel when someone advises us to "forgive and forget" shows just how deep our pain has burrowed. And though people who advise us to do so may have good intentions, forgiveness cannot be achieved on command. That kind of coercive denial could never be healing. When we're told we should simply let go of our genuine feelings of hurt and anger, we may find ourselves defending our pain and our right to continue feeling it.

FORGIVING IS A PROCESS

FOR THOSE WHO acutely feel an injury, the pain isn't in the past. The wound is still fresh. When our minds alight on the memory, it rips through our bodies and infiltrates our thoughts. In order to release the anger and hurt we carry, we must first acknowledge the painful things that happened to us. We can't change the past, but we can grieve what was lost.

To forgive, we may need to open our minds to a fuller exploration of the context in which the events occurred, and feel compassion for the circumstances and everyone involved, starting with ourselves. Grief helps us to relinquish the illusion that the past could be different from what it was. We're in charge of our own forgiveness, and the process takes time, patience, and intention.

For Michelle, one of my students, it took years for her to work through a constellation of difficult feelings before she was able to finally forgive her former husband. "My now-ex-husband and I went through an excruciatingly painful, messy separation," she recalls. "The distress and anger and sense of loss were visceral and all-consuming. We didn't even speak for the first six months after we parted, except to pass our three children back and forth at the door. In that space of anger and avoidance, there seemed to be no passageway into peace."

A few years after they separated, Michelle attended a meditation retreat with the goal of releasing the "toxic" energy that continued to possess her. "First, I had to forgive and let go of the past and cultivate compassion for myself, for him, and for us," she says. "I did a lot of screaming and crying. Afterward, I felt exhausted, but hardly better."

The surprise came on her way home when she stopped by her

ex's house to pick up their children. He quietly took her aside. "I've been thinking that I have to get over us," she remembers him saying. "I don't want to turn into one of those bitter, angry people who at eighty years old still complains about something that happened in the past. We have three children together. The things that we liked and loved about each other are still there, so maybe we can build on that."

"It's difficult to convey just how profound that moment felt to me," Michelle says now, considering that the two had hardly been speaking. "It was the first time in my life I had the experience of shared consciousness, a raw certainty that my internal processes had somehow been part of his consciousness, too. In any case, it was a beginning, and we took baby steps from there."

Now, Michelle reports, she and her ex are very good friends. They recently decided that their kids should live full-time in one house and that the two of them would take turns going between the children's home and another shared house. The arrangement is working smoothly, she says, adding, "We enjoy our friendship, our co-parenting. We laugh together, we complain together, we are very supportive of each other's goals, and that includes our own separate romantic lives.

"We both saw through the layers of the past and pain to something greater that we shared, and we cultivated it," she concludes. "That is love."

TO FORGIVE DOES NOT MEAN TO FORGET

WE'VE ALL HEARD the idiom "Forgive and forget," as if processing pain inflicted upon us by others is a quick and easy job. The phrase is an imperative and renders the idea of forgiveness compulsory; in order to heal, we must enter a state of denial and effectively avoid the pain that we have been experiencing.

But, of course, forgiveness is a process, an admittedly difficult one that often can feel like a rigorous spiritual practice. We cannot instantaneously force ourselves to forgive—and forgiveness happens at a different pace for everyone and is dependent on the particulars of any given situation. What we can do is create space for ourselves to forgive—and, perhaps ironically, part of that involves allowing ourselves to wrestle with our feelings of anger and pain to begin with. Once we are honest about our feelings, we can invite ourselves to consider alternative modes of viewing our pain and can see that releasing our grip on anger and resentment can actually be an act of self-compassion.

Telling the story, acknowledging what has happened and how you feel, is often a necessary part of forgiveness. Without that, we live in an artificial reality that is frozen in time, and sometimes woven from fabrication. I have a friend who believes that a central reason for her divorce is that she spoke the truth after her ex-husband's parents died and he waxed on about his perfect, idyllic childhood. "But you put your drunken parents to bed each night," she would point out. "You dropped out of college to do that." Her words undermined the story he was telling, and his need for a rosier past took precedence over the love between them. It also took precedence over his ability to forgive his parents, and the chance for love alongside the pain of his broken dreams.

At times, reality is love's great challenge. When our old stories and dreams are shattered, our first instinct may be to resist, deny, or cling to the way things were. But if we loosen our grip, often what fills the space is a tender forgiveness and the potential for a new and different kind of love.

Helen Whitney, director of the documentary *Forgiveness*, has said, "We talk about forgiveness as if it were one thing. Instead, we should talk about forgivenesses. There are as many ways to forgive as there are people needing to be forgiven." In other words, there are an incalculable—even infinite—number of situations in which we can practice forgiveness. Expecting it to be a singular action—motivated by the sheer imperative to move on and forget—can be more damaging than the original feelings of anger. Accepting forgiveness as pluralistic and as an ongoing, individualized process opens us up to realize the role that our own needs play in conflict resolution. We cannot simply "forgive and forget," nor should we.

Recognizing that there are many possible forms of forgiveness enables us to explore the possibilities for forgiveness, and what we need to forgive. When we respond to our pain and suffering with love, understanding, and acceptance—for ourselves, as well as others—over time, we can let go of our anger, even when we've been hurt to the core. But that doesn't mean we ever forget.

A student of mine had been molested by her father when she was younger than seven years old. He had been arrested and jailed after that, and now, as an adult who had had no contact with him for years, she struggled with the idea that to be a good person she had to go see him. She came to me privately and asked if I thought it was necessary for her to meet with him. She was frightened at the prospect, but thought it might be obligatory, a necessary step in her healing. I told her I didn't think she should feel compelled or coerced to do anything.

Confrontation might be right for some people, but not for others. Only the person who has been harmed can know what's right for her—and achieving clarity can take a long time. In my student's case, there were many possible reasons for her feeling that confrontation was obligatory. Perhaps she wanted to feel more empowered or realize firsthand that the little child inside of her was not to blame for what happened. Since her father had been jailed, perhaps she was also dealing with some level of guilt for his suffering. But the bottom line is that no one should feel pressured to confront an abuser. Healing comes in many ways, and no one formula fits all. Some people write letters to an abuser and mail them, while others write letters and burn them to ashes. Still others may prefer to role-play their confrontation scene with a therapist or trusted friend.

Forgiveness is a personal process that doesn't depend on us having direct contact with the people who have hurt us. We don't have to meet them for coffee or invite them to Thanksgiving dinner. We don't have to engage with them in any way.

Understanding this came as a relief to Marjorie. After attending one of my talks, she described how the practice of lovingkindness had helped her to forgive a once-close friend who had sent her a cruel, damning letter. But just as important, Marjorie said, the practice of self-compassion had enabled her *not* to include the friend in her current life.

A decade earlier, Marjorie's teenage daughter had attempted suicide and was admitted to a mental hospital. The friend, who had been Marjorie's closest confidante for many years, had been an important person to Marjorie's children, as well. After the suicide attempt, the woman wrote a letter blaming Marjorie for her daughter's problems. She criticized Marjorie's child-rearing, her performance at her job—even the way she hugged. At a time when Marjorie most needed kindness and compassion, her friend only added to her pain. After a short, tense conversation, Marjorie and the woman stopped speaking.

Six years later, when Marjorie's daughter was well and succeeding in college, the friend e-mailed Marjorie. Even the sight of the woman's name in her e-mail queue caused Marjorie's blood pressure to spike. Bristling with anger, she opened the message, expecting it to contain more hurtful remarks. She was stunned when she read how much her friend missed her and how sorry she was for what she'd said. But Marjorie was still so angry, she was unmoved by the note. She was furious that this person had the nerve to ask for reconciliation after having caused her so much pain.

Yet over the next few weeks, Marjorie began to remember how close her friend had been to her daughter, including the special times they'd shared. She came to appreciate that her friend, who had no children of her own, had experienced her daughter's crisis almost as profoundly as Marjorie had. As she allowed more and more space for the fullness of this event to unfold in her mind, Marjorie's ill will diminished, and she made her friend the focus of her lovingkindness meditation. Marjorie began to wish her friend well and hope that she would prosper.

At the same time, she wasn't prepared to include the woman in her life; she knew she couldn't again trust her with the intimate secrets they'd once shared. A month later, Marjorie wrote back thanking her for her e-mail, adding: "Know that I forgive you completely and hold no bad feelings for you. I wish you well. Forgiveness leaves us both free to move on."

Ultimately, we forgive others in order to free ourselves. What happens in our hearts is our field of freedom. As long as we carry old wounds and anger in our hearts, we continue to suffer. Forgiveness allows us to move on.

Like Marjorie, we may forgive someone who has hurt us, yet choose not to resume a relationship with that person. There is no need to think, *Well, I've got to get over this so you can be my best friend again.* But if we can find a way to forgive and free our hearts, in effect we're saying, *Life is bigger. We're bigger and stronger than the hurt we've suffered.*

Forgiveness can also be bittersweet. It contains the sweetness of the release of a story that has caused us pain, but also the poignant reminder that even our dearest relationships change over the course of a lifetime. Regardless of the decision we reach about whether or not to include someone in our present-day life, in the end, forgiveness is a path to peace and an essential element of love for ourselves and others.

ALL IN THE FAMILY

WE ALL ARE, or have been, sons and daughters. In an ideal world, we have warm, loving relationships with our parents or those who raised us. We feel seen, supported, and loved unconditionally by them. As we grow older, they respect our choices and accept us for the people we have become.

Yet for many of us, our families of origin didn't provide the sort of safe harbors we might fantasize about or hope to create for our children. So often we carry the scars of our early experiences into adulthood. In his book *Telling the Truth*, the American theologian Frederick Buechner wrote: "You can kiss your family and friends good-bye and put miles between you, but at the same time you carry them with you in your heart, your mind, your stomach, because you do not just live in a world but a world lives in you."

It took me years of meditation practice to realize that forgiveness would need to play a role in my coming to terms with my childhood: my mother's sudden death when I was nine, my father's disappearance when I was four, and his reappearance, brought down by years of mental illness, when I was eleven. Though neither of my parents deliberately deserted me, nevertheless, I was, in effect, abandoned by them, and to me, it felt like cruel rejection.

My opening to forgiveness first took the form of being able to connect to something bigger. Years into my practice, I was sitting a retreat and the despair of my childhood loneliness and fear surged up and filled me. But as I sat, trying to accept what I was feeling, I also suddenly knew that no matter what I might have gone through or might yet go through, I was capable of love that was big enough to hold whatever sorrow or brokenness might arise.

Rilke wrote, "So you must not be frightened. If a sadness rises up before you larger than any you have ever seen, if restiveness like light and cloud shadows passes over your hands and over all you do, you must think that life has not forgotten you."

I was rocked by the sense of not having been forgotten by life itself. From that understanding, I saw so much more deeply that my parents would have done anything to protect me and couldn't. Sometimes parents or caregivers are unable to protect their children because of ignorance, circumstances, illness, addiction, their own history of abuse, or just really bad luck. But I saw that there *is* love in this world—not of my making or contrivance, or my parents', but raw, natural, present—no matter what.

That's what gave me the strength to not feel so impoverished and to look at my mother and my father not through the lens of abandonment but with much deeper compassion and forgiveness.

OPENING TO CHANGE OVER TIME

I MEET MANY adults who have long histories of tense, fractious relationships with their mothers or fathers—or both. In some cases, contact between these adult children and the older generation remains sporadic and strained for decades, with bitterness and resentment on both sides. For as long as she remembers, my friend Ellen had a hard time with her mother, Charlotte, a woman she describes as angry, narcissistic, and extremely judgmental.

"For most of my life, she was so disapproving of me, I cut off contact with her for long periods of time," Ellen says. "I was a child of the sixties, and she just never got me. Even after I started practicing lovingkindness meditation, it felt impossible for me to open my heart to her. I stayed away from her as much as I could."

Eventually, however, life intervened. Ellen's father passed away; Charlotte, who was living on her own in Florida, fell and broke her hip; and Ellen's brother and only sibling refused to get involved. "At first, the idea of becoming my mother's caregiver seemed like a sick joke, one of those crazy, karmic twists of fate I might have found amusing if it hadn't been happening to me," recalls Ellen. "Every cell in my body was screaming, 'No!' I'd never felt safe around my mother. Still, there she was, ninety years old, all alone, with a broken body. I had to ask myself: Even if I don't feel love for this woman, what kind of human being would I be if I turned my back on her? How could I live with myself? After all, even though she was a lousy mother, she did give me life, and I was grateful for that." Ellen wound up arranging Charlotte's move to a retirement home a few miles from her house in Boston.

"I have friends, also the daughters of difficult women, who had major rapprochements with their mothers, but I never dreamed that such an opening could take place between Charlotte and me," Ellen says now. "I didn't even want it to happen. I didn't want to forgive her, because that would mean letting her into my life, and that felt too dangerous."

Ellen need not have worried—at least not initially, because Charlotte was furious with her. She yelled at Ellen and called her a bully. She accused her of stripping her of her independence and turning her into an invalid. Once again, Ellen became the target of her mother's rage. And though she did what was necessary—taking Charlotte to doctors' appointments, seeing that she was well taken care of, making perfunctory visits—she says she did it all with a shuttered heart.

Psychologist and author Mary Pipher once said that it's human nature to love who and what we care for. And, much to her surprise, that's what happened to Ellen. Slowly, almost imperceptibly, over the few years Charlotte had left, Ellen let down her guard and grew to genuinely love her mother.

"I don't know if it was her increasing frailty and awareness that she wasn't going to live forever or my ongoing practice of loving-kindness, but a seismic shift took place in both of us," Ellen reflects. "For the first time, I began to feel truly seen by my mother. On Mother's Day a few weeks before she died, she wrote me a card telling me how much she loved me and she thanked me for taking such good care of her. I don't think I'd felt that depth of love coming from her since I was very young, and maybe never at all."

As Charlotte lay dying, Ellen realized that all her life she had regarded her mother only in relation to herself, not as a separate person—a woman who was fiercely creative and intelligent but unfulfilled, and who came of age at a time when so little was expected of women. "As I sat by her side not trying to do anything but be present, everything that had divided us came unhooked, and we forgave each other for everything," says Ellen. "Even though I resisted becoming my mother's caregiver, I shudder when I think of what a terrible loss it would have been for both of us if we hadn't had that chance to find our way home to each other. In the end, Charlotte and I—and the great mystery of life itself—were so much bigger than our differences, there was nothing left but love."

"DON'T GET AHEAD OF YOURSELF"

OUR RELATIONSHIPS ARE also deeply impacted by our ability to forgive life for being as it is: ever changing, outside of our control. Even as we live with the knowledge that each day might be our last, we don't want to believe it. It's human nature to want to do all we can to stave off the inevitable. Our resistance to accepting the truth that we and those we love will someday die is deeply rooted in us and the source of some of our greatest suffering. Yet when we're able to open to the truth of our most shattering losses, at times we find moments of unimagined grace.

Mary, a writer in New York, and Jack, her television producer husband, live and swear by that phrase. "It may sound simplistic, but we're constantly saying it to each other," she reflects. "I don't know how we would have gotten through the last forty-six years if we hadn't deliberately practiced not looking ahead, because so often, the future has been terrifying." In 1970, a year after they met and two months before they planned to be married, Jack, then thirty-six, and Mary, twenty-four, went body-surfing off the coast of Long Island. When a giant wave rolled in, Mary dove under it while Jack took the wave and was flung hard against the shallow beach. He broke his neck, and the doctors predicted he'd never walk again.

Thankfully the doctors were wrong, and eventually Jack did walk, first with crutches, then canes, and eventually on his own until years later, he needed a walker. The couple's wedding took place one year after the original date.

But, Mary says now, "I had to let go of the old Jack. I was still in love with him, but he wasn't the same man as before. In many ways, the accident defined our life, but at the same time, we chose not to let it." Jack and Mary were determined to live as close to a normal life as possible, and they raised two daughters, traveled widely, and worked hard at their respective professions. Over the years, however, Jack's physical challenges became more pressing and limited what they could and couldn't do. "At each stage, even as life got more constrained, we both managed to maintain a certain amount of independence and look at the glass as half-full," says Mary.

"Our life now is just like meditation. No expectations. Which is not to say we never get depressed, because we do. Still, I wouldn't trade places with couples who are physically intact but can't stand each other. If Jack and I didn't communicate as well as we do and have such deep love for one another, ours would be a completely different story."

Through it all, she says, "Three things have kept me relatively sane—my daily meditation practice, yoga, and therapy. Meditation doesn't change the fact that the situation sucks, but it has given me the capacity to deal with it and to stay in the present as much as possible. Jack and I both know that we don't know what lies ahead. We're not in control. We just need to remember to remember."

CHAPTER 18 PRACTICES

Forgiveness meditation

Meditating on forgiveness is not terribly different from lovingkindness or sympathetic joy practices, as all of them invite us to be with our emotional states without judging them and to use the meditation as the anchor of our attention. These practices require courage, as we are not denying our suffering or the harmful actions we've taken.

Forgiveness is not passive, but an active gesture of releasing feelings like anger, guilt, and resentment, all of which deplete us if we become lost in them. Forgiveness demands presence, reminding us that we are not the same as the feelings we possess in a given situation, nor is the person who we've harmed or who has harmed us.

Traditionally, the meditation is done in three parts: first, you ask forgiveness from those you have harmed; next, you extend forgiveness to those who have harmed you; and the final practice is that of self-forgiveness, for all of those times we harm ourselves with judgmental habits of mind.

1. Sit comfortably, and allow the breath to be natural. Begin by silently (or audibly) reciting phrases of forgiveness for those you have harmed. You may try, "If I have hurt or harmed anyone knowingly or unknowingly, I ask their forgiveness."

2. Notice what comes up. You may find that offering forgiveness to one person may catalyze memories of another tough situation or person. Don't push these feelings or thoughts away—but maintain your focus on the practice, and don't get lost in guilt or self-blame about your distraction. As other thoughts arise, send your forgiveness in these new directions.

3. Next (after however long you want to spend on the first part of the reflection), you can begin to offer forgiveness to those who have harmed you: "If anyone has hurt or harmed me, knowingly or unknowingly, I forgive them."

4. Once again, thinking about past painful experiences may trigger emotion. As these feelings, images, and memories bubble to the surface, you may simply recite, "I forgive you."

5. Finally, we turn our attention to forgiveness of ourselves. Most of us have experienced self-blame—at work, in relationships, or simply because we have habitually kept ourselves in cycles of perfectionism. "For all of the ways I have hurt or harmed myself, knowingly or unknowingly, I offer forgiveness."

Creating space

One of my students tells me that she often asks herself, "Am I opening or am I closing?" when she gets into arguments with close friends, family members, or her significant other.

To her, "opening" in this case is the act of allowing dialogue, of seeing others' perspectives, of moving toward resolution; "closing," by contrast, may be withdrawing, seeking to perpetuate an argument. The very idea of contraction makes me think of how New Yorkers literally contract their bodies during winter—shoulders hunch forward and arms clench in an effort to stay warm. It is our nature to "close" when we want to protect ourselves.

But as we saw in Marjorie's story, creating more space around pain is fruitful. When we expand in the face of suffering, we can feel more—such as where the pain registers in our bodies, or what might have been going on for the other person. We may even wonder about our roles. This exercise is one of self-exploration. Consider the following questions as tools for staying open, expansive, and spacious during or after conflict.

–Where in my body do I feel anger? Sadness? Resentment? Guilt?

–When I try to relax my body, how do my emotions respond?

–What do I know about the other person's experience that

may have contributed to this conflict? Childhood wounds? Past relationships?

–What are some of my past experiences that resonate with this one? What did I learn last time?

–How would I react to myself if I were the other person during this conversation? What was my tone of voice like? My body language?

–What might have happened if I expressed myself differently? (Here you may want to consider various alternative scenarios.)

Note that these questions aren't meant to send you into a rabbit hole of rumination and regret about the past; rather, you can think of them as exercises in curiosity and creativity. Visualize each question as a way of creating more space and perspective.

SECTION 3

INTRODUCTION

✳

The Wide Lens of Compassion

I N THIS FINAL SECTION, WE consider whether we can learn to
see and feel the love that is waiting to be born between ourselves
and all others—from the salesperson we know only peripherally to
strangers we see only once and even to those whose behaviors may
oppose us, near or far. What would it look like to bring greater attention and compassion to these more remote—or perhaps seemingly
inconsequential or even negative—relationships?

The love we develop for ourselves keeps this aspiration from being shallow idealism or martyrdom. The love we may have for another is a testing ground for giving and receiving, another strength we take into love for all. And the love we develop for all of life helps us shape a practice of love for life itself.

I have a good friend who looks at me like I'm crazy whenever I talk about loving everyone. "Are you kidding me?" she asks. "Love everybody? I have enough trouble loving the people I already love! And now I'm supposed to love people I don't care about, not to mention people who do terrible things?"

I get her point. We live in a world punctuated by horrifying acts of violence, in which entire groups of people are marginalized by virtue of race, class, religion, nationality, and sexual preference. How is it even possible to imagine loving all? And what about the truly difficult people in our daily lives—the colleague who takes credit for our ideas, the spendthrift relative who's always asking for a loan, the neighbor who cut down our tree. Not to mention the random thorns in our side who spike our blood pressure and pull into parking places that should have been ours. There are days when we can feel good simply about staying calm.

I find myself inspired by the perspective my friend and fellow author Jason Garner offers: "At times it can seem glib, naïve, or perhaps even stupid to talk about loving all beings. When we look around our world, with wars, terrorist attacks, people killing each other over things like race, religion, and gender—so many incidents of beings inflicting pain on one another—how can we possibly hold a space for loving everyone? But this is, in fact, exactly why we must . . . We're called to practice a love that is more courageous than all the terror we see in our world, because if we aren't bold in our love, then the hate wins out. And there is nothing more stupid than that. So we love one another even when it's seemingly impossible; we look for the humanity behind the acts of hatred; we find our own pain in the pain of the world; and we meet it all with an intensity of love that is fitting of our intense times."

ENLARGING THE PICTURE

JACQUELINE NOVOGRATZ, BESTSELLING author of *The Blue Sweater: Bridging the Gap Between Rich and Poor in an Interconnected World*, recounts how the story of her beloved blue sweater, given to her by an uncle when she was a little girl, inspired her to start Acumen, a non-profit social venture fund that addresses global poverty. One day while jogging in Kigali, Rwanda, Novogratz spotted a small boy wearing the blue sweater—still bearing her name tag—that she'd donated to her local Goodwill a decade earlier, more than five thousand miles away. "I've held that story as a metaphor for how interconnected we are, how our action and our inaction can impact people we might never know and never meet, every day of our lives, all around the world," she says.

For that, we need to set an intention, even at times when we're not *fully inhabiting* what we know to be true. There's no denying that it takes effort to set the intention to see our fundamental connectedness with others. In a certain sense, the path of least resistance in life is survival, getting by—doing the least to complete what's necessary to put food on the table and stay safe.

If we stretch ourselves to open our minds, to see our shared humanity with others, we allow ourselves to see the existence of community and generosity in unexpected places. We just need to challenge ourselves to opt for the path that may take a little more effort but actually helps us let go of our conditioned resistances.

Yet it's also true that we miss a lot when we push for unity at the expense of understanding the differences in context, experience, hopes, and fears we each may have. It's all too easy to slip into a "we're all alike at the core, so we should all get along" kind of statement. It's not real love if we don't also honor our differences—as long-term couples and friends find out, and as communities and workplaces also find out.

Just think about what it's been like when you are in a place—a group, an event, a training session—where you have the feeling "I belong here," in contrast to what it's like when you are in a place where you sense you don't belong—the uneasiness, the uncertainty about social cues, the dread of inevitable humiliation.

What about being in an environment where you've been told outright you don't belong? Then our anxiety wouldn't seem so much about the flight-or-fight syndrome built into our biology from long, long ago . . . it would feel (and in fact be) awfully current.

So the question arises—along with our oneness, can we also recognize the vast relativity of experience and make room for it? The combination of realizing our distinctiveness along with our unity is seeing interdependence.

Today, with unprecedented threats to our planet and divisions among people, awareness of our interdependence is no longer optional. It's critical that we widen our attention to include those we encounter as we go about our daily lives, including our dry cleaner and the stranger sitting next to us on the subway. We extend our sense of inclusion even further to people we may have disagreements with, people whose actions we disapprove of, even those who may have harmed us or those we care for. We don't have to like what they've done, and we might take very strong action to try to prevent their doing it ever again, but as our experiences of the universality of suffering grows, our sense of interconnectedness deepens, and we begin to wish others could be free in a new way—in spite of their actions, their beliefs, or their positions in the world.

GETTING TO COMPASSION

AS MODERN NEUROSCIENCE has discovered, we're wired for empathy. We literally have brain circuits focused on "feeling with" others. "It's a genetic imperative for us to care," says James Doty, M.D., a professor of neurosurgery at Stanford University. It's essential to the survival and flourishing of our species.

But the neural circuits related to empathy aren't always activated, especially when we're feeling anxious or stressed. And at other times, we may feel so much empathy for another's pain that we lose our own sense of equilibrium.

In 2004, neuroscientist Tania Singer and her colleagues published an important paper showing that pain-sensitive regions in the brain get activated when we empathize with someone else's pain. In other words, when we say, "I feel your pain," we're voicing the literal truth. But this is not always a good thing.

Singer, who is director of the Department of Social Neuroscience at the Max Planck Institute for Human Cognitive and Brain Sciences in Leipzig, Germany, now calls empathy a "precursor to compassion," but notes that too much of it can have negative consequences. In an interview with the Cognitive Neuroscience Society, she explained, "When I empathize with the suffering of others, I feel the pain of others; I am suffering myself. This can become so intense that it produces empathic distress in me and in the long run could lead to burnout and withdrawal. In contrast, if we feel compassion for someone else's suffering, we do not necessarily feel their pain, but we feel concern—a feeling of love and warmth—and we can develop a strong motivation to help the other."

What's more, Singer said, even the neural networks underlying empathy and compassion are different; the former increases painful emotions, while the latter is associated with positive feelings.

This has a lot of implications for burnout, a distinct kind of exhaustion often characterized by loss of motivation, stress, anger, depression, and dissatisfaction. As a meditation teacher, I often lead retreats for caregivers—mothers, fathers, sons, daughters, spouses, nurses, doctors and hospice workers, therapists, chaplains, and many others. People in positions or professions of caregiving can be particularly vulnerable to burnout, as they tend to empathize with and take care of others without necessarily refilling their well with self-care.

Ellen, who works at a school for students diagnosed with mental illnesses—spanning mild anxiety to severe schizophrenia—is prone to burnout at her job. "I am often in a classroom full of emotional expressions, including anger, anxiety, muteness, screaming, throwing chairs, tuning out with an iPod, tears, and more tears," she tells me. Ellen is passionate about her work and committed to her students, but describes herself and her fellow teachers as getting "pummeled" by the student body's resistance to rule enforcement.

Unsurprisingly, Ellen explains that she feels not only frustration and fatigue on the job but often also a sense of hopelessness. When I asked Ellen how she finds meaning each day or if she relies on any self-care routines to replenish her energy, she responded by telling me that she is renewed by the sense of emotional openness between her and her students. "The only real hope I could see is when those kids sincerely felt that you cared about them and believed they could be better and saw some potential in them."

And in addition to offering students encouragement and support, Ellen admits vulnerability of her own: "And we also told them, 'I feel that way, too, sometimes'; 'It is really hard for me to get to work some days, too' . . . Telling them the truth, showing them that we can share the same feelings . . . has made a difference to them and, I think, given them hope. And it gave me hope to give them hope."

The authenticity that Ellen brought to her relationships with students—and that they gave her in return—helped nourish her, despite the exhaustion and frustration she felt. Her meditation practice fostered that emotional openness, helped her not to be engulfed by the pain of her students, and taught her how to return to a place of steadiness in those times she did get overwhelmed. Like Ellen, we can be compassionate while also strong; understanding while also savvy. Healthy boundaries require balance.

While we discussed the importance of healthy boundaries in close relationships throughout section 2, here we will go on to explore how we can be more skillful with compassion and empathy when it comes to challenging relationships and groups of people that we may not know intimately.

We see that compassion is not just a feeling but a skill that can be learned and applied in our lives in surprising ways. While we typically think of this skill as benefiting others, compassion can also be thought of as an attitude toward living, one that fosters self-care. As I've mentioned before, there's a strong link between compassion and both physical and mental health. When we act compassionately, our vagal tone—or the neural connection between the brain, heart, and other organs—increases. This, in turn, leads to the release of oxytocin, the feel-good neuropeptide that calms the sympathetic nervous system, including the fight-or-flight—that is, fear—response. As a result, our heart rates and blood pressures drop, inflammation is reduced, our immune systems are strengthened, we're less prone to stress—and we may even live longer. Researchers have actually proven that strong social relationships predict a 50 percent increased chance of longevity. What's more, the greatest advantages come not from receiving love but from offering it to others.

Until we can relate to our own pain with kindness and acceptance, we're more likely to defend ourselves against the pain of others. This self-defense may mean we shut down when we perceive others are in need, acting out of a self-protective impulse to numb ourselves to any pain at all.

Or perhaps we do, in fact, engage with the pain of others, but are inclined to offer support out of a desire to receive validation, praise, or love to soothe our own pain. If we turn away from our own pain, we may find ourselves projecting this aversion onto others, seeing them as somehow inadequate for being in a troubled situation. And, paradoxically, when we truly allow ourselves to feel our own pain, over time it comes to seem less personal. We start to recognize that what we've perceived as *our* pain is, at a deeper level, *the* pain inherent in human existence. In fact, it is awareness of both our shared pain and our longing for happiness that links us to other people and helps us to turn toward them with compassion.

Kevin Berrill, a clinical social worker and bereavement counselor who teaches mindfulness to oncology patients and their families, says that he's able to sense the difference between empathy and compassion in himself when working with clients. "I'm aware that I'm best able to serve when I'm in a compassionate place," he says, noting that, over the course of his career, there's been a shift from a tendency to feel another's pain to simply be present with it. "I love my work the most when I'm in that state of flow. I don't try to offer solutions or fix anything prematurely. I feel calm and peaceful and fully engaged. I can hold another's pain without drowning in it," he explains, adding that he can go through a wrenching session and come out feeling awake and alive. Berrill attributes the movement from empathy toward compassion to his own practice of mindfulness. And, he says, "When I'm in that place of compassion, I feel a deep sense of kinship and affection for the people I'm working with. I find myself loving them."

Yet when we talk about compassion and love for others, we must also talk about love for ourselves. This isn't simply because opening ourselves up to others feels good (which it does). Rather, we need to think of the relationship between loving ourselves and loving others. Unless we remember to take care of our own needs and respect our own boundaries, we may end up feeling depleted, exhausted, and so burned out that we endanger our physical and psychological well-being.

Alas, this lesson is often overlooked. During a discussion following a recent talk I gave on compassion, Eileen raised her hand. Eileen, a second-grade teacher and single parent who is the primary caregiver for her ailing mother, described her constant feelings of guilt with a look of worry on her face. "There's so much suffering in the world, I feel like I should be doing more all the time," she began. "But between caring for my mom and my kids, and teaching all day, I just don't have the time or energy."

I was grateful to Eileen for sharing her concerns. So often, well-intentioned students interpret the teachings on compassion to mean that they must be helping others rigorously, 24-7, regardless of the toll that may take on them. But most of us, including me, are *not* saints, nor should we expect ourselves to be. We all have our limits. In order to avoid burnout and practice true compassion, it's important to remember that we can only do what's possible for us; when we strain to do more, we risk feeling resentful or making ourselves ill. What's more, the capacity to give to others varies from person to person, depending on multiple factors, such as availability, energy, and resources. Ultimately, compassion has more to do with the attitude we bring to our encounters with other people than with any quantifiable metric of giving.

US VERSUS THEM

ALTHOUGH A GLOBAL society in which lovingkindness and compassion rule is a worthy aspiration, our common tendency is to see the people around us as "other," fundamentally different from us. So often out of our fears, we find ourselves relating to particular individuals or entire groups of people with antipathy, prejudice, or just indifference.

In fact, a recent body of research shows that people with the most wealth and social status pay scant attention to those with less power. The *haves* tend to lack compassion for the hardships the *have-nots* endure. Writing in *The New York Times*, psychologist Daniel Goleman said, "Social distance makes it all the easier to focus on small differences between groups and to put a negative spin on the ways of others and a positive spin on our own." But, he added, "In contrast, extensive interpersonal contact counteracts biases by letting people from hostile groups get to know one another as individuals and even friends." This kind of camaraderie is far more common among people who live in proximity and, out of necessity, come to rely on one another.

Ultimately, there are a whole host of cultural assumptions that encourage us to act according to this mentality. For one, we live in a competitive, individualistic culture, where success is often seen as triumphing over others; alternatively, we think that repressing parts of ourselves that are culturally undesirable (such as emotional states like anger and anxiety) will lead to happiness. So rather than doing what social psychologist Jonathan Haidt refers to as stepping outside of our "moral matrix" and seeing ourselves as fundamentally related to everyone else, we think we have no choice but to meet anger with anger, or separate ourselves from others in order to feel a sense of freedom.

Of course, the opposite often becomes true. Seeing others as an objectified "them" makes us feel stuck. If we think of others in such a static way, we also keep ourselves from ever accessing a fresh perspective—a new way of relating to our experiences, to ourselves, and to them. Respecting differences while gaining insight into our essential connectedness, we can free ourselves from the impulse to rigidly categorize the world in terms of narrow boundaries and labels.

AN INTENTION TO STRETCH

THE FIRST STEP toward feeling compassion for others is to set the intention to *try it out*. Regardless of whether we have certain fears or feelings of aversion when considering this idea, we can relish the experience of exercising our minds and hearts. While we may be biologically wired to look for differences between ourselves and others, we can also accept that there is validity in experimenting with new habits, wisdom that results from encouraging ourselves to learn and expand.

This works for groups we may harbor resentment toward, as well as individuals. The process requires patience, though; opening our shuttered hearts has its own timetable. Often we may spend a while just going through the motions, feeling as if we're getting nowhere fast. Yet with a clear intention and a willing spirit, sooner or later we experience the joy and freedom that arises when we recognize our common humanity with others and see that real love excludes no one.

There's no need to begin this process with judgment or a harsh sense of discipline. I've had students tell me that they feel bad or inadequate upon realizing that love for others doesn't spring forth from their hearts like water in a babbling brook. Finding this boundless love isn't the result of a goal-oriented search, but a practice. We experiment with what it feels like to treat ourselves with kindness when we "succeed" as much as when we "fail." We open our eyes to the suffering and joy of those we see in line for security in the airport as much as we do to our family members. We challenge ourselves to see that kindness is really at the core of what it means to be and feel alive.

None of this is easy. As I said, learning the practice of loving-kindness meditation for the first time challenged my emotional fabric in ways I didn't expect. As I practiced offering phrases of lovingkindness to myself, then to benefactors and to acquaintances, to difficult people, and—finally—all beings, I began noticing just how much I was conditioned to entangle myself in judgments, assumptions, fears, and stories. This act of noticing itself is part of real love. We see that we can set the intention to stretch past these habits we've gotten used to—both internally and as the result of familial, circumstantial, and overarching societal factors. Not because we are doing something phony or because we are trying to force ourselves to be hypocritical or pretentious. We stretch because, as human beings with capacity for real love, we can. We learn to move and breathe in a new way, until we realize one day how much stronger we are.

19

PRIMING THE PUMP

✳

Healing yourself is connected with healing others.

—YOKO ONO

A FRIEND WHO SHOPS AT the same small grocery store as I do recently mentioned how shocked he was to realize that he never paid much attention to the woman who rings up his purchases day after day. "She might as well be a cash register with arms," he said. He determined that the next time he went into the store, he would give the clerk his full attention.

He reported back a few days later. "The first thing I noticed was that she was singing along to something on the radio and that she has a beautiful voice. And when I told her that, she gave me a radiant smile."

Listening to my friend, I realized that I, too, hardly noticed the woman—did she often look a bit sad? I began to imagine my next trip to the store: I'd tell her I'd heard she had a beautiful singing voice and make her day. But when I actually went in and looked for her, she was already smiling broadly.

Of course, not everyone we encounter in our everyday lives—whether it's passersby at the grocery store or a colleague at work—will have a beautiful voice or a warm smile to convince us immediately to love others. But there is immense power in the act of showing up for life—in paying attention to other people, to experiences, sounds, and sights. Loving others, whoever they may be, is about seeing and recognizing the basic wish to be happy, in ourselves and in others. This wish to be happy is something we share, and simply acknowledging that is the foundation of real love.

OPPORTUNITIES AROUND
EVERY CORNER

OFTEN WE'RE SO caught up in the stories playing out in our own minds that we miss precious opportunities to connect with others that would enrich our days, as well as theirs.

Sometimes we think of compassion as a gift—something we're either born with or not—and/or that it's something we have to work very hard to attain. But I think of compassion as the natural result of paying attention. Attention is the doorway to true compassion.

Yet attention is certainly not automatic—it takes intention and effort. Sometimes, we don't even realize our own inattention until we start tuning into our lives with greater awareness. Only then can we see clearly and make more intentional choices about how to move forward with greater compassion.

My friend Jason tells a story about a sudden realization he had about the man who helps him tend his family's garden. "We were grateful for his work but never really engaged with him beyond it," Jason explains. "One day I accompanied him on a trip to the dump. As we drove, he informed me that he was going to be gone for a month. When I asked him where he was going, he told me that he was going to India to promote his book. It turned out that he was an author of spiritual books, that he studied as a young person in ashrams in India and the United States, and that we had several friends in common. I was embarrassed that I had failed to see him as a person. Here I was, writing and sharing about spirituality and love, while failing to see the person right in front of me who was doing the same. It was a great reminder for me to see people, not labels or preconceived judgments." Jason's writing and spiritual work are both built on his deep interest in learning about, understanding, and practicing love, compassion, and mindfulness. He was able to realize his lack of attention toward his family's gardener by really tuning into his process of awareness. Recognizing our interdependence, the idea that we all count and deserve to be happy, is a practice—something every single one of us must do again and again.

We are all vulnerable to moments of forgetting—failing to see the intricacies of others, their virtues, interests, and other qualities. This typically has nothing to do with a deliberate lack of compassion; instead it's related to the fact that we're conditioned to keep to ourselves, to notice "strangers" only when they threaten or oppose us. Many of us find it easier to focus on problematic situations and troublesome relationships—a picture assembled with blinders on. We favor these blinders, though. We think blinders are the smart choice because we don't want to be distracted by what is going well. It can feel foolish to our vigilant minds if we rest in reflecting that our friends and family are, for the most part, healthy, have homes, eat well, and are doing what they can to improve their lives. When we're feeling low, it is especially hard to cast aside that problem-centric tunnel vision to find peace. At such times, paying attention to the good requires both intention and creativity, an interest in seeing things in a new way.

WHEN EFFORT IS EASY

PRACTICING KINDNESS DOESN'T require us to add extra items to our daily to-do list. It's simply a matter of learning to be where we are at any given moment with an open heart. When we're truly present, the occasions for expressing care and compassion emerge spontaneously. And, rather than adding more stress to our lives, they have a way of calming us—and everyone around us.

Paying attention helped my Irish friend Bart lighten a situation that could easily have become a travel nightmare. "I was on my way home to Ireland with three friends," he recalls. "Our plane from the West Coast was delayed in Chicago, and we didn't get to New York until after midnight. We had missed our connection, our luggage was nowhere to be found, and we were exhausted. But as bad as we looked—and we looked bad—I thought that the woman behind the airline service desk looked even worse.

"I had a banjo with me, and it occurred to me that it had probably been quite a while since this woman had been serenaded," he says. "Seeing from her badge that her name was Irene, I broke into a rendition of 'Good Night, Irene.' My companions started singing along, as did some of her co-workers. By the time the song was over, Irene was beaming. She told us, 'I am the best person in the whole company at finding luggage. Never fear, I will find yours!' My friends and I went off happily to get some rest."

Instead of becoming angry and lashing out at the airline representative, as many frustrated and weary travelers might have done, Bart's awareness and sensitivity to others changed the emotional energy of the situation for all concerned. The result was relief and goodwill in the moment—not to mention the prompt return of the group's missing luggage.

NO GESTURE IS TOO SMALL

WE HAVE COUNTLESS opportunities every day to practice random acts of kindness that express our common humanity: holding the door open for someone entering a building right behind us, giving up our seat on a bus to a mother with a small child, making friendly eye contact with the receptionist at a doctor's office. A simple smile exchanged with the driver in the lane next to ours can make sitting in rush-hour traffic less onerous. Stopping to help someone in need to cross the street instead of racing to our next destination is a way to acknowledge that, at times, we are all vulnerable.

Such small, seemingly insignificant offerings can make a big difference in people's lives, including our own. Scientific studies have shown that acts of kindness and generosity are linked to greater life satisfaction and stronger relationships, as well as to better physical and mental health. "People who engage in kind acts become happier over time," says Sonja Lyubomirsky, Ph.D., a psychology professor at the University of California–Riverside and author of *The How of Happiness*. "When you're kind to others, you feel good as a person—more moral, optimistic, and positive," she says.

She also assures us, "No particular talent, measure of time, or amount of money is required. The deed need not be grand or complicated. Moreover, if you're ever at a loss about *what* act of kindness, generosity, or charity to carry out, you need to look no farther than your home, your workplace, or your community."

My student Chloe told me a story about a time she was unable to stop crying in a crowded subway car, en route to midtown Manhattan. Chloe was visiting New York City and was in the midst of going through a devastating breakup from a five-year relationship.

It was rush hour, and Chloe was riding uptown to meet her mother, who was also in town for the weekend. The subway was densely packed, and people on board were palpably grouchy from a long day of work and the humid, crowded train. Chloe was embarrassed—even ashamed—about her public emotional display. And yet when she got off the train, a quiet woman sitting by the door offered her a tissue and a gentle smile. "It changed my entire mood," she told me.

Often, it seems that we reach out to those we don't know with kindness when we are able to see their vulnerability come to the surface. Growing up, we're not taught that it's socially acceptable to disclose emotional information to others—and yet sometimes a tear streams down your cheek in the subway or at work. I've found that situations like these help catalyze compassion in others—which can be a helpful reminder of our shared humanity, no matter how isolated and infrequent they may be.

REAL LOVE WELCOMES CONFLICT

MORE OFTEN THAN not, however, we find ourselves confronted by other people who remind us how difficult it can be to feel a sense of universal love. Even when people who challenge or oppose us aren't out to hurt us or threaten us directly, they can still make us feel attacked, criticized, and combative rather than calm. After all, we're conditioned to regard self-defense as virtuous. Responding with kindness to tough everyday situations—from the person who cuts you off in line to the competitive co-worker—doesn't quite feel like the most reasonable answer. And yet situations of conflict can be the greatest opportunity to tap into a more universal feeling of love.

Evelyn, a pharmacist, tells the story of an irascible customer, a Mr. Smith, whose abusive outbursts she dreaded. "It got to the point where I heard myself say, 'I hate him,'" she recalls. "I was disturbed that such strong feelings were being triggered, so I decided

I had to send him lovingkindness. This became my practice for several months. When he came in ranting, I was respectful and tried to hold the space for him to be heard. It came to my attention that he was an alcoholic and living in his car. There was definitely compassion growing in my heart, but here's how I really learned the power of lovingkindness.

"It was Mother's Day, and I was running into my local CVS to buy a card for my mother. I saw Mr. Smith in the parking lot and, worst of all, he saw me. He came over to talk and said he would be waiting for me to come out. What did he want? It was my day off. I saw him in the store and started slinking around so he wouldn't see me. I was stalling, hoping he would just go away. Finally, I had to leave.

"He found me as I was walking to my car, and he reached out to give me a box of Russell Stover chocolates and wish me a happy Mother's Day. I was shocked. I wanted to say, 'No, you can't afford this. You can't spend your last few dollars on me.' But I knew that if I refused his generosity, I'd be committing the greatest insult to his humanity, so I accepted the gift and thanked him.

"To this day, whenever I think of this exchange, my eyes fill up with tears. This is how I came to understand the true meaning of lovingkindness, which is meant to open our hearts. When our hearts are open, there's space for everyone and everything. My encounter with Mr. Smith made me feel that any one of us could be living in our car. I was no longer separate from him. I could relate to him as an equal human being, and I felt an interconnectedness with others that I had never felt before."

As Evelyn discovered, the first step toward feeling compassion for others is to set the intention. Regardless of our fears or feelings of aversion, we can take joy in the possibility of stretching ourselves—not in a coercive way in which we judge ourselves as bad, but gently, with kindness and self-acceptance.

Considering the neutral cast of characters

As I wrote in the introduction to this section, I realize the idea of love for all others can be off-putting to some. Often when I teach about practicing lovingkindness for all others, I hear a chorus of reactions something like this: "How can I possibly make a difference? I'm too [take your pick: insignificant, busy, old, young, exhausted, overcommitted, stressed out]. I know I should meditate and exercise, eat a healthful diet, and get plenty of sleep while also meeting deadlines at my high-pressure job. Sorry, but I just don't think I have it in me to love everybody, too!"

It's true that the word *everybody* or the phrase *all others* can feel overwhelming. So for this exercise, I invite you to get more specific in thinking about who some of these omnipresent others are. Consider those individuals we encounter every day in our lives, but who we may not consider essential to us—or even necessarily good or bad.

1. Draw a vertical line down the center of a piece of paper.

2. In the left-hand column, write down the names of neutral people in your life, or descriptions of people whose names you don't know. Examples include the dry-cleaning clerk, the delivery person from your favorite takeout restaurant, a person you see often on your morning commute, and so on.

3. In the right-hand column, write down a short intention for how you'd like to shift your behavior toward this person. Perhaps you choose to smile casually at your subway companions rather than look away or down at your cell phone. And on occasion, you may forget your intention or

act absent-mindedly. There's great importance in forgiving yourself so that you can gain resolve and begin again. Remember that connecting with others, even in these small ways, is proven to boost our own quality of life.

Street meditation

Many associate the word *meditation* with a formal practice—sitting in lotus pose, incense wafting, perfect quiet, and dim lighting. Yet one of my favorite ways to practice meditation is on the move—sitting in the back of a cab, walking around New York City, waiting in line to buy groceries at the supermarket.

At every moment, we can integrate the practice of paying attention with a little more focus and intention—to the breath, to our sensations, to others, to ourselves.

The practice of lovingkindness is a wonderful way to practice in everyday life. While traditional lovingkindness meditation practices begin by directing lovingkindness to the self and then move gradually outward—first to a benefactor, a friend, then to a neutral person, a difficult person, and finally all beings—you can begin the street practices here with neutral people.

1. As you walk around, wait in line, shop at the mall or grocery store, silently repeat phrases of lovingkindness to those you encounter along the way. These may be people you have short conversations with such as a cashier, or people who pass you by and may not notice you're there.

2. Note that you needn't focus on one person for several minutes. You may choose to direct one, two, or three phrases of lovingkindness to a specific individual in your surroundings and then shift your focus to another person you encounter next.

3. As you go about your normal activity, stop intermittently to take stock of how you're feeling. Do these street practices expand your sense of perspective? Do you feel lighter, happier? You may even want to reflect on this at greater length later in the day.

Some phrases to consider are:

- *May you be healthy.*
- *May you be strong.*
- *May you live with ease.*
- *May you have mental happiness.*
- *May you be free of struggle.*

CHALLENGING OUR ASSUMPTIONS

✳

It is only with the heart that one can see rightly;
what is essential is invisible to the eye.

—ANTOINE DE SAINT-EXUPÉRY

NOT LONG AGO, A WRITER friend was shocked to realize how quickly and unconsciously he sizes up other people. His aha moment came over dinner at a restaurant following a talk he'd just given at a midwestern university. He was enjoying his meal with friends from the English department when a woman approached their table.

"She was rather dowdy looking," my friend recalls. "I automatically assumed she lived in a rural area, probably on a farm. I also pegged her as someone who hadn't had much education.

"She told me how much she'd enjoyed the lecture, especially the part about Proust. I thanked her and was turning back to my friends when she blew my preconceptions right out the window. This plain-looking woman, about whom I had rushed to judgment, announced that although she thinks there are some decent translations, she much prefers reading *Remembrances of Things Past* in the original French."

We all do it. We hastily judge every day of our lives, without even being aware that that's what we're doing. It can take an encounter like the one my friend had with the Proust maven to wake us up to our habit of automatically labeling others and plugging them into categories of our own devising. We fabricate stories about them based on little or no information. This is how our species tries to manage the world around us. When we know (or think we know) that someone is one of *us*, as opposed to one of *them*, we rest more easily at night.

BIAS IS REAL

RATHER THAN BEAT ourselves up for labeling others (or deny that we do), we need to understand bias in order to be able to work with it. Bias is a basic human trait that's part of our wiring for survival. Bias helped early humans size up strangers quickly and decide who was a threat and who could be safely admitted to the cave. Those who made the right choice survived, reproduced, and passed the trait on to their children. Bias continues to be our human inheritance, and we're strongly conditioned to think of others in terms of stereotypes.

At times, snap judgments do protect us from danger—we sense we're being followed as we walk down a dark street at night, so we change our route home. If we are part of a particular group—

because of our ethnicity, sexual preference, appearance—we can wisely understand our vulnerabilities in certain situations. For example, I don't have a single African American friend, of any socioeconomic class, who has not spoken to their male child about being very, very careful if stopped by police—and increasingly, their female child, too.

Yet we can also see that automatically and perpetually fearing strangers can be a hurtful and damaging habit. A strong sense of justice and ethics helps to tamp down unwarranted fear of those whom we reflexively view as somehow different, and stops us from overreacting. And rather than flatter ourselves that we can become completely bias-free, we can find ways to work more skillfully with our evolutionary programming and cultural conditioning.

But sometimes our primitive fear response takes over, and we may overreact without even being aware of it. This may provide us with a fleeting sense of control in a chaotic world, but it also isolates us and narrows our experience of life. We start to inhabit a world of mental projections, filled with shadows and ghosts bred in the mind. In other words, we're brainwashed by our knee-jerk reactivity.

HOW WE JUDGE OTHERS

RESEARCH SHOWS THAT most of us make split-second assumptions about people based on superficial differences in appearance. The U.S. epidemic of tragic killings of unarmed black men by police officers starkly underscores the point.

This is not just a white-versus-black issue. Rhonda Magee, a professor of law at the University of San Francisco, tells this story on the Greater Good Web site: "When I was promoted to tenured full professor, the dean of my law school kindly had flowers sent to me at my home in Pacific Heights, an overpriced San Francisco neighborhood almost devoid of black residents. I opened the door to find a tall young African American deliveryman who announced, 'Delivery for Professor Magee.' I, a petite black woman, dressed for a Saturday spent in my own home, reached for the flowers, saying, 'I am Professor Magee.'

"The deliveryman looked down at the order and back up at me." Magee explains that while she was not exactly sure what caused the deliveryman not to believe she was the gift recipient, she was sure that her looks had something to do with it. "It seems inescapable that his confusion had something to do with features of my social identity," she elaborates. Magee recalls feeling like the man perceived her social identity as a black woman to be "inconsistent with the identity of 'professor' and 'resident' of a home in an upscale neighborhood."

More often than not, we hear about racial biases in the United States within the context of white-versus-black racism, police brutality, and the relationship between race and mass incarceration. But there are also everyday, insidious ways that race clouds our judgment and determines our decisions and reactions. Of course, as shown by Magee's story, bias is not just experienced by white people. "As the story of my encounter with the black deliveryman indicates," Magee concludes, "none of us is immune: Black people may be as conditioned as anyone else by stereotypes and unconscious expectations."

RECALIBRATING HOW WE RESPOND

BECAUSE WE LIVE in a richly diverse world in which, more and more, we depend on one another, isolating ourselves is simply not an option. "We are social creatures and need to be in relationship with others," john a. powell, a law professor and researcher on race at the University of California–Berkeley, told *Mindful* magazine. "Yet we have ways of denying our interconnectedness, different ways of marginalizing each other. A lot of times we do things we aren't consciously aware of. It causes suffering all around." And, he adds, "Perhaps most damaging of all, bias can be internalized and make the subjects feel and perform as if the biases about them are true."

Though bias may be most obvious with regard to race or ethnicity, our assumptions affect all areas of our lives, from gender inequality in the workplace to discrimination against members of the LGBT community to flagrant ageism—all well-documented examples. But we may also judge others on factors hidden even from ourselves.

This was an important discovery for a student at a lovingkindness retreat I taught in downtown Oakland some years ago. She had decided to practice walking meditation by going to the nearby railway station and sending lovingkindness to random passengers getting off a train. Once there, she noticed a man heading in her direction, and for reasons she could never pinpoint, she took an instant dislike to him. But before she was able to get away, he approached her and began speaking.

"I've never done anything like this in my life," the man said. "But you look like such a kind person, and I'm having a hard time; I'd like to ask you to pray for me."

My student was stunned by the gap between her negative projections and the actual flesh-and-blood human being who stood before her. Of course, she readily agreed to pray for him—and now remembers him as one of her most valuable teachers.

Sometimes our sense of being threatened grows out of a feeling of deficiency in our own lives. Carolyn was a struggling single mother of two young children when she found herself getting angry with a newcomer in her yoga class. It all began when the woman arrived early and took Carolyn's usual spot in the front row. The next week, she did it again, and by the third week, Carolyn was silently seething at this woman, who appeared to be at least ten years younger and twenty pounds thinner than Carolyn, and, judging by the large diamond ring flashing on her finger, as rich as Croesus.

"I hated her," Carolyn recalls. "I knew it was wrong, but I just hated her. Not only did she have what I imagined to be the perfect life, she had a perfect body and could hold the hard poses much longer than I could. And though at the time I was practicing lovingkindness, I decided that this was one person I did *not* have to love."

After about six weeks, the woman stopped coming to class, and Carolyn more or less forgot about her until she showed up several months later. That morning, Carolyn was back in her old spot in the front row and the woman set her mat down right next to Carolyn's.

"I couldn't even look at her," Carolyn says. "I felt myself stiffen and spent the whole class obsessing about how unfair it was that her life was so easy and I had to work so hard just to feed my kids. But then, at the end, while we were doing corpse pose, I heard her weeping. I looked over and saw that her whole body was shaking. After class, she came over and apologized. 'I'm so sorry if I disturbed you,' she said. 'I've been having kind of a rough time.'

"Her face was all splotchy, and she looked so drawn and thin that I asked her what was wrong. She told me, between sobs, that her four-year-old daughter had died of leukemia three weeks earlier.

"I was stunned. I'd made up this whole story about her and her perfect but shallow life, when the reality was so incredibly sad. Everyone suffers, no exceptions. We'll never know what other people's life really is like until we put ourselves in their shoes. Looking back, it was crazy that in my mind I was so mad at her, when in reality I knew absolutely nothing about her."

Simply disliking someone because of your own sense of deficiency is also a strong tendency. Theresa says, "I remember taking a visceral dislike to a guy who used to wait with his group for the other therapist who shared my therapist's office. He was always regaling the other group members with his troubles, his hypoglycemia, whatever. I never exchanged a word with him, but I would seize up with judgment just seeing him. It was quite a while before I realized I was jealous because he felt so free to seek the attention and care of the group."

Sometimes our stereotypes hit even closer to home. As Mother's Day approached, my friend Doris couldn't help imagining a celebration that matched her own Hallmark ideal: she and her daughter, Cora, would get dressed up and go out for brunch at a table adorned with spring flowers.

The reality was that Cora had dropped out of college to join a punk band and was scraping by as a barista. And Cora had invited her to a crummy theater in a bad neighborhood for a special Mother's Day showing of an eighties movie called *Repo Man*—all arranged by her punk friends. Doris regretted it the minute she said yes.

But to her surprise, they had a wonderful day. Cora made a sumptuous breakfast for the two of them at her tiny apartment, and they sat around talking until movie time. The theater was filled with tattooed and pierced young people—and their mothers. There were even flowers and free beer for the mothers, and Doris was delighted to meet some of the other punk-rock moms. She found herself filled with joy. Because Doris had not insisted on her own preferences, Cora had invited her into her own world and expressed her love in a way that felt authentic and real.

TEARING DOWN THE WALLS

FOR MORE THAN half a century, social scientists have been testing ways of breaking down the barriers between potentially hostile groups. "Intergroup contact" has emerged as the most powerful way to reduce bias—specifically, prolonged opportunities for people to get to know one another as individuals, rather than as faceless members of a group. According to a 2006 analysis led by Thomas E.

Pettigrew, a professor of social psychology at the University of California–Santa Cruz, more than five hundred studies have shown that even in areas where ethnic groups were in conflict and held negative stereotypes of one another, individuals who developed close friendships in the other group exhibited little or no prejudice. They seemed to recognize that people once seen as *other* are in many ways *just like me*.

Some of these studies have documented that such friendships also contribute to "self-expansion." Whenever we learn or experience something new, our minds literally grow, and we begin to include aspects of our friends into our own sense of ourselves. Researchers caution that this does not apply to casual contact—if we simply have a Muslim co-worker or "know a trans man," for instance. The growth comes from ongoing cooperation and meaningful communication.

However, one study showed that even using our imagination creatively can begin to break down unconscious biases. A group of white participants watched a five-minute video of two men—one black, one white—in which the men performed identical activities, but where the black man was clearly the target of discrimination. Those who were asked to imagine the perspective of the black man showed less automatic bias than others who were asked to remain objective. The results underscore the value of "putting oneself in another person's shoes," according to psychologist Andrew Todd, the study's lead author.

Ultimately, in order for us to get a handle on our biases and fears, both conscious and unconscious, we must become intimately familiar with the stories we tell ourselves about other people. Mindfulness "is an excellent strategy for recognizing and softening the harmful effects of unconscious bias—that and learning to be at ease with uncertainty," UCLA professor of psychiatry Daniel Siegel told *Mindful* magazine. "For the human brain, being uncertain can often be interpreted as danger. With mindfulness training, the brain can learn to rest in uncertainty without freaking out."

Vinny Ferraro, a meditation teacher in the San Francisco Bay Area who works with young people and the adults who care for them—teachers, social workers, correction officers, parents—discovered the power of mindfulness the hard way. The son of an incarcerated father and a mother who died young, Vinny spent time in prison and suffered from addiction before turning his life around, largely through meditation. He has now taught mindfulness to more than one hundred thousand young people.

"The beginning of the conversation is if we can imagine at least for a minute that we do not know what is going on for other people, to suspend our belief that our truth is the only/whole truth, and to realize that all beings see through a lens of their own conditioning," Vinny also told *Mindful* magazine. When people really open up to one another, the walls come down. "If we all got real, basically we would all fall in love with each other," he added.

Think about a time when you had a negative first impression of someone that changed as you got to know the person. A friend, Rachel, admitted, "I was horrified the first time I met my friend Judy in the ladies' room at work: 'Why on earth did they hire this loud, wildly dressed woman with the shrieking laugh?' Turned out she was just what I needed, and we now have almost forty years as BFFs."

I have seen this, too, again and again. When we start to look beyond our conditioned responses and recognize that many of our perceived differences are built on social constructs forged in the mind, we clear a pathway to love.

CHANGING HOW THE STORY ENDS

ON SEPTEMBER 11, 2015, performer, storyteller, and stand-up comedian Aman Ali posted an entry on Facebook about what happened in his high school classroom on the afternoon of the attacks on the Pentagon and the World Trade Center. It was already clear that these were terrorist acts, and there was talk about which country the United States should bomb in retaliation. When the teacher left the room, one of Ali's classmates stood up and proclaimed, "We should bomb Afghanistan back to the Middle Ages where they belong." Then he turned on Ali and said, "I bet it was your father flying that plane."

"And as if it was some kind of Pavlovian reflex," Ali recalls, "I grabbed him by his shirt and came inches away from punching him in the face so hard that I probably would have altered the structure of his face. The only thing that stopped me milliseconds before doing it was the look he gave me.

"He had a smug smile on his face as if he was telling me, 'Yep, I knew it.'"

Ali stopped short of reinforcing the kid's stereotype of violent Muslims, but his reactivity haunted him for years.

"To this day I randomly have nightmares about this incident, thinking about his smile telling me, 'Yep, I knew it,' again and again and again. What if I was the only exposure to Muslims he ever had? What if that's the opinion he carries about Muslims for the rest of his life?"

It was on September 11, 2015, that Ali awoke to find a Facebook message from his high school nemesis, apologizing profusely for the hurtful things he'd said back in 2001.

The two men spoke on the phone later that day for the first time since they'd graduated. It turned out that during the intervening years, Ali's former classmate had served two tours of duty with the U.S. Army in Afghanistan. "The endless supply of love, hospitality and goodwill he got from people there were a constant reminder of that hateful moment as an ignorant teen [when] he wanted to bomb this country mercilessly and the hurtful things he said about my dad," Ali wrote.

"I deserved to be punched," the classmate told Ali over the phone. "Sometimes I really wish you did."

"And that's when I realized I'm really glad I didn't," said Ali. "Because we never would have been able to have this conversation fourteen years later."

REFLECTION

A LOT OF the way we look at and think about others—especially those who are different from us—is encoded unconsciously. We adopt behaviors and attitudes based on what we know, and oftentimes, we don't push back on it.

A friend tells me, "Growing up in western Mass, I heard a lot more anti-Catholicism than anti-Semitism. And I still shudder to think about the experience of the lone black girl who was enrolled in my high school senior year. We were all called together by the headmistress before she came and lectured about behaving 'properly.' But she was given a single room, and there was no discussion that I remember about including her or making an effort to get to know her. Maybe she did make a couple of friends, but I still imagine her surrounded by a wall of cool politeness."

Today, consider the following: What did you hear about other groups growing up? What was implied by the behavior of your family or school toward other groups? Do you think that conditioning affects you now?

CHAPTER 20 PRACTICES

Intentions as everyday practice

Each day in the morning, write down your intention for the day, built on the foundation of challenging your assumptions with love. Perhaps your intention is "I will notice every time I judge another." Perhaps your intention is "I will notice every time I judge another, and explore why." You may resolve to practice generosity by offering a small possession to someone unexpected. The options are infinite, but some helpful prompts are listed below:

–I will notice every time I judge another.

–I will send thoughts of lovingkindness to those who challenge me today.

–I will notice my judgments of others and reflect on them.

–I will smile at someone on the subway / in the grocery store / on the street.

–I will act kind toward someone at work who challenges me.

–I will make a list of my most common judgmental or biased thoughts and spend time reflecting on them.

Taking a walk in someone else's shoes

There are plenty of times in the day when we encounter people who are different from us—checking out of a store, engaging with servers at a coffee shop or restaurant, riding the subway, taking a taxi, giving a ticket to the clerk at the mall parking lot. Often, many of us simply don't engage with these people or even look them in the eye—not out of ill will but because we don't take the energy to tune into our interactions with intention.

This practice can be done every day, all day, as much or as little as you want. The following "steps" are not meant to be done in one sitting or session, but provide a guide to taking a metaphorical walk in someone else's shoes with different levels of engagement.

1. Start by noticing people you see around you each day, and take a moment to consider their stories. Ask yourself

questions about them. Be curious—consider that all people have memories of childhood, foods they may like and dislike, colors they prefer, or times of day that feel evocative. Opening up to people who could otherwise be faceless passersby is a powerful practice.

2. As you consider the stories of others, you may want to offer them phrases of lovingkindness: *May they be happy, peaceful, healthy, strong.* You can choose your own version of these sayings.

3. As you look around in an everyday setting and take the time to consider the shared human experience between yourself and others, even those who are very different, you may find it both fun and useful to imagine their lives. If you are sitting on the subway, for instance, perhaps you choose to create an imagined life for the person across from you rather than playing a game on your smartphone. We do this not to form conclusions about someone but to remind ourselves that all lives contain joys and sorrows.

Meditation: Lovingkindness for someone that we find difficult

Offering lovingkindness to others who have behaved badly doesn't mean that we condone their actions or that we're trying to pretend it doesn't matter. It may matter very much, but we can have the courage and the willingness to open, to remember the potential of change, to realize that we ourselves are freed by wishing them well.

We usually begin with someone who is only mildly difficult for us, somebody we find somewhat annoying or irritating, or someone we're a little bit afraid of. We don't begin right away with the person who has hurt us the most in this life. It's common to feel resentment and anger, even toward a mildly difficult person, but we undertake this practice in a spirit of adventure. What happens when instead of going over and over our old grievance, we pay attention to this person in a different way, wishing they could be free of some of the suffering that binds them, wishing they themselves could be filled with the spirit of lovingkindness and compassion?

So if there is a difficult person that comes to mind, you can visualize them, say their name, see what happens as you offer the phrases of lovingkindness to them, phrases like, "May you be safe. May you be happy. May you be healthy. May you live with ease." Remember, you're not trying to manufacture any emotion or feeling. And if you feel swamped or strained, then go back to simply offering lovingkindness to yourself. Think of yourself as deserving of love and care, and generate the phrases for yourself. But over time, try to spend some time with this difficult person, even if you need to change the phrases to seem less jarring, like, "May you be filled with lovingkindness. May you find clarity and well-being" (after all, they would be less difficult if they themselves were happier!).

And for the last few minutes of this sitting, you can be spontaneous and just see who comes to mind: someone you care about deeply, someone you have difficulty with, a stranger, someone you just met. Allow them to arise in your awareness one at a time and make the offering of lovingkindness to them, people, animals, whoever it might be.

And once you have ended the session, pay attention throughout the day to see how this meditation practice may be having an effect.

LOVE EVERYBODY

✳

The more you understand, the more you love;
the more you love, the more you understand. They
are two sides of one reality. The mind of love and
the mind of understanding are the same.

—THICH NHAT HANH

A FEW YEARS AGO, I met Myles Horton, who founded what
was then called the Highlander Folk School (now known as
the Highlander Research and Education Center), a training center
for the civil rights movement, whose students included activist Rosa
Parks. Myles asked me what I did, and when I told him about
teaching lovingkindness meditation, he said, "Oh, Marty"—as in
Martin Luther King, Jr.—"used to say to me, 'You have to love
everybody.' And I would say, 'No, I don't. I'm only going to love the

people that deserve to be loved.' And Marty would laugh and say, 'No, no, no. You have to love everybody.'"

Sometimes when I tell this story, people reply, "Well, look what happened. He got assassinated." As if this were a case of cause and effect, and King would not have been killed if he hadn't tried to love everybody. But how do we know that? If Martin Luther King had been hateful, vicious, and small-minded, would he have been safer? Would we be safer? How far would the movement have gotten if he hadn't insisted on meeting hatred with love?

Neither Myles Horton nor the friend who raises an eyebrow whenever I talk about love for all others is alone in their skepticism. A student once told me that she hates lovingkindness practice because it seems so phony: "It reminds me of a forced Valentine's Day when we're actually angry or fearful, but cover over our true emotions with false sentiment." I explained that true compassion requires honesty and insight. It's not a matter of feeling sorry for someone or denying our own emotions.

Many other people regard wholesale kindness and love as signs of weakness. They think, *If I love indiscriminately, I'll lose my ardency, my power. Other people will take advantage of me and I'll be seen as a pushover. Worse, I'll become a pushover.* Why should we send wishes for happiness to those who oppose us, disagree with us, and stand in our way? Hasn't it been drummed into our heads that we should stand up for ourselves, whatever other people think?

The answer is yes—because this is what we've been taught and conditioned to believe. There are no popular TV shows, movies, or books that depict heroes who respond to villains non-violently; we are taught to think about ethics of good/bad, wrong/right in terms of force, power, and often clear-cut violence. We don't have many contemporary role models of cultural figures who have been able to come up with peaceful models of opposition, ideological approaches to protest that are backed by powerful forces, other than violence.

Loving everybody is part of the lovingkindness practice, and certainly something we can think about when it comes to dealing with difficult people in our everyday lives—a cranky boss, a demanding friend, an unfriendly server at a restaurant. But this chapter is meant to show outstanding examples of love for all, people who have found a new vocabulary, approach, and set of behaviors for how to respond to urgent and real instances of violence and threat. Happily, in forty years of practicing and teaching lovingkindness, I've discovered that instead of turning us into pushovers who lack clear boundaries, this practice makes us stronger so that we live more in tune with our deepest values. Loving all others asks us to open our hearts and embrace our shared humanity with people we don't know well (or at all). However, it does *not* require getting personally involved with everyone we meet. It does *not* require us to agree with their actions or views—or to confess our love to strangers on the street. It *never* requires that we sacrifice our principles or cease standing up for what we believe. The primary work is done internally, as we cultivate love and compassion in our own hearts.

I'd also be the first to acknowledge that this work is never done. After the publication of *Lovingkindness*, people often said to me, "It must be incredible to love everybody all the time!" I had to tell them that although I believe that universal love is possible, I don't live every day overflowing with love. I remember complaining to a friend about someone we both knew, and she said, "Haven't you read your own book?" Recognizing when our actions don't match our aspirations can also be an act of love.

Inspiring figures don't have to be used as cudgels against our own sense of worth, though we may veer toward that kind of conditioning and need to be sensitive to that tendency. Inspiration points us to a bigger world than the one we may have been inhabiting, where we suddenly can see that human beings can go through so much and still be kind. They can create, or care, or act in a way that belies an ordinary sense of constriction or limitation. They can know love is a power, and work toward being free. We can see a path, a way, and say, "If there is a path, I, too, can walk on it."

CHOOSING LOVE OVER HATE

MALALA YOUSAFZAI IS the youngest ever winner of the Nobel Peace Prize. The daughter of an education activist and school owner in the Swat Valley of Pakistan, Malala began to speak and blog about education for girls when she was twelve. In 2012, when she was just fifteen, she was shot in the head by a Taliban gunman who boarded her school bus and asked for her by name. The Taliban explained that their real target was Malala's father, but her assassination attempt was still a part of their larger plot to secure power in Swat by demoralizing advocates of education and peace—such as the members of the Yousafzai family. Fortunately, Malala ended up making a full recovery in England, and has since become an inspiring advocate for the rights of women.

In 2013, Malala appeared on *The Daily Show* with Jon Stewart to tell her story. Stewart asked her to describe her reaction when she first learned the Taliban wanted her dead. She replied: "I used to think that the Talib would come, and he would just kill me. But then I said, 'If he comes, what would you do, Malala?' Then I would reply to myself, 'Malala, just take a shoe and hit him.' But then I said, 'If you hit a Talib with your shoe, then there would be no difference between you and the Talib.'"

Despite her young age, Malala's wise heart already knew that "an eye for an eye" retaliation, even with those who sought to harm her, would only hurt her further. When we think, speak, and act from a sense of awareness and compassion, we see that there are many ways to respond to threats and accusations. It's not as though Malala's instinctual reaction to danger was necessarily to be loving and accepting of her attackers; but she had the perspective to recognize that hitting the Talib with her shoe would mean perpetuating the cycle of violence and fear further, playing by the same rules as those who opposed and endangered her.

By recognizing that retaliation would both fuel the cycle of violence and cause her to carry the burden of pain, anger, and fear in her own heart, Malala gave herself freedom and courage, reinventing the rules of the game the Taliban tried to "play" with her. When we allow ourselves to consider the consequences of our actions with a wider lens, we also realize the profound link between how we relate to others and our own sense of harmony and well-being.

What is perhaps ironic is that the resolve of Malala's non-violent emphasis on dialogue and education proved to be more disarming than any violent retaliation. Her goal was not to kill or harm those who were threatening her life as a result of the cause she stood for but to support the cause regardless of the outcome on her safety. Her peaceful form of protest showed the Taliban—and the rest of the world—that her activism had nothing to do with ego, but rather those who could benefit from her sacrifices. With stories like Malala's, we have living proof of how such acts of love can be fiercely powerful.

INCLUSION IS THE FACE OF LOVE

SOMETIMES THE ACTIONS committed against individuals or a group of people are so agonizing that the idea of including the perpetrators in those we wish to be free seems not only impossible but an outrageous mockery of justice. Yet we can find people who show us that anger and compassion are not mutually exclusive in the brave and willing human heart. In these cases, a determination not to be defined by the actions of others does not sacrifice a fundamental loyalty to justice—it bolsters it.

South Africa's Truth and Reconciliation Commission is a powerful example of this in action on a historic scale. The commission was established in 1995 under Nelson Mandela's government to investigate the violations that took place during apartheid, as well as to provide support and reparation to victims and their families. The chair of the commission was Archbishop Tutu. At the core of the commission's work was radical honesty—victims told what had been done to them or their loved ones in the presence of the perpetrators, and the perpetrators had to acknowledge what they'd done with the victims present. Now most people credit the commission with preventing a nationwide bloodbath of retaliation.

On his Web site, the Forgiveness Project, Tutu explains how this kind of letting go, or forgiveness, benefits those who have suffered: "To forgive is not just to be altruistic. It is the best form of self-interest. It is also a process that does not exclude hatred and anger. These emotions are all part of being human . . ."

Tutu further clarifies that forgiveness can bring about self-improvement: "If you can find it in yourself to forgive, then you are no longer chained to the perpetrator. You can move on, and you can even help the perpetrator to become a better person too."

The effect of allowing ourselves to connect with "the enemy," the Other, is a radical act of love, and one that is as much about peace as it is about self-love. I was moved recently by an article in *Haaretz* written by an Israeli mother, Robi Damelin, reflecting on the murder of her son by a Palestinian sniper. Damelin wrote her story in *Haaretz* in response to outrage in Israel, which was prompted by a national radio show host making a comparison between the grief of Israeli mothers and Palestinian mothers when their children are withheld by the other side. Damelin is a central member of a grassroots organization called the Parents Circle–Families Forum, which brings together Palestinian and Israeli families who have lost loved ones due to the conflict. In the article, she asks powerful rhetorical questions: "What makes you think that the tears on the pillow of a bereaved Palestinian mother are of a different color or substance than those of a grieving Israeli mother?" Her answer is that "grief knows no borders." These kinds of organizations offer clues as to how we might go about recognizing the power of reconciliation—rather than revenge—amid real and urgent conflict.

Certainly, such brave acts of reconciliation shouldn't be used as a substitute for social change or as a Band-Aid to help sustain the status quo. Nor should we make overly idealized, unreal figures out of people who are able to go there or blame those who are not so able. But these stories show the hard work of justice when it is so much greater than merely a more polite way of saying *revenge*—and the role of the hard work of love, feeding it all the while. It's our own work.

CHAPTER 21 PRACTICES

Revisiting your role models

This exercise is about revisiting some of the role models you have had throughout your life—and adding some new ones to your list.

Is there someone in your life who has inspired you, who has opened your mind, perhaps gently or perhaps swiftly, so that you feel a different sense of possibility?

See if you can bring that person here. Keep in mind that just because you consider someone a role model doesn't mean that you necessarily follow his or her worldview at all times. And although we owe a lot of gratitude to those who have inspired us, it can also be an emotional trap for us to expect ourselves to follow in their footsteps at all times. To do so simply makes us feel inadequate—and goes against the expression of self-love and self-respect that we've been cultivating.

For this practice, you may want to close your eyes and softly visualize your role models, and feel the effects they have had on you. You may also choose to write their names down and perhaps reflect on a few admirable qualities that you associate with these particular individuals.

These names need not exist in isolation in your thoughts or in your notebook. By taking the time to reflect on the people who inspire you to act with more love and compassion, you are taking strides toward greater mindfulness in your own actions, thoughts, and words.

Visualizing togetherness

Robert Thurman, professor at Columbia University, uses a powerful (though admittedly humorous) image to teach how anyone can practice living with compassion. "Imagine you're on the New York City subways and these extraterrestrials come and zap the subway car so that all of you in it are going to be together forever." If someone is hungry on the subway car, we help get them food. If someone begins to panic, we do our best to calm them down. The truth is that everyone on the subway car is in it together—so coexisting peacefully and with a basic understanding of shared humanity makes it more pleasant for everyone.

You may choose to close your eyes or rest your attention softly below you as you consider this image. You may try introducing particularly challenging people into your subway community, to see what difficulties come up as you remind yourself again and again that you are all alike and deserve love and compassion. If your focus begins to wander, you may silently repeat phrases of lovingkindness to yourself, to all others, and perhaps to specific difficult people as you visualize the scene.

Meditation: lovingkindness for all beings

We offer lovingkindness to all beings everywhere in order to touch the immensity of life. This is an expression of our capacity to connect to and care for all of life, through focus on phrases like, "May all beings be safe, be happy, be healthy, live with ease."

You can use these phrases or any phrases that are meaningful for you. What would you wish for all beings everywhere? Remember the feeling tone is one of offering or gift-giving.

We offer the phrases of lovingkindness to all beings everywhere, then all creatures, all individuals, all those in existence. Each way of phrasing this opens us to the boundlessness of life.

And when you feel ready, you can end the session. Notice if there is a sense of spaciousness or expansiveness and how it affects you throughout the day.

CREATING COMMUNITY

✳

The moment we choose to love we begin to move
towards freedom, to act in ways that liberate
ourselves and others.

—bell hooks

A FEW YEARS AGO, MY friend David was severely depressed. Like many people struggling with depression, he felt lonely and disconnected from the world. I suggested that he might break through his feelings of isolation by volunteering for a cause he believed in. He immediately warmed to the idea and offered his services to an organization that delivers meals to homebound people who are ill. But when David showed up the first day and the manager handed him a sharp knife for slicing sandwiches, there was a problem. David's hands trembled, a side effect of the medication he was taking, and he had difficulty doing even this simple task. The manager soon noticed and switched David's assignment from slicing sandwiches to wrapping them, a job he could handle easily. David was so touched to be seen and cared for and given a job he could do with pride that he was motivated to keep coming back. "I went from feeling lost in the dark tunnel of my mind to being part of a loving community," David says now. "Working with this wonderful group of people helping others was a critical turning point in my recovery."

Like David, we all yearn for connection. Yet we often tend to withdraw when we're suffering. Perhaps we feel we don't have the energy to be with other people, or we wish to spare them our pain. But withdrawal only adds to our sense of isolation. It can require enormous willpower to reach out when the impulse is to turn off the lights and hide beneath the covers, but it can also be an act of great self-compassion. So often it's only when we connect with other people that our moods lift and we start to come home to ourselves.

As Barbara Fredrickson has said, our daily moments of connection with others are "the tiny engines that drive the upward spiral between positivity and health."

And yet loneliness has become epidemic in our country. In his book *Bowling Alone*, published in 2000, political scientist Robert Putnam documented our declining participation in once-popular community groups from the PTA to civic and church organizations to, well, bowling leagues—all of which he saw as the bedrock of a democratic society. Since then, disconnection has continued to grow as our cable channels proliferate, our moves become more frequent, our commutes longer, and our neighborhood ties weaker. In a recent study published by *American Sociological Review*, researchers studying the existence (or lack thereof) of community in America found that one in four people reported not having anyone that they could really talk to.

DO-IT-YOURSELF COMMUNITIES

EVEN AS OUR social landscape changes, my own experience suggests that religious institutions, meditation and other spiritual centers, and twelve-step programs continue to provide a crucial sense of belonging—and many people are also finding creative new ways to connect that suit their needs and interests.

Sometimes it's a sense of need or shared vulnerability that brings groups together. "Many years ago, when I was a single mom recovering from alcoholism, the home my nine-year-old daughter and I were renting had a gas explosion one week before Christmas," my student Matty writes. "Fortunately, we were out at the time, but we returned to discover that where we lived had been declared 'not fit for human habitation.' Unable to lose any time from my minimum-wage job, I quickly located an apartment in town and managed to move what could be salvaged. The little money I'd put aside for Christmas presents was needed for a rent deposit and moving expenses. There would be no holiday turkey that year.

"Then, on Christmas Eve, while I was cooking dinner, a police officer knocked loudly on the door. Panic struck my heart. I feared that some part of my past might have caught up with me. My daughter, so pleased by my sobriety, gave me a look, as if to say, 'Oh, Mama, what have you done now?' When I opened the door, a very gruff cop told me to put on my coat and come downstairs. My daughter and I followed him down several flights of stairs in silence. When we got to the police car, he said, 'I was asked by Santa to make a special delivery.'

"The entire car was filled with presents! When I asked him who was responsible, he just repeated, 'Santa.' I told him I hoped this blessing would be returned to him many times over. My daughter was overjoyed. All the toys were tailored to her interests. All the clothes were a perfect fit.

"I knew the gifts had to have come from my AA group. No one

else knew us in our new town. It was just the most benevolent thing to receive such kindness. At nine, my daughter no longer believed in Santa, but she had to reconsider that year.

"The AA group had also arranged to have an open house over the holidays for members without families. People volunteered to keep it going night and day. My daughter and I took a shift in the middle of the night. We served food and kept the coffeepot going.

"As the years went on, my finances improved and I became more secure in my sobriety. We had all we needed: plenty of gifts, turkey dinners, and friends to share them with. But once in a while, we looked back and recalled our best Christmas was when we were loved by strangers and gave love back to strangers. That love shown to me inspired me to remain sober, and I have not had a drink for thirty years."

Matty's story shows the transformational impact community can have, especially in trying times. And yet I also see rich communities being created all the time in relatively everyday contexts: in book groups, community gardens, writers' and artists' circles, progressive dinner parties, and neighborhood associations for aging in place. I have friends who meet monthly to read poetry aloud, another friend who has started a meditation group to address environmental concerns, and still others who have volunteered for rescue work in places like Haiti and New Orleans.

One of the best things about the create-your-own-community movement is its flexibility, and I recommend that people start small. Intention is necessary, but formality and large numbers are not.

A few years ago, some friends and I decided to launch what we call the Turn Left Community. It all started when my friend told a few of us that he confronts two choices when he wakes up in the morning: the computer to the right of his bedroom, and the meditation cushion in a room to the left. If he turns to the right, he feels compelled to check his e-mail, but if he turns left and meditates first, he says, he can deal much more skillfully with the pressures of his high-powered job. There are five of us Turn Lefters, and we check in with one another every day by e-mail. The subject line is always turned left. Then, if you wish, "I just did thirty minutes." Or, "I only did five, I have an 8:00 A.M. meeting, mea culpa!" or maybe just "I'm in Seattle—it's raining." It's all said in a lighthearted, conscious way, and our responses and interactions provide endless grist for our own unfolding awareness.

Somewhat more formal than my Turn Left posse, *Kalyana mitta* (KM)—or spiritual friends—groups have taken off throughout the mindfulness world. Not everyone can get to a meditation center regularly, but they can gather locally to sit, discuss books, and share their own spiritual journeys. My friend Barbara and her husband recently relocated from DC to California, and for them, one of the toughest aspects of the move was leaving their KM group. "A core group of seven of us met in our living room every other week for twelve years," Barbara reflects. "We sat together, shared our stories, supported one another through illness, our kids' crises, our parents' deaths, and other major life transitions. We cried together and laughed uproariously. There was a level of intimacy and trust in that group that's hard to replace."

CAST A WIDE NET

IN THE HANDS of creative groups, social media can serve as a virtual community organization. For example, CaringBridge provides a place for people who are ill and their loved ones to communicate directly with their chosen circle of family and friends. This takes the pressure off caregivers, who don't have to make multiple phone calls or send individual e-mails whenever there's a new development.

Following surgery for cancer, author and longtime meditator Joyce Kornblatt wrote this to her CaringBridge circle: "What this space for medical updates has unexpectedly turned into—a community of wisdom, love, and generosity from so many of you—has been a precious gift to me."

Another meditation student, Susan McCulley, told me this story: "Five months ago, two days before Christmas, a close friend's only daughter was killed in an auto accident. From that moment, waves of grief and love rippled out from person to person. Our community calls it 'the Invisible Net of Love,' meaning that we are all always surrounded by love, but we don't notice it's there until we reach out. Not just people close to the family, but acquaintances and strangers reached out to offer their support. They also reached in to recognize that this could have happened to any of us (and still could) and that we all know (or can imagine) the pain of losing someone we dearly love. On her last day, it happened that the girl and her mom had brownies for breakfast: it was the first day of Christmas break, and they wanted to celebrate. Two months after her death, to honor what would have been her seventh birthday, the girl's mother invited her Facebook circle to celebrate their dear ones by having brownies for breakfast. And on that day, more than thirty-eight thousand people around the world started their day with a brownie. Love is a net that connects us."

SEEING THROUGH SEPARATION

WE'RE ALL PART of countless ephemeral communities as we move through our days: the fellow travelers on our plane, train, or bus; the audience at a concert or movie; the glum crowd waiting in rows of chairs at the DMV. For the most part, we don't identify our brief shared occupation of time and space as a community. Yet most of us can also recall a time when an unexpected occurrence created a spontaneous bond among strangers. These are the times when we suddenly recognize the unshakable truth of our interdependence.

For a meditation student named Shirley, the catalyst was a massive snowstorm that brought her town to a standstill. After several freezing hours at home without power, Shirley headed to a nearby diner, hoping for some warmth and a quiet corner where she could read. But the place, which had a backup generator, was soon buzzing with customers, and Shirley reluctantly volunteered to share her table. Then, as she recalls, something shifted. "I offered to share some of my scrambled eggs, and the ice in me began to melt." Before long, Shirley and the others at her table were squeezing in even more cold and hungry refugees from the storm. "Thus," she concludes, "the way from separate discomforts to holy gatherings: from grumpy attitude to gratitude, finding that the unbearable becomes lessened when shared compassionately."

Such compassionate sharing is the subject of Rebecca Solnit's remarkable book *A Paradise Built in Hell: The Extraordinary Communities That Arise in Disaster*. Solnit investigated five disasters in depth, from the 1906 earthquake in San Francisco to 9/11 and Hurricane Katrina, and discovered that ordinary people typically responded to calamity with spontaneous altruism, resourcefulness, and generosity. Rather than panicking, neighbors and strangers came together to rescue, feed, and house each other. As she interviewed survivors, "it was the joy on their faces that surprised me," Solnit writes. "And with those whom I read rather than spoke to, it was the joy in their words that surprised me." She concluded that the joy revealed an unmet yearning for community, purposefulness, and meaningful work. "The desires and possibilities awakened are so powerful they shine even from wreckage, carnage, and ashes . . . These accounts demonstrate that the citizens any paradise would need—the people who are brave enough, resourceful enough, and generous enough—already exist."

And then there are those moments of illumination when we glimpse our connectedness in the most everyday circumstances. Author Alix Kates Shulman describes her experience this way in her memoir *Drinking the Rain*:

I was sitting alone on the downtown subway on my way to pick up the children at their after-school music classes. The train had just pulled out of the 23rd Street station and was accelerating to its cruising speed . . . Then suddenly, the dull light in the car began to shine with exceptional lucidity until everything around me was glowing with an indescribable aura, and I saw in the row of motley passengers opposite the miraculous connection of all living beings. Not felt; saw. What began as a desultory thought grew into a vision, larger and unifying, in which all the people in the car hurtling downtown together, including myself, like all the people on the planet hurtling together around the sun—our entire living cohort—formed one united family, indissolubly connected by the rare and mysterious accident of life. No matter what our countless superficial differences, we were equal, we were one, by virtue of simply being alive at this moment out of all the possible moments stretching endlessly back and ahead. The vision filled me with overwhelming love for the entire human race and a feeling that no matter how incomplete or damaged our lives, we were surpassingly lucky to be alive. Then the train pulled into the station and I got off.

CHAPTER 22 PRACTICES

The many facets of connection

The writer Wendell Berry said, "The smallest unit of health is a community." On physiological and psychological levels, connecting with others improves our health and state of being. We are better able to let go of stress, to feel supported, and to find a sense of wholeness even as we move through our busy lives.

Sure, we may not all have concrete groups we feel a part of in our daily lives, but we can create the sense of support engendered by community at any point in our day—simply by learning to pay attention in a new way.

Here are five simple ways to find a sense of connection and community in your every day (regardless of whether or not you're with a group of people!):

1. Pay attention to the intention behind each of your actions throughout the day. If you hold the door for someone, do you just want to be polite, or are you expecting validation? Not every intention will be so concrete, so be mindful of more elusive expectations or desires that may fuel your behavior.

2. As you go about your day, make eye contact with people you encounter and give them a smile. They may not see you, they may not smile back—but you may make someone's day.

3. Resolve to forgive yourself each and every time you make a mistake or forget something. By cultivating kindness and self-examination internally, you will be better prepared to act with awareness in your relationships with others—even those with whom you don't actually engage.

4. Before eating a meal, take a few breaths and reflect on the extended community that was involved in bringing the food to your table. There were the farmers who grew the food and the farm owners who employed those workers. There were the people who transported it and stored it. There were those who sold it in the grocery store. The list goes on.

5. As you practice bringing awareness to each emotion, thought, and experience you have throughout your day, there will inevitably be moments of greater difficulty—

frustration, disappointment, anger, resentment. As these states arise, and as you may react to them as being "bad," try to reframe your judgments into recognition of your vulnerability—your "suffering" or "pain," things you share with all other beings. How does the shift make you feel?

FROM ANGER TO LOVE

✳

Nothing is absolute. Everything changes, every-
thing moves, everything revolves, everything flies
and goes away.

—FRIDA KAHLO

YEARS AGO WHILE I WAS writing a blog post on my computer at IMS, an e-mail from a student landed in my queue.
This young man wanted to know about the nature of anger. I wrote
back explaining that becoming lost in anger cuts us off from other
people. It limits our perspective and makes us see ourselves and the
rest of the world with tunnel vision. When we're angry (not when
we're merely feeling it, but when we are overcome by anger), it often
seems like the only thing we can pay attention to is the person or

thing we're angry at. Anger also tends to make us put people in boxes, so we lose sense of our connectedness as living beings; instead, we collide with the world, kicking whatever it is we think got in our way.

Just after I clicked Reply, the computer crashed, and my stress hormones started pumping. As I tried to calm myself down, I realized that the most computer-savvy person at IMS was on vacation. My panic over missing my deadline quickly turned to anger—anger at the person who wasn't available to help me, anger at myself for not being able to fix the problem, anger at the computer, anger even at the fact that I was getting angry!

Flashes of anger like these can seem automatic. But in the midst of this quick reaction, I sat with my feelings. I made an effort to notice what my mind was doing. Did sitting with my feelings mean that the anger suddenly went away? Definitely not! But by inviting myself simply to notice what was coming up, I gave myself space to see that my anger was creating tunnel vision. I remembered that I had actually urged our computer person to take a break from work. I had even helped to arrange his trip. And a little later, as my panic subsided, I managed to fix the computer snafu.

Anger at a person or a computer has a different flavor than outrage at injustice or violence. The sheer heartbreak that fills us as we witness intense suffering can naturally call forth an inchoate cry of "No!" that we know as anger. However natural it might be to feel angry, it is still useful to examine what it's like to be repeatedly overcome by anger and the consequences both to ourselves and to others.

Most of us are familiar with the strange, addictive quality of anger—how it fills our minds and how the rush of energy that accompanies it makes it hard to turn off. As the Buddha said, "Anger, with its poisoned source and fevered climax, is murderously sweet." When someone or something makes us angry, our bodies and minds effectively have an "immune" response, much like inflammation in the body. We instinctively try to self-protect, similar to the way blood rushes to the site of a bee sting.

But when anger becomes chronic, we start to see everything through a narrowed lens. So how can we resolve problems when our vision is constricted and we feel separate from others? Can we learn to recognize ourselves in one another even when our minds and bodies are on fire? Though the energy of anger might lead us to action, it can be so interlaced with fear and tunnel vision that we recklessly lash out, hurting ourselves in the process.

Yet if we learn to recognize and let ourselves experience anger when it arises, we can use its energy productively and avoid becoming embittered and consumed by it. Paying attention actually dissolves anger's toxicity and allows us to detect the fear, grief, and feelings of helplessness that a surge of fury often masks.

LETTING GO AS LOVE

INTENSE MOMENTS OF anger can arise in everyday contexts, and those feelings can do quite a fair bit of damage. A friend of mine tells me often about how much she learns from the controversies in her New York co-op apartment building. "We only have four units," she explains, "and there's no board to hide behind. I've had very painful, disruptive conflicts with the people downstairs—the kind of thing that makes your stomach churn and keeps you awake all night." Undoubtedly, we've all been there—hot with anger at our roommate who leaves the toothpaste open on the bathroom sink; overwhelmed with frustration at the landlord who doesn't return our calls; irritated by the people on the beach listening to a blaring radio. Despite the relative banality of these examples, the intensity of these feelings of anger is real.

Finding a way to let go—with love, both for yourself and others—doesn't mean you stop feeling angry. And yet holding on to the feelings and allowing them to become heavy and inflexible hurts us more than anyone. We do not have to love everyone who lives in our apartment building or forget about how annoying it is that our roommate is sloppy. We can acknowledge that we're frustrated, choose to take an action, and then let it go.

In the last chapter of section 2, "Forgiveness and Reconciliation," I wrote about the process of grief and forgiveness, and their relationship to seeing one's life as a part of something bigger. Recognizing that all of our lives are interdependent—that our landlord counts as much as we do, and that she or he wants to be happy as much as anyone else—is a radical act of love in and of itself. This creates a strong foundation from which we can practice letting go.

Practicing lovingkindness for all beings, including those we feel angry at or wronged by in everyday life, doesn't mean we suddenly feel positive. Rather, it's a way we can reformat our relationships. It's like changing the channel. As you increase your ability to see and to love, it will feed into your next interaction and to how you see the world. You are sending this person lovingkindness for the benefit of all. In these situations, we aren't necessarily explicitly transforming anger into activism, but we are similarly using the energy of our anger toward collective well-being.

START WHERE YOU ARE

I HAVE SEEN time and again that anger is a special quandary for people who devote their lives to helping correct the world's injustices. We often need a giant jolt of energy, as in outrage, to open our eyes and shake us out of complacency. Many of us have enough to do just to manage our own lives day to day, let alone get passionate about someone down the block or half a world away. The work, though, can make you vulnerable to chronic rage. In fact, for many activists, cultivating anger feels like part of their job description.

It takes profound courage to shift such entrenched feelings. As my friend Mallika Dutt, founder of the global human rights organization Breakthrough and an activist for thirty years, recognized, anger was undermining her physical and psychological health, as well as her ability to help others. She told me, "Many of us who do this work carry trauma from our own lives, along with the pain and trauma of the people we've worked with. When you focus on the horrible things people do to one another, in a way you're constantly re-traumatizing yourself. What we don't learn in advocacy training is how to heal our own trauma and find ways to take care of ourselves as we hold space for other people and their pain."

But five years ago, around the time we met, Mallika says she felt a deep sense of fatigue and began questioning *how* she was doing the work. After decades of work to end violence against women, she said, "I don't know how to turn the anger off. It is manifest in my organization, in my relationships. I need to be able to develop a different relationship to it." This, coupled with the breakup of her twenty-year marriage, led to a time of personal crisis. "That got me started on the spiritual path that I had previously avoided," she says. "In the process, I began to explore emotions other than anger and fury and a pervasive sense of injustice. I opened up more to compassion, connection, and love."

Her spiritual journey, including the study of shamanism and other indigenous traditions based on the interconnectedness of all life, has enabled her to heal her own trauma and approach her work from a place of love and compassion. Now, she reflects, "As I watch the world around me struggle with finding solutions to the problems we face, I feel increasingly grounded in the idea that love is an essential component of the pathway forward. If you begin with the understanding that we're all connected, then the solutions have to include everyone and everything on the planet."

Mallika emphasizes that working toward social justice from a position of love does *not* mean rolling over. She points out: "Martin Luther King Jr. wrote that famous speech about love and power . . .

He talked about how love without power can be anemic and how power without love can be ruthless. For me, it's really about how one steps into power and how one can exercise power from a space of love."

When we recognize that we can impact the world from a position of love and strength, we free ourselves from the notion that we must always meet injustice with a clenched fist. We develop critical wisdom about our anger and realize our profound sense of choice in approaching change we want to see. "Critical wisdom is fierce . . . yet at the same time subtle and tender," wrote my colleague Robert Thurman in *Love Your Enemies*. We *can* meet hatred with love. But to be able to do this, like Mallika, we must also turn our attention inward and learn to hold our own emotions and experience with compassion. As she says, "The self-care piece is critical. If you don't take care of yourself, you can't show up effectively for other people."

THE DISARMING POWER OF LOVE

AI-JEN POO IS the director of the National Domestic Workers Alliance, an organization working to build power, respect, and fair labor standards for nannies, caregivers for the elderly, and housekeepers in the United States. In a realm where efforts to create change are frequently fueled by animosity and conflict, she says, "I believe that love is the most powerful force for change in the world. I often compare great campaigns to great love affairs because they're an incredible container for transformation. You can change policy, but you also change relationships and people in the process . . . I think that you can love someone and be in conflict with them."

Ai-jen Poo is a unique activist for many reasons, one of which is her prodigious ability to help people find common ground. Her organization, Caring Across Generations, helps workers build on their shared values of family and the recognition that we all at one time need care.

I went to the launch of Poo's book, *The Age of Dignity*. Before she spoke, we were asked to turn to the person sitting next to us and share a story of having been the recipient of someone's care. The first person who came to my mind was one of my meditation teachers, who was incredibly nurturing and loving. (Remember, I had gone to India when only eighteen, out of a fractured, traumatic childhood. My teachers basically re-parented me.) I was uncertain as to how the notion of meditation teacher as caregiver would go over as a cultural concept with my partner, but it turns out she was from Nepal and was right there with me.

We so often just take for granted the care we have received, and we take for granted those who are providing the care. Poo is basically calling for a shift in consciousness, lifting up love. She says, "I've always believed it's important to make the invisible visible. And valuing that which has been taken for granted is something that I've always instinctually known is the key to the kind of society I want to live in and raise my children in."

Poo first became involved in the labor movement by volunteering for a domestic violence shelter, one that specialized in creating community for Asian immigrant women. Looking back on the origins of her work, Poo tells *The Nation* about her "growing hunger for getting at the root causes of the issue"—an insidious mix of poverty and gender-related oppression. One of Poo's goals in developing the organization Caring Across Generations was to expand the notion of "workers' issues" to include pay discrimination, childcare, schools, and housing—issues women typically deal with, and which are indispensably important when it comes to workers' needs to feed their families while also holding a steady job. Her organization frequently partners with other national organizations such as 9to5, in addition to other race-and gender-related non-profits.

Ai-jen Poo isn't simply trying to help workers catalyze the right fights—between each other, and between them and their employers; rather, Caring Across Generations seeks to build a support system for progress and reforms—to benefit all parties in a collaborative way. This model stands in stark contrast to the typical union actions of pitting workers against one another. "I learned that there is no such thing as an unlikely ally," Poo has said in another interview with *The Nation*. While her work may be sustained, in part, by steadfast commitment to resisting the status quo, it's clear that she recognizes the disarming strength of love and connection.

LEAN IN WITH LOVE

BROTHERS ALI AND Atman Smith and their partner, Andres "Andy" Gonzalez, founders of Baltimore's Holistic Life Foundation, jokingly refer to themselves as "love zombies." I first met them several years ago at the Omega Institute at a conference on mindfulness and education, and simply fell in love with them. I felt that they loved me, too, which many, many people would say about their own experience—I've heard from their students, trainees, colleagues, and supporters, "They reminded me of the love that does exist," "They showed me I was worthy of something," "I stopped thinking it was weird to say 'I love you' because of them." And much more like that.

Though Ali and Atman grew up in West Baltimore (the same inner-city neighborhood where a young man named Freddie Gray died in police custody in 2015), they weren't your typical boys from the hood. Their father and uncle taught them yoga at an early age, and the siblings attended a private Quaker school. But even the neighborhood was different in those days. "There was more of a sense of community, including an informal mentoring system, with the older guys being role models for the younger ones," says Atman. "Then crack came and wiped out a generation of people. They used or sold drugs, got locked up, or died. I think that's why the gang explosion happened. No one was holding kids accountable the way they did when we were growing up."

Ali and Atman met Andy at the University of Maryland–College Park. Together, the three young men practiced yoga and devoured books on spirituality. After college, they moved back to Baltimore and delved even more deeply into yoga, meditation, breath work, and self-inquiry. Then one day Ali and Atman's mother asked her sons and their friend if they'd like to teach football to twenty "bad kids" at the school where she was a teacher. But when the three met with the principal, they asked if they could teach yoga instead, and she told them they could try. "The kids were crazy and off the hook," Andy recalls. But, he adds, "After just a few weeks, the teachers and staff said to us, 'We don't know what y'all are doing, and we don't really care. Whatever you're doing is working, so please keep it up.'" Fast-forward fifteen years and the majority of that first group of "bad kids" is now on the Holistic Life Foundation staff, which has mushroomed from the original three to twenty-five.

"We saw an opportunity, and we jumped on it," says Andy. "There was suffering all over, and we wanted to make a difference. We focused on underserved communities—inner-city kids, drug rehab centers, mental health facilities, homeless shelters, and homes for the elderly—where these practices weren't available. We wanted to provide them for free. Our after-school program started with twenty kids; now we serve a hundred and twenty every week. I imagine that five to ten years from now, those kids will come back and our army of love soldiers will keep spreading and spreading."

Ali tells the story of Ja'Naisa, one of the kids in the after-school program, who had a history of getting into fights with her peers. "Boys or girls, it didn't matter, they would make fun of her, and she'd knock them out," he says. But then one day in the gym when another girl made a disparaging remark about her, Ja'Naisa grabbed her and slammed her against the wall. "She looked at the girl, then at us, then back at the girl and said, 'You'd better be glad I meditate,'" recalls Ali. "Then she walked to the corner and meditated for a while. When she was done, she got up, smiled, and went to play with her friends."

In the wake of the riots following the death of Freddie Gray in Baltimore in 2015, the Holistic Life team organized a citywide event they called "Be More Love." "There was so much friction and anger, the only way we saw to counter that angry vibe was with a loving vibe," explains Atman. "So we brought people from diverse backgrounds together in the area where the uprising happened. We had people from more affluent communities who had never been to West Baltimore. They were seeing some of the things they'd only seen on TV. And people from our community came, including the kids in our program. We led a group lovingkindness meditation and people sent love to themselves, to Freddie Gray's family, to victims of police brutality, and victims of violence everywhere."

"We wanted to get past the anger and move toward the healing," adds Ali. "The anger did bring a lot of problems to light, but love was the cohesive force."

Ali acknowledges, "Anger can be the spark for the fire. But then you have to create a controlled burn. Instead of a forest fire that will bring down the whole forest, you have to imagine a controlled fire burning up the invasive species and weeds, and letting everything else flourish. It's the same with anger . . . You need to say, 'Okay, I'm angry.' And then adjust your focus to come from a place of love, empathy, and compassion."

There will always be people and situations that ignite our outrage—for good reason. Yet when we stop resisting our anger and relate to it with awareness, we free ourselves from anger's stranglehold. By allowing ourselves simply to feel what we feel, we release the expectation that painful states of mind such as anger will consume us. They can arise, and we can let them go—like the tides of the ocean or the waxing and waning of the moon. It's a practice of not holding on, of choosing not to identify. In this way, the energy we have to try to make a difference becomes cleaner and stronger.

CHAPTER 23 PRACTICES

The many sides of anger

It's often hard to see anger as being a complex feeling. After all, when something makes us angry, we tend to feel inundated in a static state of being, and we fixate on it. But when we practice being more mindful of anger as it arises, we can actually prevent ourselves from getting lost in the state of tunnel vision and instead can see that anger is multi faceted—it contains emotions like anxiety, fear, sadness, and even love.

Recognizing these elements of anger makes it seem more complex, but also more manageable. Anger is not solid and irrepressible but part of our changing system of feelings and conditions, an alive system that is ever shifting and ephemeral.

1. To familiarize yourself with the multifaceted nature of anger, list all of the emotions that you have experienced when feeling angry with another person, a situation, or even yourself.

2. As you brainstorm, it may help to close your eyes and visualize a specific instance of feeling angry. What emotions come up? You may want to write down some of the emotions that came up prior to the peak of your feelings of anger.

3. As you breathe in and out, think about how the anger felt in your body. Did your muscles tense? Did you feel an urge to cry? Remember that anger and stress produce the

stress hormone cortisol, which raises blood pressure and accelerates heart rate.

4. Try to focus on some of the other more psychological nuances of anger (frustration, impatience, insecurity, and so on).

The art of self-intervention

Anger is uncomfortable—but it's also addictive! In tough situations, anger emerges as a defense mechanism, a tool to help you energize so you can handle whatever catalyzed the feeling. We convince ourselves again and again, whenever we get angry, that the inner fire of anger will help us deal with whatever or whoever injured us. Little do we know that we often injure ourselves even more deeply by allowing the toxicity to take over.

The good news is that we can intervene in moments of anger as we learn that letting anger control us is often the greatest enemy of all. So the next time you are in a situation that sparks a reaction of anger, try out this practice of self-intervention.

1. Recognize your anger as it arises. Suppressing anger just makes the feeling more intense and insurmountable.

2. Consider whether there is anything concrete you can do or say to make the situation better (such as leaving the room where a heated conversation took place, or taking a walk to cool down).

3. If there's nothing you can do in the moment, keep your attention on the simple recognition of your anger. The simple gesture of directing your mind to managing the situation with mindfulness prevents you from tunnel vision. This is an act of self-care.

4. If it feels impossible to tolerate the discomfort of your anger, try opening your perspective. Think of all the things you're grateful for in the moment. This may help you change your perception of the situation at hand.

Believe it or not, accepting ourselves—angry as we may be—is an act of compassion, of love. These moments will always come and go again and again. The greatest question, then, to ask is, how can I alchemize this anger into some act of love?

24

SAY YES TO LIFE

✳

*You are born alone. You die alone. The value of the
space in between is trust and love.*

—LOUISE BOURGEOIS

I BOARDED A TRAIN IN New Delhi once bound for Bodh Gaya
and a silent meditation retreat—that is, I assumed that at the end
of the seventeen-hour journey, I would alight close to the legendary
town where the Buddha achieved enlightenment. And so I crawled
into my tiny compartment and fell asleep. But when I awoke, ready
to disembark on holy soil, I discovered that while I slept, the train had
reversed course and returned to Delhi. There was some problem

with a stubborn cow on the tracks—or maybe it was a whole herd. I never knew for sure.

And so before taking my place on a meditation cushion, I received a reminder of one of the most profound lessons of mindfulness training: *Don't pick a fight with reality.* Even then, as young and naïve as I was, I realized that I could respond to the situation in one of two ways: I could be anxious and upset about perhaps missing the start of the retreat, or I could be open to what was happening and view it as a surprising adventure that I could learn something from, though at the time I couldn't say what. And as it turned out, I need not have worried about being late. Unknown to me until we arrived, the teacher I was heading to Bodh Gaya to sit with—the renowned S. N. Goenka—was on the same train!

In the four decades since my train trip to nowhere, I have been reminded again and again that we don't have to go anywhere to approach life with the sense of adventure and openness that I felt that morning in Delhi. It's just a matter of saying *yes* to life.

Saying *yes* to life is enlivening and invigorating.

Saying *yes* to life frees up our energy to be present with whatever is happening.

Saying *yes* to life is the gateway to unimagined adventures and possibilities—as readily available to us in our living room as on a trek across India. It's a matter of how we relate to our unfolding experiences.

OPENING TO THE MOMENT

SUSAN, A MEDITATION student, wrote me this: "When I'm feeling disconnected or lonely or anxious, I do my best to remember to pay attention to details. While paying attention does have a calming effect, I realize that paying attention—exquisite, extraordinary attention—is a way of falling in love. I can fall in love with the intricacies of a maple seed. I can fall in love with the sharp sound of the blue jays and squirrels fighting nearby. I can fall in love with the tension in my heart and throat when I think about the uncertainty of the coming months. This is a love that I consciously choose and that transforms any moment from one I'm rushing through or impatient with or not noticing to one I'm in love with."

The more we open to our present circumstances—our internal experiences, as well as our relationships with others and the world around us—the more we create the conditions for happiness to blossom. Eventually, we come to realize that, in fact, everything we need to be happy is here right now, when we say yes to life.

Saying yes to life doesn't mean that we have to like what is taking place at every moment. And in fact, we grow and can make ourselves happier even by just noticing those moments when we find we are saying *no* to life. One fall, I was in Santa Fe for a retreat with the Tibetan teacher Tsoknyi Rinpoche. One rainy afternoon, I pulled into the parking lot of my hotel and noticed crowds of people trying to photograph the sky. I looked up, and there was an incredible rainbow. I hopped out of the car to join the others in documenting the moment, but by the time my old iPhone turned on, the rainbow had disappeared. Instead, there were luminous pink clouds in the sky. And yet I was disappointed. I fixated on the fact that I had neglected to buy a new iPhone. A few moments later, two women left the hotel and walked past me. I heard one of the women gasp. "Wow. Look at those amazing clouds," she said to the other. It was at that moment that I realized I could be saying yes to life, and I did. I was able to laugh at my habit of disconnecting from the beauty of life by clinging to old tendencies, stories, judgments, and criticisms. But as I laughed, I let go. I settled back into the moment, and I allowed my *no* to become a *yes*. Those clouds were extraordinary!

When we open to *this* moment and don't judge it or try to change it, even when we're suffering and wish it were otherwise, we tap into the spaciousness of mind that allows us to move forward skillfully, with discernment and joy. In other words, every aspect of our experiences is included. No unwanted thought, emotion, or bodily sensation is left behind. This is wholeness.

CURIOSITY AND AWE

JUST AS WE looked earlier at ways we can reclaim these qualities in personal relationships so that they transform us rather than just seeming mawkish and clichéd, so, too, can we reclaim them in our relationship to life itself.

Awe doesn't ask our permission to wow us; it just smacks us in the face with something bigger without bothering to argue us out of our tedium. Awe can come in a single glance, a beautiful sound, a heartfelt gesture. Think of how we can slog along in our little tunnel of daily life, back and forth, and then one day pass a lilac bush in bloom. The fragrance catches us first and then the beauty of the full blossoms. In pausing to appreciate it, we receive a reminder of the spectacular. Much like that, awe can bring this invigorating sense of novelty into everyday relationships that might otherwise feel stale or dull.

Curiosity is the place where awe is born, and it starts with heightening our senses. We may suspect life holds many mysteries, but only by paying attention can we access the grandeur and subtleties that make each person different and each encounter something fresh. By using our senses and paying a different kind of attention to the world around us, we may see that people we took for granted are more complex than we think they are. If we are able to open the mind to investigate, we may also discover some people are much simpler than the story we had constructed around them. Curiosity brings us the unexpected. It is the antidote to those times when we find ourselves in a rut, unable to take in anything new because we just can't risk disrupting the dreary order of the day to day. With that frame of mind, curiosity looks like it would take too much energy. *What, on top of everything else, you want me to question my reality? Honestly, I haven't got the time for awe or wonder.*

Instead of gripping tightly to a fixed idea of how things are and how they should be, we can train our mind to hold those notions lightly and begin each day ready to explore. We do not need to face the world demanding that it prove us right. Instead, we can say to it: *Surprise me.* We can become excited by the possibility that if we keep our eyes open, we open our hearts to something new. To have the kind of openness that cultivates awe does not mean we have to be credulous and sentimental, but the ironic stance—to act unimpressed because we fear looking foolish—has us experiencing our own lives at a distance. If, instead, we open our hearts to real love, we allow ourselves to feel the wonder of life, which research says is vital to sustaining our connection to the world and to one another.

Awe comes on a spectrum from being inspired by something quite small to springing from the soaring and majestic. On one end is "Aw!"—the sound we make when we notice something that reminds us of the struggles we all share and how we take them on with a full heart, endeavoring to do the best we can. "Aw!" comes out of the mouth almost without us noticing, the automatic connection to the heart we spontaneously experience when we see a child taking his first brave steps, his little hands steadied by those of his beaming grandmother. The toddler is joyful in the newness of his body and excited by his growing capabilities, and the grandma is joyful in guiding another child to step fully into this life. Awww! We see a spring-loaded puppy bound after a stick, we get an unexpected call from a friend who remembers that this is the anniversary of our mother's death, we watch as a teenager on the subway who looks for all the world like a character from an angsty dystopian novel pops up from his seat when an elderly man hobbles onto the train car.

This very sound—"Aw!"—captures our amazement at the simple things, the wondrous moments that happen between people all the time.

The other end of the spectrum is *awe* with an *e*. This awe may be revealed in the small things, the tiny personal triumphs, but what we get a glimpse of is a sense of the immensity of the world in all its possibilities, the vastness of its expanse and our piece in the unfolding of it all. This awe generates its resonance through a connection to the grand and limitless. In our experiences of real love with ourselves, with another, with the world, we get the full spectrum of awe, from the commonplace to the infinite, with someone who is very close at hand or with all of life.

Two psychology professors, Paul Piff and Dacher Keltner, performed an experiment about the significance of awe, a quality they defined as "being in the presence of something vast that transcends our understanding of the world [and] shifts our focus from our narrow self-interest." In one experiment, they brought study participants to a grove of eucalyptus trees on the edge of the University of California–Berkeley campus. Piff and Keltner hoped to demonstrate how experiencing awe makes us more collaborative, accepting, and more strongly bound to one another.

They gave the study subjects the choice of looking up at these magnificent trees, many of which are more than two hundred feet tall, or looking instead at the concrete façade of a science building that stands just east of the grove. While the participants were contemplating their options, the professors staged a mishap. They had someone walking on the path through the grove stumble and drop a handful of pens. Those who had spent a minute, just a minute, looking at the trees were more helpful to the person who tripped, picked up more of the scattered pens, than those who had been gazing at the building. The lines of the building stirred the rational mind, the researchers concluded, but not the heart. When the heart and the mind were opened by gazing at the trees, the sense of awe reinforced those people's instincts to be less self-interested, kinder, and more helpful to a stranger.

I remember overlooking the Straits of the Bosporus the first time I traveled to India. I was excited to be at the juncture of two continents. I stood in Istanbul, waiting for a ferry, and saw Europe on one side of the narrow body of water and Asia on the other—with all the mystery and possibilities it held. That instant for me was the same as it was for those in the study looking at the tall trees: I felt connected to the immensity of the world, to the limitlessness of my dreams and curiosity about what might come next.

A friend who attended Berkeley says she'd like to show me that eucalyptus grove, because when she came upon it as an undergraduate, she felt the same things she's heard me describe about standing on the edge of the Bosporus. Sometimes between classes, she told me, she would take refuge in the grove and deeply inhale the trees' menthol perfume. The temperature in the core of the grove is cooler than the rest of campus, and in the morning, the fog lingers there, giving the stand of trees a mystical quality. Two forks of Strawberry Creek, a waterway that runs through Berkeley, merge in that grove. Breathing in the scent of the trees, hearing the sound of water running over the rocks in the creek bed, she felt her body releasing into the sensation that she was a cluster of atoms among other atoms, supported by the world and also a vital and integrated part of the web of life. This humbled her, yet also connected her to the infinite scale of life. As joy coursed through her body, she embraced it and subsequently felt the chatter in her mind lessen. She felt less stressed and more available, emotionally, to the people in her life. My friend was experiencing what the researchers described as awe's impact—imbuing people with humility and a different sense of themselves, one that is part of something larger.

In my friend's case, she sought out this experience intentionally, as a way to bolster her connection to herself and the universe and to replenish her energy for those she loved. We can train our minds to be like my friend's: finding delight in everyday life will elevate us, too, and help us fully see ourselves and those we love. I like what the actress Rashida Jones has observed about her parents, music producer Quincy Jones and actress Peggy Lipton, because it suggests that she is awed by awe. "My parents are the coolest of the cool on every single level," Rashida said in an interview, "and it's because they have a deep appreciation for every moment of their lives."

TRANSFORM *NO* INTO *YES*

THE MORE WE cultivate mindfulness, the more clearly we see and appreciate what's right in front of us, unclouded by judgment or expectation. And the more we cherish the life around us, the more we cherish ourselves. It's a powerful equation.

It wasn't until she moved into her new apartment that Donna noticed the post office across the street. She'd relocated to the small city in search of peace and quiet, but the post office and adjacent parking lot bustled with activity. Donna was angry with herself for not having realized this before signing the lease. But she didn't want to move again, so she decided to pay attention both to her resistance and to the commotion outside her window.

First came the morning when members of a large family leaped out of a large van and the mom yelled, "Okay! Everyone show me your passport photographs." They were clearly headed for an adventure, and Donna felt a wave of excitement for them.

Soon she noticed the elderly man who came once a week to collect his mail. Stooped and slow, he leaned on a cane as he made his way across the parking lot. Donna's first reaction was to worry about her own mobility as she aged. But then she saw that as he made his way back to his car, he would stop and painstakingly pick up trash. Donna imagined that he wanted to help make the world a better place for as long as he could. Her view of her own future brightened.

Another day, she watched an old Toyota screech into the lot and a mom, cell phone crushed between shoulder and ear, wrangle her sleeping toddler out of his car seat. In a rush, she bumped the boy's head against the car frame, and he woke up screaming. With that, she dropped the phone and, holding her son to her chest, kissed his head and murmured words of comfort until he calmed down.

Donna felt uplifted by these fleeting, ordinary moments. Even if none of the people she observed later recalled the events she'd witnessed, she would recall them, and they fueled her happiness. They helped her remember trips she'd taken, the joyful yet stressful years spent raising her children, and her own tender aging. Watching the flurry of people come and go made Donna aware of how everyone struggles daily to be happy. Best of all, she realized that if she could extend this compassionate awareness to strangers, she could grant it to herself, as well.

For some, of course, the day-to-day hurdles are large, to the point of threatening the life we have dreamed of and worked for. After a car accident led to the amputation of her right foot when she was sixteen, Indian dancer Sudha Chandran, who had been training to dance since early childhood, took three years to recover. On the Facebook page for a portraiture project entitled *Humans of Bombay*, Chandran shared her story: "I remember people would come home and say things like, 'It's so sad your dreams can't come true,'" she recalls in a blog post. But she decided to relearn how to dance: "It was a slow and painful process," Chandran elaborates, "but with every step I learnt, I knew that this is what I wanted."

On the day of her first performance following the accident, the headline in the morning paper read, LOSES A FOOT, WALKS A MILE. Chandran hasn't stopped dancing since.

While Chandran undoubtedly experienced frustration, disappointment, rumination, and regret during her process of reframing her relationship to dance, she was open to seeing what could be relearned, and became more resilient. In the end, the greatest triumph may not be that Chandran is dancing again but that she had the immensity of heart to try. I always think of that heart when I reflect on her quotation, "You don't need feet to dance."

THIS FLEETING WORLD AS A
BUBBLE IN A STREAM

TIME IS BOTH the implacable thief who steals away the gifts of life and the sacred messenger who bestows them.

Even as we live with the knowledge that each day might be our last, we don't want to believe it. Yet when we're able to open to the truth of even our most shattering losses, we find moments of unimagined grace.

Rosemary, an interior designer and longtime practitioner of Tibetan Buddhism, lost her husband, Jonathan, to cancer a few years ago, ten years after the initial diagnosis. "We got the news the day of our wedding anniversary," Rosemary recalls. "I was devastated and thought we should just go home and weep. But Jonathan wouldn't hear of it. He said, 'Rosemary, we have no idea what's going to happen. We still have to celebrate our lives. Let's not let cancer make us special; let's just go on being who we are.'" Jonathan chose to see his life as ordinary throughout the course of his illness, which included massive amounts of chemotherapy and a difficult stem cell transplant. "We're all experiencing loss and change every moment," he told Rosemary. "Mine is just more noticeable."

Although she had been preparing for Jonathan's death for some time, when it happened, she felt crushed. "I think the hardest thing when you're a new widow and you've had this loving exchange is that suddenly you're unplugged and there's no love coming in and no love going out," Rosemary says. "It's as if you've been plugged into an electrical socket and then the power goes out forever. I knew it was going to be hard, but I didn't know I'd feel like I'd fallen off a cliff."

Rosemary was helped through the weeks and months following Jonathan's death by family, friends, and a widows support group. The group, she notes, helped her open to her grief in a way that felt both deeper and safer than when she was on her own. And her spiritual community, which had been a source of enormous support to both Rosemary and Jonathan throughout his illness, also played a key role in helping her through her grief. "Being with people who knew Jonathan made a huge difference," she says. "When they were around, I felt there was a bridge from where I'd been to where I was then and where I was going. It was a long bridge, and I didn't feel like I was on the edge of a cliff anymore."

At a certain point, though, Rosemary says she had to stop focusing on her loss. "The pain was so strong, I felt like I was being taken down by it," she explains. "I believe that as important as it is to allow yourself to grieve, you also have to set boundaries. You can't just let yourself sink. Sometimes you have to go for a walk or call a friend or watch a movie. And then one day you wake up and decide that you don't want to live in the past. Jonathan had such an innate sense of courage about living life no matter what, I wanted to honor him and the life we shared."

Now, three years later, says Rosemary, "It's as if all the love I gave to my husband can go out to the entire world, and the whole world is my husband."

Hearing Rosemary's story made me think of a time years ago when I went to see my Tibetan teacher, Nyoshul Khen Rinpoche, in Taiwan. I loved Khenpo (as he was known) deeply and was overjoyed at seeing him again, but I was concerned because he appeared especially frail and ill. He was never really in great health, but this time he seemed considerably worse.

After the visit, we went back to our hotel, close to where we had met him. My traveling companions and I planned to see Khenpo again in a few days, but knew that during the interim he had moved somewhere else. When the day of our second visit arrived, a group of us, holding flowers and offerings, were waiting outside our hotel for taxis to take us to the new place. I was feeling incredibly sad. It seemed that now all I could think was, *Oh no. This could be the last time I ever see him.* The prospect was devastating, and I was deeply upset.

After the taxis picked us up, every one of them got completely lost in the streets of Taiwan. In that time of fruitlessly driving around, my attitude toward seeing Rinpoche suddenly shifted. I started thinking, *I'd give anything to see him one more time. One more time would be the best thing in the entire universe! It would be the greatest gift I could ever have!*

As it turned out, the taxis eventually found the right address, and we were able to see Rinpoche. Contrary to what I feared, he lived many more years, and I saw him many more times. But that experience taught me a valuable lesson, as I saw clearly how "one more time" can be the best prospect imaginable or the worst, depending on how I related to it.

In mindfulness, we are talking about a sense of an expanded present. Our protestations, our clinging to the past, our efforts to control the future may arise, but they are strongly attenuated by remembering to simply be with what is. We drop through our reactions to a space of profound, grateful connection—that is love of life itself. Always keep in mind that in reality, what we might have in this moment with a friend, with a place, with a dance, with a poem, *is* the one more time. Treasure it.

Love and loss and grief, letting go and embracing love and life again, form the tender, inexorable, but natural rhythm of our days. In opening to this rhythm, we find within ourselves the unshakable love we have been searching for. To this, too, we learn to say *yes*.

If love is an ability, a nascent power curled within me, isn't it then also a responsibility? My own responsibility? This is something

I wrestle with often. The kindness or cruelty with which I treat myself once I've made a mistake, the way I take shame to heart or hold it in perspective, my ease of laughter and caring and encouraging myself, or consoling myself when my heart is broken—is that all up to me?

How about when I meet a stranger or owe a debt of gratitude, run into an old friend who is a friend no longer, see my heart open under the admiring gaze of another, or feel myself disappearing as I strive to endlessly please them—is my response really in my hands?

What about when life deals me a bad blow, when I am reeling from unfairness or cruelty, when my body betrays all I care about or my neighbor betrays all I care about or my country betrays all I care about? "Love is a strength, not a weakness," might be my favorite saying, but what about those times when I am tempted to, in effect, cross my fingers behind my back before uttering it? Is the love that ensues or doesn't—love for myself, for another, for life itself—also up to me?

I think it is up to me. It is up to each one of us. And I think that working toward fulfilling that promise is the most amazing thing we can do with our lives.

TAKEAWAYS FROM EACH SECTION

Section 1 Takeaways

–The capacity for love exists inside ourselves.

–We can find freedom from the negative stories we tell ourselves.

–Finding self-love can emerge from testing the borders of our judgments and assumptions.

–We are always changing and have incalculable potential.

–Perfectionism is an unproductive use of attention. Self-hatred will not make us "better."

–Acceptance is what allows us to realize that all experiences are opportunities to learn and grow.

–Through lovingkindness for ourselves, we can learn to accept—and love—our imperfect selves.

Section 2 Takeaways

–Once we identify the expectations, assumptions, and habits of mind that we carry around about loving others, we can open ourselves up to real love.

–A great foundation for loving others is maintaining a level of curiosity; we can always learn more about those we are close to.

–In a relationship with another person, fairness is not a fixed principle of right and wrong but a mutual willingness to reassess the situation and adopt a fresh perspective.

–Whenever we are close to another person, there will always be a space that separates us. With mindfulness, we are able to explore that space with a sense of possibility, rather than fear.

–Letting go is essential in love—it is the opposite of clinging to expectations about how things *should* be and allows us to accept others (and ourselves!) as they are.

–Recognizing that no one else can complete us actually enhances our capacity to love and receive the love of others.

–Mindfulness enables us to see the conflict with a fresh perspective so that we can feel emotions like anger without getting lost in them.

–Sympathetic joy takes our attention away from our own preoccupations and allows us to see that joy is available in many more places than we have yet imagined.

–Forgiveness is a path to peace and a powerful element of love for ourselves and others.

Section 3 Takeaways

–Compassion isn't a gift or talent—it's the natural result of paying attention and realizing the infinite opportunities to connect with others.

–When we make very small efforts to engage in random acts of kindness, we actually make life less stressful and more pleasant for ourselves, as well as for others.

–Extending lovingkindness toward others (even those we may not know or like) doesn't make us into pushovers, but stronger and more authentic versions of ourselves.

–The first step toward being able to show compassion for others is to set the intention to do so; we can take joy in the act of stretching ourselves with kindness and self-acceptance.

–When our fear response takes over and we isolate from others we perceive as different or threatening, we actually restrict our own sense of identity.

–When we look past our conditioning, we see that many differences we latch onto are built on social constructs.

–We may not be part of an official group, but we all share certain everyday communities—a train car, the line at the DMV. In these common moments, we can recognize our profound interdependence.

–It takes immense courage and openness to alchemize feelings like anger into love and hope.

–When we learn to stop resisting tough feelings like anger, we can engage our feelings with awareness; once we do that, we see that these feelings are not permanent.

–Approaching life with a sense of adventure is always available to us, no matter where we are.

ACKNOWLEDGMENTS

✳

I'm very grateful to Bob Miller of Flatiron Books for always championing love, Carole Tonkinson of Bluebird for seeing so completely what I wanted to say, and my agent, Joy Harris, for being the best of agents and best of friends.

As in all things in my life, it takes a village and this did. Many people offered their stories, poems, quotes, and images of love. They are really the heart and soul of the book.

Danelle Morton helped me greatly in understanding the structure of the book, then collecting stories from people and crafting them to help the structure come alive. Lise Funderburg illuminated a clear path through the sticky terrain of love for another, whether parent, child, lover, colleague, or pet dog!

Lily Cushman became my assistant just after I began working on the book, and brought all my work to a whole other level of presentation, creativity, and impact.

Barbara Graham is a tremendously talented writer who put aside her own work to help me when I needed it most. Her broad knowledge of research findings about topics like meditation, trauma, and gratitude, combined with her humor and kindness and fundamental know-how of the mechanics of writing, made her contributions invaluable.

Charlotte Lieberman worked with me for a long time on this project, first helping me move from the sweeping beginnings of a scary blank screen to envisioning the book, then interviewing lots of people to capture their stories, helping me respond to editorial suggestions through several iterations, and doing whatever excruciatingly detailed work was called for, like seeking permissions to use quotations. And it is excruciating.

I had always wanted to work with Toni Burbank as an editor, and I finally got to. She is a legend, and deservedly so. My ceaseless travel and teaching commitments made me, I'm sure, a difficult case. Toni was always brilliant in pointing out what needed to be done despite that, and that brilliance is reflected throughout the book.

Of the many friends I am blessed with in this life, I can only mention a few: Joseph, Gyano, Steve, Elizabeth, Willa, and Josey are like my fam. Jeff, Jerry, and Jennifer provide unwavering support. My meditation community offers inspiration in both contemplation and actions. And I want to give a shout-out to Jason, Christi, and Kevin Garner. They seemed to somehow be there for the most intense moments of the book—turning in the first draft, turning in the final draft—taking care of me. And when I was most discouraged about writing, feeling like I might not be able to settle for just being mediocre, and perhaps would have to just settle for that, Jason and Kevin took me to see the play *Hamilton*. I walked out knowing I had to give writing this book all that was in me. So also a thank-you to Lin-Manuel Miranda, for his amazing play, which changed everything.

NOTES

✳

INTRODUCTION: LOOKING FOR LOVE

1 we cannot live within: James Baldwin, "Letter from a Region of my Mind," *The Fire Next Time* (New York: Vintage, 1992).

SECTION 1 INTRODUCTION: BEYOND THE CLICHÉ

11 to do with accountability: Linda Carroll, interview with the author, July 2015.

13 a right to be here: James Baldwin, "They Can't Turn Back," *The Price of the Ticket: Collected Nonfiction* (New York: St. Martin's Press, 1985).

13 who can best us: Sonja Lyubomirsky, *The How of Happiness: A Scientific Approach to Getting the Life You Want* (New York: Penguin, 2007).

15 be reduced by them: Maya Angelou, *Letter to My Daughter* (New York: Random House, 2008).

17 calm, safety, and generosity: Kristin Neff, "The Chemicals of Care: How Self-Compassion Manifests in Our Bodies," SelfCompassion.org, http://self-compassion.org/the-chemicals-of-care-how-self-compassion-manifests-in-our-bodies.

1. THE STORIES WE TELL OURSELVES

28 *It Didn't Start with You*: Mark Wolynn, *It Didn't Start with You: How Inherited Family Trauma Shapes Who We Are and How to End the Cycle* (New York: Viking, 2016).

29 the one after that: L. H. Lumey et al., "Prenatal Famine and Adult Health," *Annual Review of Public Health*, no. 32 (2011).

29 more prone to PTSD: Rachel Yehuda et al., "Holocaust Exposure Induced Intergenerational Effects on FKBp5 Methylation," *Biological Psychiatry* 80, no. 5 (2015).

31 nervous system and psyche: Nancy Napier, interview with the author, November 2016.

2. THE STORIES OTHERS TELL ABOUT US

39 ten attempt it: Statistics from *2004 i-SAFE Foundation Survey*, https://www.isafe.org/outreach/media/media_cyber_bullying.

40 joyously and with cake: Frank Bruni, "Our Weddings, Our Worth," *New York Times*, June 26, 2015.

41 my relationship . . . is blessed: Paul Raushenbush, "Debating My Gay Marriage? Don't Do Me Any Favors," *Huffington Post*, October 20, 2014, http://www.huffingtonpost.com/paul-raushenbush/dont-do-me-any-favors_b_6014926.html.

3. WELCOMING OUR EMOTIONS

49 *I'm going to protect you*: Daphne Zuniga, interview with the author, August 2015.

50 health and well-being: Jordi Quodbach et al., "Emodiversity and the Emotional Ecosystem," *Journal of Experimental Psychology* 143, no. 6 (2014).

51 real love and happiness: Barbara Graham, interview with the author, March 2016.

4. MEETING THE INNER CRITIC

60 off the golf course: George Mumford, *The Mindful Athlete: Secrets to Pure Performance* (Berkeley, CA: Parallax Press, 2015).

61 she needs a rest: Mark Coleman, interview with the author, October 2016.

5. LETTING GO OF PERFECTION

66 have need of love: Oscar Wilde, *An Ideal Husband* (Mineola, NY: Dover Publications, 2012).

66 self-acceptance and self-love: Kathryn Budig, interview with the author, April 2015.

69 got a little better: Quoted in Kathy Jesse, "David Letterman, Even Retired, Keeps on Interviewing," *New York Times*, December 1, 2015, http://www.nytimes.com/2015/12/02/arts/television/david-letterman-even-retired-keeps-on-interviewing.html.

6. BECOMING EMBODIED

74 heart never lies to us: Ben Harper, "You Found Another Lover (I Lost Another Friend)," *Get Up!*, Stax Records, 2013.

7. MOVING BEYOND SHAME

81 revolution is long overdue: Margaret Cho, "Self-Esteem Rant," *NOTORIOUS C.H.O.: Live at Carnegie Hall* (New York: Wellspring Media, 2002).

9. FOLLOWING YOUR ETHICAL COMPASS

93 heals the maker: Christopher Alexander, *The Nature of Order*, vol. 4 (Berkeley, CA: Center for Environmental Structure, 2002).

95 things seemed more challenging: Quoted in Olga Khazan, "Spill the Beans," *Atlantic*, July 8, 2015, http://www.theatlantic.com/health/archive/2015/07/spill-the-beans/397859/.

SECTION 2 INTRODUCTION: LOVE AS A VERB

103 "The very essence of romance": Oscar Wilde, *The Importance of Being Earnest* (Ballingslöv, Sweden: Wisehouse, 2016).

103 peacefulness of love: Linda Carroll, interview with the author, July 2015.

104 the passion itself: Zadie Smith, *White Teeth* (New York: Knopf, 2001).

104 I rose in it: Toni Morrison, *Jazz* (New York: Knopf, 2004).

106 interaction with other people: Atul Gawande, "Hellhole," *New Yorker*, March 30, 2009, http://www.newyorker.com/magazine/2009/03/30/hellhole.

107 unwanted mental experiences: Baljinder Sahdra and Phillip Shaver, "Comparing Attachment Theory and Buddhist Psychology," *International Journal for the Psychology of Religion* 23, no. 4 (2013).

108 emotion were particularly active: Richard Davidson et al., "Lending a Hand: Social Regulation of the Neural Response to Threat," *Psychological Science* 17 (2006).

109 baby on the plane: Barbara Fredrickson, "Remaking Love," TedX, January 10, 2014.

109 people in your midst: Barbara Fredrickson, *Love 2.0: Creating Happiness and Health in Moments of Connection* (New York: Penguin, 2013).

10. BARRIERS TO FINDING REAL LOVE

111 Sufi poet and mystic: Rumi translation by Brad Gooch and Maryam Mortaz (unpublished).

114 ourselves more conscious: James Hollis, *The Eden Project: In Search of the Magical Other* (Toronto, ON: Inner City Books, 1998).

117 we cannot live within: James Baldwin, "Letter from a Region of My Mind," *The Fire Next Time* (New York: Vintage, 1992).

118 world as a whole: Erich Fromm, *The Art of Loving: The Centennial Edition* (London: Bloomsbury Academic, 2000).

11. CULTIVATE CURIOSITY AND AWE

126 considerable healing potential: Stephen Levine, *Embracing the Beloved* (New York: Anchor, 1996).

12. AUTHENTIC COMMUNICATION

131 coping is the problem: Virginia Satir, *The Satir Model* (Palo Alto, CA: Science and Behavior Books, 1991).

131 the kinder path: Quoted in Emily Esfahani Smith, "Masters of Love," *Atlantic*, June 12, 2014, http://www.theatlantic.com/health/archive/2014/06/happily-ever-after/372573/.

132 attempt to find fault: Kathlyn and Gay Hendricks, "How to Create a Conscious Relationship: 7 Principles, 7 Practices," *Huffington Post*, November 15, 2011, http://www.huffingtonpost.com/kathlyn-and-gay-hendricks/creating-conscious-relationships_b_1092339.html.

134 deeper layers as well: John and Julie Gottman, *And Baby Makes Three: The Six-Step Plan for Preserving Marital Intimacy and Rekindling Romance After Baby Arrives* (New York: Harmony, 2007).

134 can be powerfully transformational: George Taylor, interview with the author, October 2016.

139 they could give it: Mark Wolynn, *It Didn't Start with You: How Inherited Family Trauma Shapes Who We Are and How to End the Cycle* (New York: Viking, 2016).

13. PLAYING FAIR: A WIN-WIN PROPOSITION

144 make love last: B. Janet Hibbs, *Try to See It My Way: Being Fair in Love and Marriage* (New York: Avery, 2009).

14. NAVIGATE THE SPACE BETWEEN

155 room of our own: Deborah Luepnitz, *Schopenhauer's Porcupines: Intimacy and Its Dilemmas* (New York: Basic Books, 2008).

156 before an immense sky: Rainer Maria Rilke, *Letters to a Young Poet*, translated by M. D. Herter Norton (New York: W. W. Norton, 1934).

159 "The beginning of love is": Thomas Merton, *No Man Is an Island* (Boston: Mariner, 2002).

15. LETTING GO

162 I am letting go: Alice Walker, "Even as I Hold You," *Good Night, Willie Lee, I'll See You in the Morning* (New York: Doubleday, 1979).

165 neurological and emotional network: James Hollis, *The Eden Project: In Search of the Magical Other* (Toronto, ON: Inner City Books, 1998).

166 but then move on: Christine Carter, "Raising Happiness," *Greater Good*, April 29, 2014, http://greatergood.berkeley.edu/raising_happiness/.

168 quicker if they didn't: Barbara Kingsolver, *Animal Dreams* (New York: HarperCollins, 2009).

16. HEALING, NOT VICTORY

176 becomes second nature: George Taylor, *A Path for Couples: Ten Practices for Love and Joy* (self-published, 2015).

17. THE HEART IS A GENEROUS MUSCLE

188 winning an award: Shelly Gable et al., "Will You Be There for Me When Things Go Right? Supportive Responses to Positive Event Disclosures," *Journal of Personality and Social Psychology* 91 (2006).

18. FORGIVENESS AND RECONCILIATION

192 The shared world: Naomi Shihab Nye, *Honeybee: Poems and Short Prose* (New York: HarperCollins Publishers, 2008).

197 nor should we: Helen Whitney, *Forgiveness: A Time to Love and a Time to Hate*, PBS, 2011.

200 world lives in you: Frederick Buechner, *Telling the Truth: The Gospel as Comedy, Tragedy, and Fairy Tale* (New York: Harper & Row, 1977).

SECTION 3 INTRODUCTION: THE WIDE LENS OF COMPASSION

212 our intense times: Jason Garner, interview with the author, July 2016.

213 around the world: Jacqueline Novogratz, *The Blue Sweater: Bridging the Gap Between Rich and Poor in an Interconnected World* (Emmaus, PA: Rodale, 2010).

215 to help the other: Quoted in "Feeling Others' Pain: Transforming Empathy into Compassion," Cognitive Neurological Society, June 24, 2013, https://www.cogneurosociety.org/empathy_pain/.

217 offering it to others: Julianne Holt-Lunstad et al., "Social Relationships and Mortality Risk: A Meta-Analytic Review," *PLoS Medicine* 7 (2010).

218 find myself loving them: Kevin Berrill, interview with the author, September 2015.

220 rely on one another: Daniel Goleman, "Rich People Just Care Less," *New York Times*, October 5, 2013.

19. PRIMING THE PUMP

227 or your community: Sonja Lyubomirsky, *The How of Happiness: A Scientific Approach to Getting the Life You Want* (New York: Penguin, 2007).

20. CHALLENGING OUR ASSUMPTIONS

236 an upscale neighborhood: Rhonda Magee, "How Mindfulness Can Defeat Racial Bias," *Greater Good*, May 14, 2015, http://greatergood.berkeley.edu/article/item/how_mindfulness_can_defeat_racial_bias.

237 biases about them are true: Quoted in Karin Evans, "Fear Less, Love

More," *Mindful*, January 7, 2016, http://www.mindful.org/fear-less
-love-more/.

240 *just like me*: Thomas Pettigrew and Linda Tropp, "A Meta-Analytic
Test of Intergroup Contact Theory," *Journal of Personality and Social
Psychology* 90 (2006).

240 study's lead author: Andrew Todd et al., "Does Seeing Faces of Young
Black Boys Facilitate the Identification of Threatening Stimuli?" *Psychological Science* 27 (2016).

241 without freaking out: Evans, "Fear Less, Love More."

241 in love with each other: Ibid.

243 fourteen years later: Aman Ali's story of 9/11, Facebook status post,
https://www.facebook.com/amanalistatus/posts/10103715731256804
?notif_t=like.

21. LOVE EVERYBODY

247 The more you understand: Thich Nhat Hanh, *How to Love* (Berkeley,
CA: Parallax Press, 2014).

251 opposed and endangered her: Interview with Malala Yousafzai by Jon
Stewart, *The Daily Show*, October 8, 2013, http://www.cc.com/video
-clips/a335nz/the-daily-show-with-jon-stewart-malala-yousafzai.

252 better person too: Archbishop Tutu, TheForgivenessProject.com.

253 real and urgent conflict: Robi Damelin, "Palestinian and Israeli Bereaved
Mothers Feel the Same Pain," *Haaretz*, February 24, 2016, http://www
.haaretz.com/opinion/.premium-1.703226.

254 be together forever: Quoted in Sharon Salzberg, "Three Simple Ways
to Pay Attention," *Mindful*, March 4, 2016, http://www.mindful.org
/meditation-start-here/.

22. CREATING COMMUNITY

257 positivity and health: Barbara Fredrickson, *Love 2.0: Creating Happiness and Health in Moments of Connection* (New York: Penguin,
2013).

257 a democratic society: Robert Putnam, *Bowling Alone: The Collapse
and Revival of American Community* (New York: Touchstone Books,
2001).

257 could really talk to: Miller McPherson et al., "Social Isolation in America: Changes in Core Discussion Networks over Two Decades," *American Sociological Review* 71, no. 3 (2006).

262 generous enough—already exist: Rebecca Solnit, *A Paradise Built in Hell: The Extraordinary Communities That Arise in Disaster* (New York: Penguin, 2010).

263 I got off: Alix Kates Shulman, *Drinking the Rain: A Memoir* (New York: Farrar, Straus and Giroux, 1995). Reprinted with permission.

23. FROM ANGER TO LOVE

271 *Love Your Enemies*: Robert Thurman and Sharon Salzberg, *Love Your Enemies: How to Break the Anger Habit and Be a Whole Lot Happier* (Carlsbad, CA: Hay House, 2013).

271 effectively for other people: Mallika Dutt, interview with the author, April 2016.

271 in conflict with them: Quoted in Mark Engler, "Ai-jen Poo: Organizing Labor—With Love," *Yes! Magazine*, November 9, 2011, http://www.yesmagazine.org/issues/the-yes-breakthrough-15/ai-jen-poo-organizing-labor-with-love.

272 raise my children in: Quoted in "An Incredible Container for Transformation: An Interview with Labor Organizer and Feminist Ai-jen Poo," *Believer*, May 9, 2014, http://logger.believermag.com/post/85221891259/an-incredible-container-for-transformation.

272 gender-related oppression: Quoted in Bryce Covert, "How the Rise of Women in Labor Could Save the Movement," *Nation*, January 10, 2014, https://www.thenation.com/article/how-rise-women-labor-could-save-movement.

273 interview with *The Nation*: Quoted in Laura Flanders, "Can 'Caring Across Generations' Change the World?" *Nation*, April 11, 2012, https://www.thenation.com/article/can-caring-across-generations-change-world.

274 we were growing up: Atman Smith, interview with the author, April 2016.

274 spreading and spreading: Andy Gonzalez, interview with the author, April 2016.

275 the cohesive force: Ali Smith, interview with the author, April 2016.

285   helpful to a stranger: Paul Piff, Dacher Keltner, et al., "Awe, the Small Self, and Prosocial Behavior," *Journal of Personality and Social Psychology* 108, no. 6 (2015).

286   moment of their lives: Quoted in Sean O'Neal, "Interview with Rashida Jones," *A.V. Club*, April 8, 2009, http://www.avclub.com/article/rashida-jones-26240.

287   what I wanted: Sudha Chandran's story, *Humans of Bombay* Facebook post, January 18, 2016, http://ow.ly/hjoe307axmx.